NAPOLEON HILL'S
MASTER COURSE

NAPOLEON HILL'S
MASTER COURSE

The Original
Science of Success

MEDIA

Published 2020 by Gildan Media LLC
aka G&D Media
www.GandDmedia.com

First Edition: 2020

Front cover design by David Rheinhardt of Pyrographx

Interior design by Meghan Day Healey of Story Horse, LLC.

Library of Congress Cataloging-in-Publication Data is available upon request

ISBN: 978-1-7225-0307-9

10   9   8   7   6   5   4   3   2   1

This book consists of edited transcripts of audio recordings of lectures given by Napoleon Hill for his Master Course. It was delivered in Chicago in May 1954 to individuals who were being trained to teach his philosophy.

Contents

1

The Definite Major Purpose

This philosophy is based on seven major premises.

The First Premise

The first premise is that definiteness of purpose is the starting point of all achievement, because it is the starting point of all individual achievements. A definite purpose must be accompanied by a definite plan for implementation followed by appropriate action. You have to have a purpose, you have to have a plan, and you have to start putting that plan into action. It's not too important that your plan be sound, because if you find that you have adopted a plan that's not sound, you can always modify it. But it is very important to be definite about what you're going after, what your purpose is. There can be no ifs or buts about it. Before you get through this lesson, you will see why it's got to be definite.

Just to understand this philosophy, read it, or hear me talk about it, wouldn't be of very much value to you. The value will come when you begin to form your own patterns out of this philosophy and put them into work in your daily life, your job, and your human relations. That's where the benefits will really come.

The Second Premise

The second premise: all individual achievements are the results of a motive or a combination of motives. You have no right to ask anybody to do anything at any time without giving that person an adequate motive.

Incidentally, that's the warp and the woof of all salesmanship: the ability to plant in the mind of the prospective buyer an adequate motive for his buying.

There are nine basic motives. Everything that people do or refrain from doing can be classified under these nine. Learn to deal with people by planting in their mind adequate motives for doing the things that you want them to do.

A lot of people who call themselves salesmen have never heard of the nine basic motives. They do not know that they have no right to ask for a sale until they have planted a motive in the mind of the buyer for buying. The nine basic motives are:

1. Self preservation
2. Financial gain
3. Love
4. Sexuality
5. Desire for power and fame
6. Fear
7. Revenge
8. Freedom of body and mind
9. Desire to create

The Third Premise

The third premise: any dominating idea, plan, or purpose held in the mind through repetition of thought and emotion, allied with a burning desire for its realization, is taken over by the subconscious section of the mind and is acted upon through whatever natural and logical means that may be available.

In that paragraph, you've got a tremendous lesson in psychology. If you want the mind to pick up an idea and to form a habit so that the mind will automatically act upon that idea, you've got to tell the mind what you want over and over and over again.

When Mr. Émile Coué came over here some years ago with his famous formula, "Day by day, in every way, I'm getting better and better," he cured thousands of people, but he didn't cure a great number more than that, and I wonder if you would know why. There was no desire, no feeling put into that statement. You might just as well blow in the wind as to make a statement unless you put some feeling back of it.

Incidentally, if you tell yourself anything often enough, you'll get to where you will believe it, even a lie. This is funny, isn't it? But it happens to be true. There are people who tell little white lies (and sometimes they're not so white as all that) until they get to where they believe in them themselves.

The subconscious mind doesn't know the difference between right or wrong. It doesn't know the difference between positive and negative. It doesn't know the difference between a penny and a million dollars. It doesn't know the difference between success and failure. It'll accept any statement that you keep repeating to it in thoughts or words or any other means.

It's up to you in the beginning to lay out your definite purpose, write it out so that it can be understood, memorize it, and start repeating it day in and day out until your subconscious mind picks it up and automatically acts upon it.

This is going to take a little time. You can't expect to undo what you've been doing overnight. Your subconscious mind bounces back by allowing negative thoughts to get into it. You can't expect that to change overnight. But you will find that if you emotionalize any plan that you send over to your subconscious mind and repeat it in a state of enthusiasm, backing it up with the spirit of faith, the subconscious mind not only acts more quickly, but it acts more definitely and more positively.

The Fourth Premise

The fourth premise: any dominating desire, plan, or purpose which is backed by that state of mind known as *faith* is taken over by the subconscious section of the mind and acted upon immediately. That state of mind is the only state of mind that will produce immediate actions through the subconscious mind. When I say *faith*, I don't have reference to wishing or hoping or mildly believing. I have reference to a state of mind wherein you can already see whatever you're going to do as a finished act before you even begin it. Now, that's pretty positive, isn't it?

I can truthfully tell you that never in my whole life have I failed to do anything that I made up my mind to do unless I got careless in my desire to do it and backed away from it or changed my mind or my mental attitude. And I'll tell you that you can put yourself in a frame of mind where you can do whatever you make up your mind to do, unless you weaken as you go along, as so many people do.

Again: any dominating desire plan or purpose which is backed by that state of mind known as *faith* is taken over by the subconscious section of the mind and acted upon immediately.

I suspect that only a relatively small number of people really understand the principle of faith and know how to apply it. Even if you do understand it, if you don't back it up with action and make it a part of your habit life, you might just as well not understand it, because faith without deeds is dead, faith without action is dead, faith without absolute, positive belief is dead. I don't know how you're going to get any results through believing unless you put some action back of that belief.

Incidentally, if you tell your mind often enough that you have faith in anything, the time will come when your subconscious mind will accept that, even if you tell your mind often enough that you have faith in yourself. Have you ever thought what a nice thing it would be if you had such complete faith in yourself that you wouldn't hesitate to undertake anything you wanted to do in life? Have you ever thought about what the benefits of that would be to you?

Many people sell themselves short all the way through life because they don't have the right amount of confidence, let alone faith. They amount to somewhere between 98 and 100 percent of people. They never in their whole lives develop a sufficient amount of confidence in themselves to go out and undertake the things they want to do in life. They accept from life whatever life hands them.

I have never in my whole life accepted, from life or from anything else, anything I didn't want. A lot of things were pushed over on my side of the street that I didn't like, that didn't smell so good, but I didn't accept them; I didn't become a part of them.

The greatest man I have ever known beyond any question of a doubt—and I have known many very great men—measured by his ability to apply this philosophy, was the late Mahatma Gandhi. Now there was a man who understood the principles of faith. He not only understood them, he freed India with them.

It's a marvelous thing to learn the art of depending upon yourself and using your own mind. Isn't it strange how nature works? She gives you a set of tools, everything that you need to attain all that you can use or aspire to have in this world. She gives you a set of tools adequate for your every need, and she rewards you bountifully for accepting those tools. That's all you have to do: just accept them and use them.

Nature penalizes you beyond compare if you don't accept them and use these gifts. Nature hates vacuums and idleness. She wants everything to be in action, and she especially wants the human mind to be in action. The mind is no different from many other parts of the body. If you don't use it, if you don't rely upon it, it atrophies and withers away and finally gets to where anybody can push you around. Oftentimes you don't even have the willpower to resist or protest.

The Fifth Premise

The fifth premise: the power of thought is the only thing over which any human being has complete and unquestionable means of control. This fact is so astounding that it connotes a close relationship between the mind of man and infinite intelligence.

There are only five known things in the whole universe, and out of those five, nature has shaped everything that's in existence, from the smallest electrons and protons of matter on up to the largest stones that float out there in the heavens, including you and me. Just five things: time, space, energy, and matter, and those four things would be no good without the fifth thing. Everything would be chaos. You and I never could have existed without that fifth thing.

It's universal intelligence, and it reflects itself in every blade of grass, everything that grows out of the ground and all of the electrons and protons. It reflects itself in space and in time. In everything that is, there is intelligence, operating all the time. This intelligence permeates the whole universe; space, time, matter, energy, everything.

The person who is the most successful is the one who finds ways and means of appropriating the most of this intelligence through his brain and putting it into action. Every individual has the privilege of appropriating to his own use as much of this intelligence as he chooses. He can only appropriate it by using it. Just understanding it or believing in it is not enough. You've got to put it into specialized use in some form.

I believe in miracles. But I saw a lot of miracles fifty years ago that I can explain away very easily now: they're not miracles anymore. In the final analysis, of course, there is no such thing as a miracle, because every effect has a natural cause. When we can't discover that cause, oftentimes the effect is so astounding that we call it a miracle.

To me, the most outstanding miracle is the human mind. The mind of the humblest person is capable of extending itself into proportions beyond belief and imagination. Think of a man like Henry Ford or Thomas Edison, starting out without education and building two great empires, Mr. Edison ushering in the great electrical age, Mr. Ford ushering in the great automotive age. And then think of Napoleon Hill in one lifetime, creating a philosophy that is benefiting millions of people and will benefit millions after he's gone. How could he have done that if he hadn't have made use of his mind?

It wasn't my education that permitted me to do such a gigantic thing, because I had very little. It wasn't my financial backing because of that I had none. Even Mr. Carnegie refused to subsidize me, which was one of the finest things I've ever came across, although I didn't think so at the time.

Honestly, the things that have happened are so fantastic that when my business associate Mr. W. Clement Stone and I go out to make speeches, we have to tone down the facts. If we told all of them, they would seem so fantastic, so impossible, that people who do not know of my background wouldn't believe them. Sometimes I wonder if I believe them myself.

I started with a tremendous handicap, one that I brought over with me from the previous plane as well as that which I found awaiting me when I got here. With all of that, by a series of manipulations, based upon the use of my own mind, I was able to enter, penetrate, examine, and take out the sum and the substance of what five hundred of the smartest men in this country gained by a lifetime of effort. I have put it in a shape so that the humblest person not only can understand it but can embrace it, apply it, and use it to his own benefit. Never in the history of the world has an achievement like this been produced in the life of one author. Never in the history of the world has any other author produced in simple terms a philosophy that you can live by day in and day out, wherever you are, whoever you are, and whatever you're doing.

All this goes back to the miraculous power of the human mind, but that power is going to do you no good unless you recognize it, embrace it, and use it. The main responsibility of this course is to give you a pattern, a blueprint, by which you can take possession of your own mind and put it into operation. All you have to do is to follow the blueprint. Don't just pick out the part of it that you like best and discard the others. Take it all as is.

I met a man not long ago who had made quite a huge fortune. He'd made it in a very few years, and he made it honestly. He said, "Napoleon Hill, I want to tell you something that may astound you. When I got hold of one of your books, my wife and I read the book together. My wife pooh-poohed it and didn't accept it. I wasn't as smart as she was, but I accepted it, and I became immensely wealthy."

You will find people who are very much smarter than you. They know all the answers, and they'll be reluctant to accept this philosophy. They just know it can't work for them. You will find people like that. Don't be too disturbed.

I used to become disturbed when not everyone would accept and embrace this philosophy. I got a lesson some years ago that did me more good than anything that had happened up to that time. I was complaining about the ingratitude of one of my students when a man very much older than myself said, "Look here, Napoleon Hill, about nineteen hundred years ago, a very fine man came to this world, and he had a very fine philosophy to live by. And would you believe it, sir? He didn't get a 100 percent following either. As a matter of fact, you're doing much better than he did. He only had twelve disciples, and one of them went sour on him. What does it matter if a few go sour on you? Who are you to expect that some of them won't go sour? If they do, it's their misfortune, not yours; just remember that."

Don't let people disturb you because they disbelieve. You can't expect all people to believe. If all people had the capacity to believe that you're going to have when you assimilate this philosophy, this would be a utopia. You won't be afraid of the H-bomb or of any other kind of a bomb.

The Sixth Premise

The sixth premise: the subconscious section of the mind appears to be the only doorway of individual approach to infinite intelligence. I want you to study that language carefully. I said it "appears to be." I don't know if it is. I doubt if you do, and I doubt if anyone knows it definitely. A lot of people have a lot of different ideas about it, but from the best observations that I have been able to make through thousands of experiments, it appears to be true that the subconscious section of the mind is the only doorway of individual approach to infinite intelligence, and it is capable of being influenced by the individual through the means described in this and subsequent lessons.

The basis of approach is faith based upon definiteness of purpose. That one sentence gives you the whole key to that paragraph. Faith based upon definiteness of purpose. Do you have any idea why you don't have as much confidence in yourself as you should have? Have you ever stopped to think about that? Have you ever stopped to think about why it is, when you see an opportunity coming along or what you believe to be an opportunity, you begin to question your ability to embrace it and use it? Haven't you had that happen to you many times?

If you've had a chance to be closely associated with people who are very successful, you'll know that that is one thing that they are not bothered by. If they want to do something, it never occurs to them that they can't do it.

I hope that in your association with Napoleon Hill Associates, you'd come to know my distinguished business associate Mr. Stone better, because if I ever saw a man that knows the power of his mind and is willing to rely upon that mind, Mr. Stone is that man. As a matter of fact, it's rubbing off on me. I thought I had a great supplier, but believe you me, I can go to Mr. Stone anytime and have my batteries recharged too. What a grand thing it is to be around somebody who has complete control of himself, who has everything under control. I don't think Mr. Stone has any worries. I don't believe he would tolerate a worry. Why? Because he has confidence in his ability to use his mind and to make that mind create the circumstances that he wants to create. That's the condition of operation of any successful mind, and that's going to be the condition of your mind when you get through with this philosophy. You're going to be able to project your mind into whatever objective you choose, and there'll never be a question in your mind as to whether you can do what you want to do or not. Never a question in the world.

The Seventh Premise

The seventh premise: every brain is built of a receiving set and a broadcasting station for the vibrations of thought. This fact explains the importance of moving with definiteness of purpose instead of drifting, since the brain may be so thoroughly charged with the nature of one's purpose that it will begin to attract the physical or material equivalents of that purpose.

I want you to go over the previous paragraph, analyze it, read it many times, and get it into your consciousness. The first radio broadcasting and receiving set was the one that exists in the brain of man. Not only does it exist in the brain of man, but it exists in a great many animals. I have a couple of Pomeranian dogs, and they know exactly what I'm thinking, sometimes before I know. They're so smart that they can tune on me. When we start off for an automobile ride, they know whether they're going or not. You don't have to say a word, because they're in constant attunement with this through telepathy.

Your mind is sending out vibrations constantly. If you're a salesman and you're going to call on a prospective buyer, the sale ought to be made before you ever come into presence of the buyer. Have you ever thought of that? If you're going to do anything requiring the cooperation of other people, condition your mind so that you know the other fellow is going to cooperate.

Why? First, because the plan that you're going to offer him is so fair and honest and beneficial to him that he can't refuse it. In other words, you have a right to his cooperation. You would be surprised to know what a change there will be in people when you come sending out positive thoughts over this broadcasting station of yours instead of thoughts of fear.

If you want a good illustration of how this broadcasting station works, say you need a thousand dollars really badly. You've got to have that thousand by the day after tomorrow, or they're going to take back the car or the furniture. You just have to have that thousand dollars. You go down to the bank, and the moment you walk inside of the door, the banker can tell that you just have to have it, and he doesn't want you to have it.

Isn't that funny? No, it's not funny. It's tragic. You carry the matches around in your pocket oftentimes and set your own house afire. You broadcast your thoughts, and they precede you. When you get there, you find that instead of getting the cooperation you want, the other person reflects back to you that state of doubt, that state of mind that you sent out ahead of you.

I used to teach salesmanship. I made my living that way for a long time while I was doing the research on this philosophy, and I have taught over thirty thousand salesmen. Many of them now have become members of the Million Dollar Round Table in the life insurance field. And if there is one thing in this world that has to be sold, it's life insurance. Nobody ever buys life insurance. It has to be sold. The first thing that I taught those people under my direction was that they must make the sale to themselves before they try to make it to the other fellow. If they don't do that, they're not going to make a sale. Somebody might buy something from them, but they'll never make a sale unless they first make it to themselves.

Another thing that I'll call to your attention: Sometimes you feel moody, you feel a little bit blue. You don't know what the trouble is. Do you ever feel that way?

I don't anymore. If you're in a bad frame of mind, study yourself carefully and trace down the cause of it. Did you know that you're constantly picking up the vibrations being released by other moody people, people who are in a state of frustration? Did you know that now their world is in a state of chaos? People are talking about the total destruction of mankind. They're looking and praying for the day when the H-bomb will come along and wipe out whole cities. What do you expect is going to happen if millions of people all over the world keep expecting, looking for, and praying for destruction? Why do you think it's going to happen? The inevitable, that's what will happen.

This world needs a renaissance that will cause people to know the power and dignity of their own minds, so that they can keep those minds on the things that are constructive and off the things that are destructive. Every brain is a broadcasting station and a receiving set.

Some years ago, when I was first starting out, I delivered a series of lectures at the Harvard Business School. I told the students that my observations under Dr. Alexander Graham Bell and under Dr. Elmer R. Gates had been such that I believed the ether was constantly carrying sounds that we couldn't interpret with the human ear, that the human brain was constantly picking up thoughts from other brains, and that the human brain was constantly sending out thoughts that other brains are picking up in turn.

I didn't get much further than that when I heard the scraping of feet all over the room. Then I saw a broad grin break out over their faces, and then they broke out into a horse laugh. They gave me the boot.

I might go back to Harvard and that same group of men and women. I might start off by apologizing for having to be in competition with so many noises here in this room, all of the orchestras—people singing, people playing, people talking in competition with me—and would they please bear with me and not pay attention to the others? They'll just listen to me. There'll be no shuffling of the feet. There'll be no laughing if I said that this time, because you know that's true.

There's a great myriad of variety of noises here in this room right now. The ether is the medium that carried them. The ether is a medium that carries your thought from your brain to other brains. You can be so attuned with another person that you can communicate with that person by telepathy.

I wouldn't make that statement if I didn't know it was true. And how do you think I do? Only because I have experienced it. I was walking in Central Park in New York some years ago, and I imagine that at least three or four thousand other people were out there. My wife wanted me to go over to the Columbia Broadcasting Station, where I was negotiating for a program, and to be there at one o'clock for an important conference. She sent out the call mentally. I picked it up. Instead of going back to my house, I went straight to the Columbia Broadcasting Station. When I got there, I got in under the wire, with just one minute to go. If I'd had a letter delivered to me giving me that information, it couldn't have been any more definite.

I was lecturing over in New Jersey some years ago, at the Rotary Club. After the lecture was over, a lot of them gathered around, and we sat down for a bull session. An hour and half elapsed, and all of a sudden I said, "Excuse me gentlemen, I have to answer a telephone call. My wife is calling me," and I went to the phone and answered her. She said, "You're late."

I went back and said, "Excuse me, gentlemen, my wife is anxious about me because I was late; she wanted to know if anything had happened."

They said, "How did you know your wife was calling you?"

"Oh, that's a state secret," I said. I didn't go to the trouble of explaining to them because I was afraid that they would discount the fine speech I had just given them. I thought it was just as well not to tell too much.

But with you, my students, I feel I can be frank; I can take you into my confidence. I can tell you about some of the extracurricular experiences that I've had that indicate beyond any question of a doubt that your brain is a broadcasting station and a receiving set, and you can tune that brain so that it will attract only the positive vibrations released by other people. That's the point. You can train your own mind to pick up, out of the myriad of vibrations that are floating out there constantly, only the things that are related to what you want most in life.

How do you do that? By keeping your mind on what you want most in life: your definite major purpose. It's all by repetition, by thought, by action, until finally the brain will not pick up anything not related to that definiteness of purpose. You can educate your brain so that it will absolutely refuse to pick up any vibrations except those related to what you want. When you get your brain under control like that, you will be on the path; you will really and truly be on the beam.

Benefits of Definiteness of Purpose

Now let's look at some of the benefits of definiteness of purpose. I've never in my whole life suggested that anybody do anything without giving them a good reason for doing it. When I speak about planting motives in people's minds, that's not just something for you to follow; it's something that I follow too. And I can give you some very good motives for following this lesson to the letter.

First of all, definiteness of purpose automatically develops self-reliance, personal initiative, imagination, enthusiasm, self-discipline, and concentration of effort, all of these being prerequisites for any success of vital importance. That's quite an array of things that you develop if you develop definiteness of purpose, that is to say, knowing what you want, having a plan for getting it, and having your mind mostly occupied with carrying out that plan.

If you have to adopt a plan, unless you're an unusual person, you're almost sure to adopt some plans that are not going to work so well. When you find out that your plan is not right, immediately discard it, get another one, and keep on until you find one that will work. In the process of doing this, just remember one thing: that maybe infinite intelligence, being gifted with a great deal of wisdom, might have a plan for you better than the one you had yourself.

Have an open mind. If you adopt a plan to carry out your major purpose or a minor purpose and it doesn't work well, dismiss that plan and ask for guidance from infinite intelligence. You may get that guidance.

What can you do to be sure that you will get it? How can you believe that you'll get it? You can believe that you'll get it, and it's not going to hurt if you say out loud that you believe it. I suspect that the Creator can know your thoughts, but I found that if you express yourself with a lot of enthusiasm, it doesn't hurt any. And I'm sure that it doesn't hurt in arousing your subconscious mind.

When I wrote *Think and Grow Rich*, its original title was *The Thirteen Steps to Riches*, and both the publisher and I knew that that was not a box-office title. We had to have a million-dollar title.

The publisher kept prodding me every day to give him the title that I wanted. I wrote five or six hundred titles, and none of them were any good. Then one day he scared the dickens out of me. He called me up and said, "Tomorrow morning, I've got to have that title, and if you don't have one, I have one that's a humdinger."

"What is it?" I said.

"We're going to call it *Use Your Noodle and Get the Boodle.*"

"My goodness," I said, "you'll ruin me. This is a dignified book, and that's a flip title. That would ruin the book and me too."

"Whether it will or not, that's the title unless you give me a better one by tomorrow morning."

I want you to follow this incident, because it has potent food for thought. That night I sat down on the side of the bed, and I had a talk with my subconscious mind. I said, "Now, look, you old stub, you and I have gone a long way together. You've done a lot of things for me and some things to me, thanks to my ignorance, but I've got to have a million-dollar title, and I've got to have it tonight. Do you understand that?"

I got to talking so loudly that the man in the apartment above me rapped on the floor, and I don't blame him, because I guess he thought I was quarreling with my wife. I really gave the subconscious mind no doubt as to what I wanted. I didn't tell the subconscious mind exactly what kind of a title it was. I just said it's got to be a million-dollar title.

I went to bed after charging my subconscious mind until I reached that psychological moment where I knew it was going to produce what I wanted. If I hadn't gotten to that point, I'd be up there still, sitting on the side of the bed talking to my subconscious. There is a psychological moment—and you can feel it—when the power of faith takes over whatever you're trying to do and says, "All right, now you can relax; this is it."

I went to bed, and at about two o'clock in the morning, I woke up as if somebody was shaking me hard. As I came out of my sleep, *Think and Grow Rich* was in my mind. Oh boy! I let out an Indian whoop. I jumped to my typewriter and wrote it down.

I grabbed the telephone, and I called the publisher. "What's the matter?" he said. "Is the town on fire?" It was about 2:30 in the morning.

"Yes," I said, "you bet it is—with a million-dollar title."

"Let's have it," he said.

"Think and Grow Rich."

"Boy, you've got it," he said.

Yes, I'll say we've got it. That book has grossed over $23 million already in the United States and probably will gross over $100 million before I pass on, and there's no end to it. It's a million-dollar—a multi-million-dollar title.

After the thrashing that I gave my subconscious, I'm not surprised that it came around and did a good job. Why didn't I use that method in the first place? Isn't that a funny thing? I know the law. Why did I fool around and temporize? Why didn't I go to the source and get my subconscious mind heated up instead of sitting down there at my typewriter writing out five or six hundred titles?

I'll tell you why. It's for the same reason that you will oftentimes know what to do but won't do it. There's no explaining the indifference of man toward himself. Even after you know what the law is and what the score is, you fool around until the last minute before you do anything about it.

It's just like in prayer: you fool around until the time of need comes, and then you're scared to death. Of course you don't get any results from prayer. If you want to have results from prayer, you condition your mind so that your life is a prayer day in and day out. Every minute of your life is a constant prayer because it's based upon belief in your dignity, and tuning into infinite intelligence to have the things that you need in this world. If you wait until the hour of need, it's just like having a death in the family and going over to the undertaker and the graveyard man. Believe you me, they'll skin you alive, because you are in a state of grief and you haven't got any resistance. And what happens to you is nobody's business, because you didn't prepare when there was not a need.

So it is with this human mind. You've got to condition the mind as you go along from day to day so that when any emergency arises, you will be right there ready to deal with it.

Definiteness of purpose also induces one to budget one's time and to plan day-to-day endeavors which lead to the attainment of one's major purpose. If you would sit down and write an hour-by-hour account of the actual work that you put in each day for one week, and then an hour-by-hour account of the time that you wasted, you're going to get one of the shocks of your life.

Not long ago, somebody said, "Napoleon Hill, you are a terribly busy person. You're on the plane going here, there, and the other place. You're writing books, you're making lectures, you're helping Mr. Stone to run a business. You must be a hard worker."

My face turned red. You know why? I waste at least half of my time. I could put in five hours every day doing something else if I want to do it badly enough. And if I'm that deficient, what do you think you are?

Don't get mad at that; I just wanted to step on your toes a little bit. I wanted to call your attention to the fact, ladies and gentlemen, that we all are time wasters. We're not efficient. We have about eight hours to sleep, about eight hours to earn a living, and eight hours of free time in which you can do anything you want. That eight hours of free time is the opportunity time. That's the time when you can condition your mind to do anything you want to do.

Definiteness of purpose also makes one more alert in recognizing opportunities related to the object of one's major purpose. It also inspires the courage to embrace and act upon those opportunities. We all see opportunities almost every day of our lives from which, if we embraced them and acted upon them, we could benefit. But there's something called procrastination. We just don't have the will, the alertness, the determination to embrace opportunities when they come along. But if you condition your mind with this philosophy, you'll not only embrace opportunities, but you will do something better.

What could you do better than embrace the opportunity? *Make* the opportunity. One of Napoleon's generals (the other Napoleon) came to him one day. They were fixing to attack next morning. This general said, "Sir, the circumstances are not right for the attack tomorrow."

Napoleon said, "The circumstances are not right? Hell, I *make* circumstances. Attack."

I have never seen a successful man yet in any business who, when somebody says it can't be done, didn't say, "Attack, attack."

Start where you are. When you get around to that curve in the road, you'll always find that the road goes on. Attack. Don't procrastinate. Don't stand still. Attack.

Definiteness of purpose inspires confidence in one's integrity and character, and it attracts the favorable attention of other people. Had you ever thought about that? I think the whole world loves to see a person walking with his chest sticking out. He doesn't need to be too chesty, but we have this guy that tells the whole doggone world that he knows what he's doing and he's right on the way to doing it. If you are determined to get by, people on the sidewalk will get out of the way , and you don't have to whistle at them or holler at them. You just have to send your thoughts ahead with determination, and they'll stand aside and let you go through.

The world's like that. Many people are so indifferent that they let people push them around. The man who knows what he wants does a lot of pushing around, believe me, especially with anybody that gets in his way. The man who knows where he is going and is determined to get there will always find willing helpers to cooperate with.

Here is the greatest of all benefits of definiteness of purpose: it opens the way for the full exercise of that state of mind known as *faith* by making the mind positive and freeing it from the limitations of fear and doubt and discouragement and indecision and procrastination.

The very minute that you decide upon something and you know that's what you want, you know you're going to do it. All of the negatives that have been bothering you pick up their baggage and get out. They just move out. They can't live in a positive mind.

Can you imagine a negative frame of mind and a positive frame of mind occupying the same space at the same time? No, you can't, because it can't be done. And did you know that the slightest bit of a negative mental attitude is sufficient to destroy the power of prayer? Did you know that the slightest bit of a negative mental attitude is sufficient to destroy your plan? You have to move with courage, with faith, with determination, in carrying out your definiteness of purpose.

Next, definiteness of purpose makes one success-conscious. Do you know what I mean by *success-conscious*? If I said that it makes one health-conscious, would you know what I meant by that? It means your thoughts are predominantly about health. With reference to success consciousness, your thoughts are predominantly about success—the can-do part of life, and not to think no can do. Did you know that 98 percent of the people who never get anywhere in life are no-can-do people? In any circumstances that are placed before them, they immediately fashion their attention upon the no can do part, the negative part.

I'll never forget as long as I live what happened to me when Mr. Carnegie surprised me with a chance to organize this philosophy. I tried to give him all the reasons I could think of why I couldn't do it, and every one popped into my mind immediately. I didn't have a sufficient education. I didn't have the money. I didn't have the influence. I didn't know what the word *philosophy* meant. I was trying to get my mouth open to tell Mr. Carnegie that I thanked him for the compliment he paid me, but I doubted that Mr. Carnegie was such a good judge of human nature in picking me to do a job like that. Although that's what went on in my mind, there was a silent person looking over my shoulder who said, "Go ahead, tell him you can do it. Spit it out."

I said, "Yes, Mr. Carnegie, I'll accept the commission, and you can depend upon it, sir, that I will complete it."

He reached over and grabbed me by the hand. He said, "I not only like what you said, but I like the way you said it. That's what I was waiting for."

He saw that my mind was on fire with the belief that I could do it, even though I hadn't the slightest asset to give me a beginning other than my determination to create this philosophy.

If I had wavered in the slightest, if I had said, "Yes, Mr. Carnegie, I'll do my best," I am sure that he would have taken the opportunity away from me instantly. He would have indicated that I wasn't determined enough to do it.

But I said, "Yes, Mr. Carnegie, you can depend upon me, sir, to complete it," and you are living this here. You're living with the fact that Mr. Carnegie didn't pick wrongly.

He knew what he was about. He had found something in the human mind, in my mind, that he'd been searching for over years. He found it. I didn't know its value, but I found out its value later. I want you to recognize its value, because you have that same thing in your mind—the same capacity to know what you want and to be determined that you'll get it, even though you don't know where to make the first start.

Think of Mme. Marie Curie starting out to find radium. All she knew was that theoretically there should be radium somewhere out there in the universe. Talk about looking for a needle in a haystack— that's looking for a needle in the universe, searching for radium—and all she had was a theory. She put so much faith back of that theory that she developed, refined, and brought forth the first radium ever produced in the world. Isn't it marvelous that the human mind could do a thing like that?

Next to that achievement, your petty oppositions and problems are as nothing, nothing at all. These problems that we worry about day in and day out are nothing in comparison with the problems that faced Marie Curie or Thomas A. Edison when he was working on the incandescent electric lamp, or Henry Ford when he was building his first automobile. It took a tremendous amount of faith. It took continuous faith, definiteness of purpose, before those great men of achievement could achieve.

What makes a great man or a great woman? Greatness is the ability to recognize the power of your own mind, to embrace it and use it. That's what makes greatness. In my book of rules, every man and every woman can become truly great by the simple process of recognizing his or her own mind, embracing it, and using it.

2

Applying the Principle
of Definite Major Purpose

Here are instructions for applying the principle of definite major purpose, and these instructions are to be carried out to the letter. Don't overlook any part of them.

Write Out a Statement

First, write out a clear statement of your major purpose, sign it, commit it to memory, and repeat it at least once a day in the form of a prayer, or an affirmation if you choose. You can see the advantages of this, because it places your faith and your Creator's squarely back of you.

I've found from experience that this is the weakest spot in students' activities. They read this, they say it's simple enough, they understand it; what's the use of going to the trouble of writing it out? But you must write it out. You must go through the physical act of translating a thought onto paper, you must memorize it, and you must start talking to your subconscious mind about it. Give that subconscious mind a good idea of what you want. It won't hurt any if you remember the story I told about what I did to get my million-dollar book title.

Give your subconscious mind to understand from here on out that you are the boss. But you can't expect the subconscious mind or anything else to help you if you don't know what it is you want, if you're not definite about it. Ninety-eight out of every hundred people do not know what they want in life and consequently never get it. They take whatever life hands them. They can't do anything about it.

Now in addition to your definite major purpose, you can have minor purposes, as many as you want, provided they are related to or lead you in the direction of your major purpose. Your whole life should be devoted to carrying out your major purpose in life.

Incidentally, it's all right to be modest when you ask for what you want, but don't be too modest. Reach out and ask for the things that you're sure you're entitled to. But in asking, be sure that you don't overlook the subsequent instructions I'm going to give you.

Second, write out a clear, definite outline of the plan or plans by which you intend to achieve the objective or purpose, and state the maximum time within which you intend to attain it. Describe in detail precisely what you intend to give in return for the realization of the object of your purpose. Make your plan flexible enough to permit changes anytime you are inspired to do so, remembering that infinite intelligence may present you with a better plan than yours; oftentimes it will if you are definite about what you want.

Have you ever had a hunch that you couldn't describe or explain away? You know what a hunch is? It's your subconscious mind trying to get an idea over to you. Oftentimes you are too indifferent even to let the subconscious mind talk to you for a few moments. I've heard people say, "I had this darn fool idea today," but that darn fool idea might have been a million-dollar idea if you had listened to it and done something about it. I have great respect for these hunches, because there is undoubtedly something outside of yourself trying to communicate with you. I have a great respect for these hunches that come to me, and they come to me constantly. I find that they are all related to something that my mind has been dwelling upon, something that I want to do, something that I am engaged in.

Write out a clear, definite outline of the plan or plans, and state the maximum of time within which you intend to attain them. That timing is very important. Don't write out as your definite major aim that "I intend to become the best salesman in the world" or that "I intend to become the best employee in my organization" or that "I intend to make a lot of money." That's not definite. Whatever it is that you consider to be your major objective in life, write it out clearly, and time it: "I intend to attain X within Y number of years," and then go ahead and describe what it is.

Then, in the next paragraph down below, write, "I intend to give so-and-so in return for the thing that I request," and then go ahead and describe it.

Do you have any idea of what it is that you would have to give in return for whatever you want in life? Do you have any idea of what I have to give in return for anything that I want in life? Incidentally, I have everything in life that I want, and I have it in abundance. I got something yesterday I didn't want, but I didn't keep it. I got a little cold in my head. But the prince of sound health got busy and did something about it. (I'll say more about the prince of sound health later.)

When you become proficient teachers of this philosophy, you're going to enrich the minds of those who come under your influence. That's what you have to give. What better thing could you give for anything in the world that you want? I wouldn't have any compunction whatsoever about asking for anything that I wanted, because I think the service I am rendering entitles me to anything I want, and I want you to feel that way too.

But don't go out like many people, wishing you could make a million dollars in the next year and not have to work too hard for it. Don't do that. Be willing to give and then start giving first.

Incidentally, even before you complete this course, it'll be a mighty fine thing if you'll get two or three of your friends together and start teaching these lessons. Take this lesson tonight: I daresay that every one of you could make a pretty good stab at explaining it to somebody, especially if you have my notes to look at while you're explaining.

Start by trying that. You will be surprised what it'll do to you, also to them. You can do a little proselyting, you can do a little practicing, and you'll find that you'll grow and develop in doing it.

Nature has a system of timing everything. If you're a farmer and you want to plant some wheat in the field, you go out, you prepare the ground, and you sow the wheat at the right season of the year. Then would you go back the very next day with a harvester and start harvesting?

No. You'd wait for nature to do her part. Whether you call it infinite intelligence or God or whatever you want, there is an intelligence that does its part if you do your part first. Intelligence is not going to direct you to or attract to you the object of your major purpose unless you know what it is and unless you properly time it. It'd be quite ridiculous if you started out with only a mediocre talent and said that you're going to make a million dollars within the next thirty days. In other words, make your major purpose within reason of what you know you are able to desire.

Keep Your Purpose to Yourself

Next, keep your major purpose strictly to yourself, except insofar as you will receive further instructions on this subject in the lesson on the Master Mind. Why do I suggest that you keep your major purpose to yourself? Do you know what your relatives will do to you or your relatives if you stick your head up one inch above what you've been doing and announce it? They'll laugh you out of the house. Mine did. For years, out of all of the people that I knew, there were only two that stood by me and gave me courage: my stepmother and Andrew Carnegie. I couldn't have survived without the faith of those two people; I couldn't have made it. You've got to have somebody believing in you. You can't get along without one. You've also got to *deserve* to have somebody believing in you.

In any case, you don't disclose your major purpose to other people, because there are a lot of people in this world who like to stand on the sidelines and stick their toes out when you go by, especially if you've got a high head and look like you're going to accomplish more in life than they are. For no good reason at all, as you go along, they stick their toes out, just to see you fall. They will throw a monkey wrench into your machinery—if they don't have a monkey wrench, they'll put sand in your gearbox—but they will slow you down. Why? Because of the envy of mankind.

The only way to speak about your definite major purpose is in action, after the fact and not before the fact, after you've achieved it. Let it speak for itself. The only way anybody can afford to boast or brag about himself is not by words but by deeds. If the deeds are engaged in, you don't need any words: they speak for themselves.

It used to be that every now and then somebody would criticize me, and I guess they still do, for that matter, but I don't even hear it anymore, let alone answer. Why? Because what I am doing speaks so loudly that what people say I'm doing makes no difference whatsoever. Let your work, let your deeds speak for themselves.

Make your plans flexible: don't become determined that the plan you've worked out is perfect just because you worked it out. You will make a mistake if you do that. Leave your plan flexible. Give it a good trial, and if it's not working properly, change it.

Condition Your Mind for Success

Next, call your major purpose into your consciousness as often as may be practical. Eat with it, sleep with it, and take it with you wherever you go, keeping in mind the fact that your subconscious mind can thus be influenced to work for its attainment while you sleep.

Did you know that I have been instrumental in working out a machine that conditions your mind for success while you're asleep? I had been lecturing about fifteen years on that. Now there are over six different machines that you can turn on and it will automatically play back to you any message to your subconscious mind every fifteen minutes until you turn the machine off. You can treat yourself for physical ailments. You can certainly treat yourself for mental ailments, lack of confidence, lack of faith. If you have anything that you want to get over to your subconscious mind, you can do it better when you're asleep. If that had not been true, I would not have been able to influence nature to improvise a set of hearing aids for my son, Blair, who was born without any ears at all. I worked through his subconscious mind entirely.

Now your conscious mind is a very jealous mind. It stands guard and doesn't want anything to get by except the things that you are afraid of and the things that you are very enthusiastic about (especially the things you are afraid of). If you want to plant an idea in your subconscious mind, you have to do it with a tremendous amount of faith and enthusiasm. You've got to arrest the conscious mind so that it steps aside and lets you go through to the subconscious because of your enthusiasm and faith.

Repetition is a marvelous thing too. The conscious mind finally gets tired of hearing you say things over and over and says, "All right, if you are to repeat that, I can't stand here and watch you forever. Go on in there and take it into sub and see what he'll do with it." That's the way it works.

This conscious mind is a very contrary thing, and it learns all of the things that *won't* work. It has a tremendous stock of things that won't work and things that are not right; it has a tremendous stock of pieces of string, horseshoes, nails, like some misers gather up. A whole stock of those things is lying around—useless trash that is gathered, impedimenta that you don't need. That's the kind of stuff the conscious mind is feeding to your subconscious mind.

Every night, just before you go to bed, you should give your subconscious mind some order for the night for the things you want done. Certainly for the healing of your body. The body needs repairing every day. When you lay the carcass down for sleep, turn it over to the infinite intelligence and request your subconscious mind to go to work and heal every cell and organ in your body and to give you tomorrow morning a perfectly conditioned body in which the mind may function.

Don't go to bed without giving orders to your subconscious mind. Tell it what you want. Get the habit of telling it what you want. If you keep on long enough, it will believe you and deliver what you ask for. Therefore you'd better be careful about what you ask for, because if you keep on asking for it, you're going to get it.

I wonder if you wouldn't be surprised if you knew right now what you've been asking for back down through the years. Have you ever thought of that? You've been asking for it. Everything that you have that you don't want, you've been asking for it, maybe by neglect, maybe because you didn't tell the subconscious mind what you really wanted, and it stocked up on a lot of stuff you didn't want. It works that way.

Your Greatest Purpose in Life

Here are some important factors in connection with your definite major purpose. First of all, it should represent your greatest purpose in life: the one single purpose which, above all others, you desire to achieve and the fruits of which you are willing to leave behind you as a monument to yourself.

That's what your definite major purpose should be. I'm not talking about your minor purposes; I'm talking about your major overall purpose, your lifelong purpose. Believe me, friends, if you don't have an overall lifelong purpose, you're just wasting the better portion of your life. The wear and tear of living is not worth the price you pay for it unless you really are aiming for something, unless you're going somewhere in life, unless you're doing something with this opportunity here on this plane.

I imagine you were sent over here to do something. I imagine you were sent over here with a mind capable of hewing out and attaining your own destiny. If you don't attain that, if you don't use that mind, I imagine that your life to a large extent will have been wasted from the viewpoint of the one who sent you over. Take possession of your mind; aim high. Don't believe that you can't achieve in the future because you may not have achieved much in the past. Don't measure your future by your past. A new day is coming. You're going to be born again. You're setting up a new pattern, you're in a new world, you're a new person. If not, why not? If you don't get that idea, if you don't use it, then you won't get anything out of this course. I intend that every one of you shall be born again mentally, physically, and maybe spiritually, with a new aim, a new purpose, a new realization of your own individual self and of your own dignity as a unit of mankind.

If you ask me what I believe to be the greatest sin of the mankind, I bet you'd be surprised at my answer. What would yours be? What do you think the greatest sin of mankind is?

The greatest sin of mankind is neglect to use his greatest asset, because if you'll use that greatest asset, you'll have everything you want and you'll have it in abundance. I didn't say you'll have everything *within reason*. I said you'd have *everything* you want and have it in abundance. I didn't put it qualifying words in there. You're the only one that can put qualifying words in there as to what you want. You're the only one that can set up limitations for yourself. Nobody else can do it for you unless you let them.

Keep Your Purpose ahead of You

Your major purpose, or some portion of it, should remain a few jumps ahead of you at all times as something to which you may look forward with hope and anticipation.

If you ever catch up with your major purpose and attain it, then what? What are you going to do? Get another one. By attaining your first one, you will have learned that you can attain a major purpose. When you select your next one, make it a bigger objective than your first. If your objective is to acquire material riches, don't aim too high for the first year. Work out a twelve-month plan within reason and watch how easily you can attain it. Next year, double it. The next year, double that.

Earl Nightingale told me not long ago that he was lying in bed reading a copy of my book some years ago, and all of a sudden, he came upon an idea that revealed to him what I'm talking about, namely the focal point at which he could take hold of himself and do anything he wanted. His success started from that very moment. He let out a war whoop, and his wife came running in; she thought somebody was murdering him.

"I found it, I found it," he said.

"You found what?"

"What I had been searching for all of my life. Right here," and he read it to her. Then he said, "Now I'm going to prove it. I'm going to find out if Napoleon Hill is a faker or if he's a real guy. I'm going to double my salary next week." And he doubled it. "Well," he said, "anything could happen once. I'm going to try it again." Then he doubled it again, and then he stopped there. He said, "From here on, I'll take it on my own."

Believe you me, Earl Nightingale is doing all right, financially and otherwise. He did a wonderful job. He got his start out of this philosophy, which gave him an idea. What was the idea? He discovered that he had the answer all the time. He didn't need to get it from my books or any other place, although it just happened that he did find it in one of my books.

I don't know where you are going to find that something I'm describing, but you're going to find it somewhere, and you're going to help every person that comes under your instruction to find that something through which they'll become self-determining.

One's major purpose should keep a few jumps ahead of him. What's the purpose of that? Why not lay out a definite purpose that you can catch up with tomorrow let's say. Obviously if you do that, your definite major purpose is not going to be very extensive, and you're not going to have the fun of pursuit.

The joy of pursuit is a great thing. If you've found success or if you've found your objective, there's no fun; you have to turn around and start over with something else. Life is less interesting when one has no definite purpose to be attained other than merely living.

The Hope of Future Achievement

The hope of future achievement in connection with a major purpose is among the greatest of man's pleasures. I couldn't describe that. I don't have the adequate words with which to describe the pleasure I get out of looking into the future and seeing the millions of people that I'm going to have the privilege of benefiting through my students and through the books that I will write. It thrills me to the marrow of my bones to contemplate the good that I may be able to do in the future. For as long as I live, I'll be doing something good for somebody in some way. There isn't anything that can take the place of that kind of hope. It's yet unattained, but it's a marvelous state of mind to be in.

Sorry indeed is the man who has caught up with himself and no longer has anything to do. I've found a lot of them. They're all miserable. I retired once and went down to Florida. I thought I'd get along all right without making any more money. I suppose I could have.

It was fine for the first six months, then I commenced to get itchy feet and itchy fingers. I started to tell the churches what was wrong with them. That really made me popular. Then I wasn't satisfied. I wasn't getting enough reaction there. The clergy wasn't fighting back enough, so I started dealing with the universities and colleges. Boy, that really put me on top.

Then I woke up to myself and discovered something I hope you will never discover. I found out that idleness was truly the devil's workshop, and I was in the middle of it. It took a series of severe jolts to jolt me out of that idea and put me back to work again. I'll never be caught going out of my way to retire anymore. No, you've got to keep active, keep doing something, keep working, keep having an objective ahead of you.

One's major purpose may, and it generally does, consist of that which can be attained only by a series of day-to-day, month-to-month, and year-to-year steps, because it is something which should be so designed as to consume an entire lifetime of endeavor. One's major purpose may consist of many different combinations of lesser aims, such as the nature of one's occupation, which should be something of one's own choice. In fact the major purpose should harmonize with one's occupation, business, or profession, for each day's work should bring an individual one day nearer to the attainment of his major purpose in life.

I feel sorry for the individual who is just working day in and day out in order to have something to eat and some clothes to wear and a place to sleep. I feel sorry for the person who has no aim beyond just enough to exist on. I can't imagine anybody who studies this course satisfying himself with sitting down. I think you want to live. I think you want abundance. I think you want everything that's necessary for you to do the things you want to do in life, including money.

Be sure that you definitely include in your purpose perfect harmony between yourself and your mate. Do you know of anything more important than that? Do you know of any human relationship more important than that of a man and his wife? No, of course you don't. Nobody does.

Have you ever seen or heard of a relationship of man and wife where there was no harmony? I know you have. Not pleasant, is it? It's not pleasant even to be around people who are not in step with one another. Well, you can be harmonious, and here is where you ought to start applying your Master Mind relationship first. Your wife or your husband should be your first Master Mind ally. Maybe you'll have to go back and court him or her over again, but that's nice too. I don't know of anything I ever did in my life that I enjoyed as much as courting; it's a wonderful experience. Go back and court the girl, or the man, over again.

I have a wife who doesn't belong in this world. I'm glad she's in it, but she really belongs in another world, because if there's anybody that knows all about me, knows exactly what to do at the right time to make me happy, she's that person. She could read my mind. She knows what I'm thinking about. I don't have to be around her, because she knows what's going on all the time. She knows when to turn on the inspiration when most needed. It's a wonderful thing to have a wife like that.

If you have a mate, and you can work up a relationship with that mate so that the mate complements you in every place where you're weak, you've got a fortune beyond compare, an asset that's beyond comparison with anything else in this world. That Master Mind relationship between a man and his wife can surmount all difficulties. They join their mental attitudes and multiply their enthusiasm, turning it on to places where each is in need of it.

Get on the Right Terms with Associates

If you're not on the right terms with your business associate or the people you work with every day, go back and rededicate yourself to the business of striking out on a new basis.

You'll be surprised what a little confession on your part will do. The confession is really a marvelous thing. Most people claim they have too much pride to confess their weaknesses. I'll tell you, it's a good thing to get some of the weaknesses out of your system by confession. Acknowledge that maybe you're not perfect, or not entirely. Maybe the other fellow will say, "Come to think about, neither am I," and then you're off to the races.

Rededicate yourself to a better relationship with the people that you come into contact every day, whoever they may be. You can do that. I know you can. How do I know it? Because I used to make about as many enemies, if not more, than I made friends. It took me a long time to find out why I was doing that. As a matter of fact, in the beginning, I didn't give a darn. If I didn't agree with a man, I'd go out of my way and let him know I didn't, and he didn't need to ask me either; I'd tell him about it. That can make you very popular—going out of your way to create an incident with somebody, or to take exception to somebody's statement, or to tell the other fellow how you know he's wrong. I just love to have a man walk up and say, "Napoleon Hill, I read your book, and I don't agree with it." I have that happen once in a while. It makes me feel very good, but not as good as it would if he walked up and told me, "Napoleon Hill, I read your book, I found myself, and I'm succeeding."

Most inharmonious human relations are due to neglect of people: you just neglect to build up your human relations. You can do it if you want to.

Your outline of your major purpose should include a definite plan for developing harmony in all of your relations and especially those in the home, where one works, and where one plays or relaxes. The human relationship leg is the most important one in connection with one's major aim, since the aim is attainable largely through the cooperation of others. Had you ever thought of that—that the things that you do in life that are worthwhile have to be done through harmonious cooperation with other people? How are you going to get that harmonious cooperation if you don't cultivate people, if you don't understand them, if you don't make allowances for their weaknesses?

Did you ever have a friend who appreciated that you were trying to reform him or change his mind about something? Do you like to have a friend come around and try to reform you? No, you don't. Nobody does. There are certain things you can do for a friend by example. That's a mighty effective way of doing it, but if you start to tell a man where he is wrong, chances are that the next time he sees you coming, he'll get on the other side of the street.

You can develop marvelous human relationships, but you can't do it by criticizing people and harping upon their faults, because we all have faults. A better thing to do is to talk about a person's virtues and his good qualities. I have never seen any person yet who was so low that he didn't have some good qualities. If you will concentrate upon those, the person you're concentrating on will lean over backwards to make sure that you're not disappointed.

Reach beyond Your Grasp

One should not hesitate to choose a major aim which may be for the time being out of his reach. Certainly when I chose my definite major purpose—the organizing and taking to the world of the first practical philosophy of individual achievement—it was way beyond my reach. What do you think kept me down to twenty years of effort and research? What do you think it was that kept me striving and struggling in the face of the fact that the majority of people I knew were criticizing me? What do you think it was? Because whatever it was, that's something you need.

You may say you need to have faith, but how do you get faith? Don't you have to have a motive? Don't you have to have an objective before you can have faith, and don't you have to put action in back of that objective? I had to have an abundance of faith, and I had to keep that faith alive by moving always as if I knew in advance that I was going to complete the task which Mr. Carnegie assigned to me.

At times it looked as if what my friends and relatives were saying about me was absolutely true. From their viewpoint and their standards, I *was* wasting twenty years of my time. But from the viewpoint of the millions of people who have benefited and will benefit by my work during those twenty years, I was not wasting my time. I was probably making the most useful application of my time of any author of this generation.

When you start out teaching, you won't start off with a bang, with big classes. You'll have to cut your eyeteeth, so to speak. You will have to break in. You will have to get confidence in what you're doing, and you'll have to become seasoned. That might take a few weeks, a few months; it might even take a year. But if you start complaining that it's taking a year before you get to where you can go out and lay them in the aisle, just remember, it took me twenty years. I didn't quit, so why would you?

Also think of the techniques that I have learned and am passing on to you, which you won't have to experience or pay for. I have paid the price that you would have had to pay if you hadn't come into this course. I spent the past ten years out on the coast experimenting on radio, television, lecturing, training, and advertising. There isn't a single thing in connection with the work that you're going to do as teachers about which I can't give you some counsel based upon actual experience. I'm going to shorten your probationary time greatly. You're not going to have to put in the twenty years that I did, and I wouldn't be at all surprised if I don't have a great number of people in this class who can start out within a matter of three or four months and do a bang-up job of teaching this philosophy.

You can't fail unless you think you can. If you think you can fail, then you can. If you stay around me long enough, I'll get you so you're not going to think you can fail. You will know you're not going to fail.

Purpose in Nature

The greatest demonstration of the principle of definiteness of purpose may be seen by observing nature. Nature moves with definiteness of purpose. If there is anything in this universe that's definite, it's the laws of nature. They don't deviate, they don't temporize, they don't subside. You can't go around them, you can't avoid them. You can, however, learn their nature, adjust yourself to them, and benefit by them. Nobody ever heard of the law of gravitation being suspended even for one fraction of a second. It never has been done and never will be, because nature's whole setup, throughout the whole universe, is so definite that everything moves with precision, like clockwork.

If you want an example of moving with definiteness, you only have to have a smattering of understanding of the sciences to see the way that nature does things—the orderliness of the universe, the interrelation of all natural laws, the fixation of all the stars and planets in an immovable relationship. Isn't it a marvelous thing that the astronomers can sit down and predetermine, hundreds of years in advance, exactly where given planets and stars will be in relationship to one another? They couldn't do that if there was not a purpose, a plan under which we're working.

We want to find out what that purpose is as it relates to us as individuals. That's why you're in this course. That's why I'm teaching you. I'm giving you the little bit that I have picked up from life and from the experiences of men so that you will learn how to adjust yourself to the laws of nature and use those laws instead of allowing yourself to be abused by your neglect of them.

To me, one of the most horrible things to contemplate is the possible collapse of natural laws. Imagine all of the chaos, all of the stars and planets running together if nature allowed her laws to be suspended. It would make the H-bomb look like a firecracker, but she doesn't do that. She has very definite laws to go by.

If you look at the seventeen principles that I will set out below, you will find that they check out perfectly with the laws of nature. Take the principle of going the extra mile. Nature is profound in her application of this principle. When she produces blooms on trees, she doesn't produce just enough to fill a tree. She produces enough to take care of all the damage from winds and storms. When she produces fish in the seas, she doesn't just produce just enough to perpetuate the fish; she produces enough to feed the bullfrogs, the snakes, the alligators, and all the other things and still have enough to carry out her purpose. She has an abundance, an overabundance.

Nature also forces man to go the extra mile or else he will perish. If nature didn't compensate a man when he goes out and puts a grain of wheat in the ground by giving him back five hundred grains to compensate him for his intelligence, we'd starve to death in one season. If you'll do your part, nature does her part, and she does it in abundance, in superabundance.

Use Autosuggestion

Let me go on to this rule: hypnotize yourself through autosuggestion into believing you will get the object of your desire. Do you ever try to hypnotize yourself? Have you ever been hypnotized?

Yes, you have. You're being hypnotized every day. I don't mean that you're being knocked out, but you're undergoing a degree of hypnotism all the time. You're responding to the law of suggestion, and that's a form of hypnotism.

Let's use hypnotism, not to charge our subconscious mind with negatives and fears and frustrations, but with the glorious things we want to do in life—the things that we want, not the things we don't want.

Take a successful man or a successful woman. Those people are able to so thoroughly hypnotize themselves that they can see achievement already finished before they even start it. It's a marvelous thing to be able to do that.

That's self-hypnosis. It means you close your eyes to all of the no-can-do part of the thing and focus your attention on the can-do part. One of the strange things about nature is that if you keep your mind focused on the positive side of life, it becomes greater than the negative side; it always does that. If you keep your mind on the positive side, it becomes greater than all of the negatives that may try to penetrate your mind and influence your life.

3

The Master Mind

The first premise of the Master Mind principle is that it is the medium through which one may procure the full benefits of the experience, training, education, and specialized knowledge and influence of others as completely as if their minds worked as one. Isn't it marvelous to contemplate that whatever you lack in education, knowledge, or influence you can always obtain through somebody who has it. The exchange of knowledge is one of the greatest gifts in the world. It's very nice to engage in business, where the exchange of money makes you a profit, but I would rather exchange ideas with somebody: give them an idea that they didn't have before and receive in return one that I didn't have.

You of course know that Thomas Edison was perhaps the greatest inventor the world has ever known. He dealt with many of the sciences all the time, and yet he knew nothing about any of them. You'd say it would be impossible for a man to succeed in any undertaking unless he was educated in that field. When I first talked to Andrew Carnegie, I was astounded to hear him say that he personally didn't know anything about the making or marketing of steel.

"Mr. Carnegie," I said, "just what part do you play?"

"I'll tell you the part that I play. My job is to keep the members of my Master Mind alliance working in a state of perfect harmony."

"Is that all you have to do?" I said.

"Have you ever tried to get any two people to agree on anything for three minutes in succession in your life?"

"I don't know that I have," I said.

"You try it someday, and see just what kind of a job it is to get people to work together in the spirit of harmony; it is one of the greatest of human achievements."

Mr. Carnegie went on to break down his Master Mind group to describe each individual and what part he played. One was his metallurgist, one was his chief chemist, one was his plant works manager, one was his legal advisor, one was chief of his financial staff, and so on down the line. Over twenty of those men were working together, and their combined education, experience, and knowledge constituted all of what was known about the making and marketing of steel at that time. Mr. Carnegie said it wasn't necessary for him to know about it. He had men all around him who did understand it, and his job was to keep them working in perfect harmony.

The Second Master Mind Premise

The second premise of the Master Mind principle: an active alliance of two or more minds in a spirit of perfect harmony for the attainment of a common objective stimulates each individual mind to a higher degree of knowledge than that which is ordinarily experienced, and prepares the way for that state of mind known as *faith*.

The human brain is a peculiar piece of machinery; I don't know that anybody understands it. However, we do know some of the things that can be done with the human brain. We know that the human brain is both a broadcasting station and a receiving station for the vibrations of thought, working on a very similar plan to ordinary radio broadcasting and receiving sets.

We do that when people get together. Whether they call themselves a Master Mind alliance or a church group or a social group, when a group of people get together to express enthusiasm and good humor, there is a meeting of the minds. That meeting steps up the vibrations of each mind, so that if there are fifteen or twenty people in the group or more, each one will tune in and have the benefit of that higher rate of vibration.

The radio principle works like this: You go to the broadcasting station, and you start talking. The broadcasting station steps up your voice millions of times until it's changed from audio frequency, that is, the frequency that you can hear with a human ear, to radio frequency, which is a frequency you cannot hear with the ear. The ether picks up the vibration and spreads it in all directions. Through the receiving set, the listeners pick up the vibration sent out at the radio frequency rate. It is stepped back down again to audio frequency, where you can hear it as it comes out over the tubes.

That's the way the radio works, and that's exactly the way the mind works. You can stimulate the mind to pick up information on a higher level than you can possibly get in the prosaic, everyday frame of mind that you usually are in.

One of the most important functions of the Master Mind alliance is that you can go in there and get your batteries recharged. You know that when driving an automobile every so often, the battery runs down, and you have to do something about it. You come out some morning, you step on the starter, and nothing happens. I know of people who get out of bed in the morning and do the same thing. Nothing happens except they feel bad, they don't want to put on their shoes, they don't want to get dressed, they don't even want to eat breakfast. What do they need?

They need to have their batteries charged, of course, and they have to have a source for it. As a matter of fact, if a man gets up in the morning feeling like that, he can have a little talk with his wife. If she's a good coordinator, she helps to charge his batteries. If the wife is not a good coordinator and lets him get away in that frame of mind, chances are he'll come home empty-handed.

The Third Master Mind Premise

The third premise: a Master Mind alliance, properly conducted, stimulates each one in the alliance to move with enthusiasm, personal initiative, imagination, and courage to a degree far above that which the individual experiences when moving without such an alliance.

In my own early beginning, I had a Master Mind alliance of three people. I had an alliance with Mr. Carnegie and with my stepmother. We three people nursed this philosophy through the stages when everybody else was laughing at me for undertaking to serve the richest man in the world for twenty years without any compensation. There was logic to what they were saying, because at that time I wasn't getting very much compensation, at least in the way of money. There came a time, however, when the laughing was on the other side of the fence, although that took a long time. There were plenty of blood and tears shed, I'll assure you, before I got to the point at which I could laugh back at the people that laughed at me.

The relationship between us three people—my stepmother, Mr. Carnegie, and myself—enabled me to offset the mockery that was thrown at me by my relatives and my friends. If you undertake anything above mediocrity, you're going to meet with opposition, you're going to meet with people who poke fun at you, and most of them will be close to yourself. Some of them will perhaps be your own relatives.

When you're going to aim above mediocrity, you need some source to which you can turn to get your batteries charged and keep them charged so that you won't quit when the going is hard and won't pay any attention when somebody criticizes you.

Criticism falls off my back just like a water off a duck's back or like a bullet off a rhinoceros's head. I'm absolutely immune to all forms of criticism: whether it's friendly or unfriendly makes no difference to me whatsoever. I became immune because of the relationship with certain people through my Master Mind alliance. If it had not been for the relationship with my stepmother and Mr. Carnegie, I wouldn't be standing here talking to you folks tonight, you wouldn't be here as students of this philosophy, and this philosophy would not be spread all over the world helping millions of people, because I had a million opportunities to quit. And every one of them looked very alluring. Sometimes it almost seemed as if I was stupid if I didn't quit. But I had this marvelous relationship. I could always go back to Mr. Carnegie, I could always run into my stepmother. We'd sit down and have a little chat, and she'd say, "Stand by your guns; you'll come out on top. I know you will."

At a time when I didn't have two nickels to rub together, as my enemies were saying, my stepmother said, "You are going to be the richest member of the Hill family far and away. I know it, because I can see it in the future." I suspect that I have more riches than all of my relatives put together for three generations back on both sides of the house. My stepmother could see that. She could see that what I was doing was bound to make me rich. I don't have reference to monetary riches. I have a reference to those higher and broader riches that you find when you can render service to many people.

The Fourth Master Mind Premise

The fourth premise: to be effective, a Master Mind alliance must be active. You can't just form an alliance with somebody and say, "We've got it. I'm lined up with this person, that person, and the other person; we've got a Master Mind alliance." It amounts to absolutely nothing until you become active. Every member of the alliance has got to step in and start pitching in mentally, spiritually, physically, financially—every way that is necessary. They must engage in the pursuit of a definite purpose, and they must move with perfect harmony.

Do you know the difference between perfect harmony and ordinary harmony? I suspect that I have had harmonious relationships with as many people, maybe more, than any person living today. But I want to tell you that perfect harmony in relationships is just about the rarest thing in the world. I think I could count on the fingers of my two hands all of the people that I now know with whom I have a relationship of perfect harmony. I have a nice, polite speaking acquaintance with a lot of people, but that's not perfect harmony. I have a working alliance with a lot of people, but that's not perfect or permanent harmony.

Perfect harmony exists only when your relationship to the other fellow is such that if he needed and wanted everything you have, you would willingly and immediately turn it over to him. It takes a lot of unselfishness to put yourself in that frame of mind.

Mr. Carnegie stressed time and time again the importance of this relationship of perfect harmony, because he said that if you don't have perfect harmony in the Master Mind alliance, it's not a Master Mind alliance. Without harmony, the alliance may be nothing more than ordinary cooperation or a friendly coordination of efforts.

The Master Mind gives one full access to the spiritual powers of the other members of the alliance. I'm not talking about just the mental powers or the financial powers, but the spiritual, thought powers. And the feeling that you have when you begin to establish permanency in your Master Mind relationship is going to be one of the most outstanding and pleasant experiences of your entire life. When you're engaged in a Master Mind activity, you have so much faith that you know that you can do anything that you start out to do. You have no doubts, you have no fear, you have no limitations, and that's a marvelous frame of mind to be in.

The Fifth Master Mind Premise

The fifth premise: it is a matter of established record that all individual success based upon any kind of achievement above mediocrity is attained through the Master Mind principle and not by individual effort alone.

Do you have any idea how far you would get in the world if in your occupation you decided to stand alone and not depend upon anybody else? Imagine how little you could accomplish if you didn't have the cooperation of other people.

Suppose you're in a profession, suppose you're a dentist or a lawyer or a doctor or an osteopath, and suppose that you didn't understand how to convert each one of your clients or patients into a salesman for yourself. Imagine how long would it take to build up a clientele. Outstanding professional men understand how to make salesmen out of every person that they serve. They do it all indirectly. They do it by going an extra mile, by going out of their way to be of unusual service, but they do make salesmen out of all of their clients. Emotional touches are the result of personal power, and personal power of sufficient proportions to enable one to rise above mediocrity is not possible without the applications of the Master Mind principle.

During the first term of Franklin D. Roosevelt in the White House, I had the privilege of working with him as a confidential advisor. It was I who laid out the skeleton of the propaganda plan that took the words *business depression* out of the headlines of the papers and instead substituted *business recovery*.

Those of you who remember what happened on that Black Sunday, when the banks were closing the following Monday morning, remember what a stampede there was in this country. All over the country, people were lined up in front of the banks to draw out their deposits. They were scared to death. They had lost confidence in their country, in their banks, in themselves and everybody else. They still had some confidence in God but didn't show much sign of it. It was a scary time, I'll tell you.

We had a meeting down at the White House, and we sat down and worked out a plan that created one of the most outstanding applications of the Master Mind that this nation has ever seen. I doubt that any nation on earth has ever had the equal of it, because it was only a matter of weeks until we had taken all that fear out of people. It was only a matter of days until salesmen on the road who had run out of funds, who couldn't get money, were laughing and not in any way scared about it.

My own funds were closed. I had money; yes, I did. This is funny. I got very smart when I found out what was coming, and I had a $1,000 bill. Nobody could change it. I might just as well have had only ten cents. It wasn't worth a nickel. But I wasn't scared, because everybody else was in the same boat that I was in. Even so, something had to be done about it.

Franklin D. Roosevelt was a great leader. He had great imagination, and he had great courage. Here's what we did. First of all, we got both houses of Congress working in harmony with the president. For the first time in the history of this nation, both houses of Congress, Democrats and Republicans alike, got behind the president and forgot about their political faiths. In other words, there were no Democrats, there were no Republicans: they were just Americans backing the president with everything he needed in order to stop that stampede of fear. I had never seen anything to equate to it in my life. I never hope to see it again, because there was a great emergency on then, and something had to be done about it.

Second, the majority of the newspaper publishers of America published everything that we sent out. They gave it marvelous space. The radio station operators gave us marvelous help despite their political beliefs. And the churches, all the denominations—that was one of the most beautiful things I've ever seen in this country: Catholics and

Protestants, Jews and Gentiles, and all of the rest pulling together as Americans.

It was a wonderful time. They all got behind the president. Every one of them made some sort of a contribution toward reestablishing people's faith in this country.

What a marvelous thing it'd be about now if some great renaissance would come along and knit together all of the forces of this nation in one grand undertaking to sell the American people. They would sell the unprecedented privileges that people enjoy as American citizens. That's what they need to be sold. You and I and all the rest of us—we are taking too many things for granted.

Did you know that there were less than thirty men down in Washington who control this country from stem to stern? You think you've got some four hundred members in the house, the lower house, and ninety-six members in the Senate? There are around five hundred representatives down there. You think they are representing you as individuals, standing up for your individual rights, and playing quite a part in affairs. Perish the idea. Around thirty men—the leaders of the political parties—are calling the cards. And for the first time in the history, I saw all of those leaders get together, come over to the White House in a friendly way, find out what the president wanted done, and then went ahead and did it. There was no bickering; there was no fighting.

I don't know what it was, but everybody in this country practically thought that Franklin D. Roosevelt came straight from heaven during these tremendous days. I thought so myself. There were some people later on who decided that maybe he came from the other place. (I wasn't responsible for that.) But during these hectic days, there wasn't any doubt in the minds of the majority of the people. I didn't come in contact with anybody who didn't think that Mr. Roosevelt was the finest man, the only man, that could possibly have handled that chaotic condition.

Don't get me wrong politically. I'm just talking about a great man who did a great job at the time when it needed to be done. He did it because he had a Master Mind alliance right out there that was unbeatable.

Master Mind Alliances

Let's look at the different kinds of Master Mind alliances. First of all, there are alliances for purely social or personal reasons, consisting of relatives, friends, and religious advisors, where no material gain is involved. The most important of this type is the Master Mind alliance between a man and his wife. If you are married, I can't overemphasize the importance of going to work immediately and rededicating that marriage to a Master Mind alliance. It will bring joy, health, and success into your life that you never dreamed of. It's a marvelous thing when a real Master Mind alliance exists between a man and his wife. I don't know of anything that equals it.

Then there are alliances for business or professional advancement, consisting of individuals who have a personal motive of a material or financial nature connected with the object of their alliances. Now I imagine that the majority of you who are studying this now will be forming your first Master Mind alliances for purely economic or financial advancement purposes, and that's perfectly legitimate. You want to improve your economic and financial conditions. You should start in immediately now to form a Master Mind alliance for that purpose.

If you begin with one person, that's all right; start out with one, and then look around until the two of you select another one. You alone can't select the third party; it must be the two of you. When you select the third party, be sure that the second one is in the call. The three of you together then will decide on the fourth, and you'll go over the matter very carefully before you make a new member of the alliance. Then the four of you will select the fifth.

In the Master Mind alliance, there's no such thing as one person dominating except in this respect: generally speaking, one person is the coordinator and leader, but he in no way undertakes to dominate his associates, because the very moment you start to dominate anybody, you'll find resistance and rebellion. Even though it's not open rebellion, it's rebellion nevertheless. And the Master Mind alliance is supposed to be one continuous spirit of perfect harmony, where you move and act as if you were only one man.

The modern railway system is a marvelous example of the application of the Master Mind in industry. There's not always perfect harmony in relationship of the employees of a railway, but there is respect for authority, as anybody knows who's worked for a railroad company. There has to be respect for authority; otherwise, railroads couldn't operate.

The American system of free enterprise is another example of the Master Mind principle. This system is the envy of the world because it has raised the American standard of living to an all-time high level, even though there's not perfect harmony. But there is motive in the American system of free enterprise to inspire every individual to do his best.

Incidentally, more and more industry and business are coming to understand that they can go a step further: instead of just having cooperation or coordination of effort between management and the workers, they can use the Master Mind principle by sharing the management problems, by sharing the profits, by sharing everything. Wherever I have been successful in influencing any business to adopt that policy, the business has made more money than it ever made before, the employees have received more wages, and everybody's happy.

One of the most extensive examples of this practice is the McCormick Tea & Spice Company of Baltimore, Maryland. That's one of my products. Before the plant that they now operate was put into operation, there were gripes, complaints, and dissatisfaction. Any foreman could fire a man without the consent of anybody else. Today it takes five times as long to fire a man in the McCormick Company as it does to hire a man. No one individual can fire anybody, not even the president of the company. Why? Because if a complaint is filed against a man, he's given a hearing by the management and by an equal number of his fellow workers. He's got a chance to try his case, in other words. If in the final analysis, they do agree unanimously to let him out, they don't just let him go and find another job; they look around until they find him a job with some other company where the particular thing that caused them to let him out would be no objection. Isn't that a wonderful thing for a firm to do?

Six Qualities of an Employee

If you want to know my idea of Applied Christianity, ladies and gentlemen, that's it. That's not just theory, but doing unto others as if you were the others—becoming your brother's keeper. What a wonderful thing it is, if you have to disassociate your relationship with anybody, to shake hands from the heart and say, "The fortunes of life just seemed to be such that we can't go farther together. Your path goes in one way and mine in another. I wish you success with all my heart." If you can say that to a person when you come to a parting of the ways and mean it, what a joyous thing it would be to you and to the other fellow, but that's not the way we part company. We usually do it with anger, pulling hair, epithets, and uncomplimentary remarks about the other fellow.

As far as I've been able to determine, Christ and his twelve disciples constituted a Master Mind alliance, which, although it was meek and with little power to begin with, has extended itself to become one of the great powers of the world.

You know what happened when one of those disciples once betrayed the master: he met with the supreme catastrophe of his life.

I have seen that same thing over and over and over again in human relations, in business, in the professions, and in the home—where somebody went sour and became disloyal. I'm helping Mr. Stone to build a great organization that eventually will be international. Do you have any idea of the first two qualities that I look for in all of the employees that we'll take on from here on out?

Loyalty and *dependability*. Dependability is at the top of the list. If a person is not dependable, I don't want any part of him in a business transaction, no matter how brilliant or well educated he may be. The more educated he is, the more dangerous he may be if he's not dependable.

And if he's not loyal, I would say the same thing. If an individual is not loyal to those to whom he owes loyalty, then to me he has no character whatsoever, and I want no part of him.

Dependability and loyalty. After those two comes *ability* to do the job. Notice that I placed ability down at third place. I'm not interested in a man's ability until I find out whether he's dependable and loyal.

Number four is *positive mental attitude*, of course. What good is a negative wet blanket around you? You could pay him to stay away and then be ahead of the game.

Number five is *going the extra mile*. And number six is *applied faith*. When you find people that come up to all of those six traits, you've really found somebody. You're in the presence of royalty.

The Rotary Clubs constitute a marvelous illustration of the Master Mind. But there is a weakness to the Rotary Club, which is why they don't 100 percent illustrate the potentials of the Master Mind.

They have no definiteness of purpose, no outstanding program. As Bill Robinson says, they come down, eat, burp, and go home. That's not meant to disrespect the Rotary Club—I was a member of the first one—but what he said about the Rotary might be true for practically all of the other clubs too. A lot of them are doing wonderful things in a small way, but they need a great overall program.

Just think what would happen if the Rotary Club, the Kiwanis, Lions Club, Exchange Club, and all of the other clubs started to proselytize to this nation. Just think what they could do. It would be terrific; the potential and power available would be out of this world. Just think what would happen if the Lions Club, for instance, would take this philosophy and sponsor it all over this nation and start study clubs in every city where there's a Lions Club. Then they could take part of the profits and use it to organize Boys Clubs in each town.

There is an idea for you: Boys Clubs. I hear a lot of talk about delinquency among youth, especially among boys. If the boys had clubs with things to interest them, they wouldn't be engaging in destructive habits. It would be a marvelous thing if all of the Lions Clubs would get back to that idea all over the world. There's already a Boys Club that I had the privilege of speaking before last week, sponsored by the Marshall Square Lions Club, and they're doing marvelous work.

In any Master Mind alliance, to get together in the spirit of good fellowship, as they do in Rotary, is wonderful, but it doesn't go far enough. They ought to have some dynamic, outstanding program through which they will be rendering useful service, helping others and helping themselves.

Forming a Master Mind Alliance

Now I want to go into the instructions for the formation and maintenance of a Master Mind alliance.

First, adopt a definite purpose as an objective to be attained by the alliance, choosing individual members whose education, experience and influence are such as to make them have the greatest value in achieving the purpose.

A lot of times I'm asked, what is the most favorable number for a Master Mind alliance, and how do you go about selecting the right sort of people for your Master Mind alliance?

The procedure is exactly the same as if you were starting into a business and you were choosing employees: what kind of an employee would you choose? You would choose one who could do the thing that you need to have done in that business.

How many? That would depend upon the volume of business you're going to do. If you're only running a peanut stand or two, you may need only one person, but if you're running a chain of peanut stands, you might need a hundred persons.

As for the qualifications for those in a Master Mind alliance, first of all, take those six points that I have already given you: they are the qualifications for your Master Mind. There must be dependability, loyalty, ability, positive mental attitude, willingness to go the extra mile, and applied faith. If you want to know what the qualifications of your Master Mind allies are, there they are, and don't settle for anything less. If you find a man that has five of those qualities and doesn't have all six of them, you'd better be wary, because they're all central in a Master Mind relationship.

You can check carefully and see that that's true. You couldn't have perfect harmony unless you are working with somebody who checked out 100 percent on all of those six fronts. You couldn't have a Master Mind alliance. You might have a working arrangement, as many people do, but it wouldn't embrace all of the potential values of the Master Mind.

Next, determine what appropriate benefit each member may receive in return for his cooperation in this alliance. Remember, nobody ever does anything for nothing.

You may say that when you give love to somebody, you don't get anything out of that; you don't do that for nothing. Let me tell you something. You get plenty out of it, because to have the privilege of loving is a great privilege. Even though the love is not returned, you still have had the benefit of that state of mind known as love, and you've enjoyed development and growth as a result of it.

There's no such thing as something for nothing. Nobody works without some sort of compensation. There are many different forms of compensation, so don't expect that your Master Mind allies are going to jump in and help you make a fortune—or help you do anything—unless they are equally participating in the benefits that come out of that Master Mind alliance.

There's the criterion that you go by: each individual must benefit approximately equally with yourself, whether it's a monetary or social benefit or happiness or peace of mind.

Then also give consideration to the nine basic motives, which prompt people to do and refrain from doing everything they do all the way through life. Never ask anybody to do anything unless you give an adequate motive for doing it.

If I went down to the bank and wanted to borrow $10,000, what would be an adequate motive for the bank to lend me that money?

Two motives, both under the heading of financial gain. The bank will be delighted to lend me as much money as I can take away if I give them three for one security. They want collateral, and they want the profit on that loan. That's what they're in business for.

Now there are other transactions that are not based upon the monetary motive. For instance, when a man asks a girl of his choice to marry him, what's the motive there?

Love? Sometimes. Theoretically, but not always. I have known a lot of marriages that had nothing to do with love on either side.

I want to tell you that when my father brought my stepmother home, he was just a farmer and he never had on a white shirt or a tie. He was afraid of white shirts and ties; he wore blue cotton shirts. My stepmother was a college woman, she was well educated, and they were as different as the North Pole and the South Pole.

She cleaned him up and put a white shirt on him and made him look like somebody. Nevertheless, it took her quite a while to do it. Finally she finally got him into the money, and he became an outstanding man. One day I said to her, "How in the world did my father ever sell himself to you? What was the motive?"

She said, "I'll tell you. I recognized that he had good Anglo-Saxon blood in his veins, so he had possibilities that I believed that I could bring out," and she did. A lot of times a woman will marry a man because she sees that he has possibilities. Sometimes it's the monetary consideration, sometimes it's love, sometimes it's one thing and sometimes another. But every time anybody engages in any transaction, there is a motive back of it, you can be sure of that.

Whatever it is that you want anybody to do, pick out the right kind of motive and plant it in the mind under the proper circumstances, and you will become a master salesman.

Next establish a definite plan through which each member of the alliance will make his contribution in working towards the achievement of the object of the alliance, and arrange a definite time and place for the mutual discussion of the plan. Indefiniteness here will bring defeat. Keep a regular means of contact between all members of your alliance.

Have you ever had a great friendship with somebody and then suddenly saw it grow cold and die? Most of us have, to be sure. What do you think was the reason for it?

Neglect. That's all—neglect. If you have very close and dear friends, the only way you can keep them is to keep in contact constantly. It may be nothing but an occasional postal card. I have one student who was a member of my class in New York City in 1928. She never has missed a single one of my birthdays to send me a card. One time she was off on vacation, and she forgot it until mid-afternoon of my birthday; she sent me a telegram congratulating me. In other words, she has been the most constant student that I've ever had out of the many thousands all over the country. As a result of that close attention that she's given me, there have been times when I had been able to help her in a business way. I got her a promotion that amounted to about $4,000 a year, which is quite a little payoff for keeping in contact.

You have to keep in contact with your Master Mind allies. You have to have regular meeting places. You have to keep them active. If you don't, they grow cold, they grow indifferent, and finally they're of no value to you.

Club Success Unlimited

You have an opportunity to benefit by the Master Mind principle first as a member of Club Success Unlimited, where all members will cooperate for the purpose of helping one another to attain his or her definite major purpose or solve personal problems. If the solution cannot be found in your club, it can be passed on to the executive staff at Napoleon Hill Associates, and in time we will have executive staff there with the answers to all reasonable problems.

Don't you see what a marvelous thing you have? You have not only just purchased the privilege of attending this course, you've purchased an alliance from here on out. If you make intelligent use of it, then that alliance is going to pay off for the rest of your lives, no matter what you do with this philosophy. But you'll have to keep the relationship alive. If you just go out after this course is over and forget about us, we will forget about you. An old saying—out of sight, out of mind—is just as true it can be. Keep up the alliance. We have valuable contacts that you can use just for the asking. When we find out what your needs are, we turn immediately to our card index of contacts, and they're all over this world. If you needed something in India, for instance, I could contact you with the most powerful men in India who would give you every consideration. If you needed something in Brazil, I could contact you with powerful men in Brazil on the telephone. I can get somebody on the telephone in a matter of a couple of hours at most. Anywhere in the British Empire, I could give you a marvelous professional or business or social contact. I could give it to you because my whole life has been devoted to building up friendly contacts: people who would go out of their way to accommodate anybody that I might introduce to them. I want you to use the valuable connection that you have here in this course. That's what the Napoleon Hill Associates are for. We're here to serve the people who are taking this philosophy and in turn help them do a better job of serving other people.

By forming your own alliance with other members of this class who are mutually agreeable for the attainment of any desired purpose, you will find some perfectly marvelous alliances.

The Power of Remarkable Women

Mrs. Henry Ford and Mrs. Thomas E. Edison are two of the outstanding examples that I use time and time again to show what a woman can do to make her husband successful. Had it not been for Mrs. Ford's understanding of the Master Mind principle (although she didn't call it with that name), Mr. Ford would never have been known, the Ford Motor Company never would have been here, and I doubt if the automobile industry would have been ushered in as it has been. It was Mrs. Ford that kept him going, kept him alert, and kept him filled with confidence in himself when the going was hard and when other people were criticizing him in connection with this contraption, as they called it, that was only designed to scare horses. Mrs. Ford sustained him through those trying hours when the going was hard.

All of you will experience such periods in your life. At some point, the going is hard for everybody. I had over twenty years of it. The marvel is that I had the endurance, spiritually and mentally and physically, to go through what I did. It must have been a great purpose. There must have been somebody looking over my shoulder that I didn't see.

4

Applied Faith

Your education, your background, your nationality, your creed have nothing whatsoever to do with your ability to achieve. It's the state of mind that you maintain. That's the thing that determines how and what and when you achieve. To me, that's the most profound thing in all of the knowledge of mankind: the fact that a person can take possession of his own mind. He can color it any way he chooses; he can project it into high places or into the gutter. He can make it a success, or he can make it a failure: just the change of his mental attitude will change it from success to failure almost instantly.

Your mental attitude will do the same thing with your physical health. Had you ever thought about that? I went down to Jackson, Mississippi, a year ago to deliver this entire Master Course in five nights for a dental group. I had to lecture four hours every night. From 8 a.m. until 12 p.m., I was writing scripts and recording radio programs for the local station. From one o'clock in the afternoon until four, I was interviewing each of my students, listening to their problems, and giving them the answers. The rest of the time I was just twiddling my thumbs, fooling around.

I had gone down there with the flu. My doctor said that instead of going on a lecture campaign, I should be going to the hospital. When the end of the week came, I had whipped the flu, and I had found out that my mind could take care of any unusual circumstance if I wanted to do it. I want to tell you that there's not enough money in the United States Treasury to pay me to undertake to do a job like the one I did down there if I had been doing it only for money. I wouldn't have submitted my physical body to that kind of a test. But I came out of it in flying colors. I had no ill effects; I've never felt better in my life. I learned a great lesson: that there are no limitations to the human mind except those that you set up in your own mind. I think that's one of the one of the most glorious and profound experiences in my whole life.

I found out something that I didn't know. Namely, that there are no limitations to what you can do to your physical body or for it with your mind.

A burning desire is the material from which faith is created. A burning desire is an obsession. Obsession means a desire that takes possession of you; it obsesses you. Now there are a lot of desires in the world, but they are not burning or obsessional desires. Most people in their whole lives have never experienced an obsessional desire for anything. We start off with faint hopes and wishes. Everybody wishes for a lot of money without having to work for it. People wish for a Cadillac when they're driving a Ford; they wish for a mink coat when they are wearing a quilted coat.

I went down to Miami, Florida, with Mr. Stone to address a convention of his state managers. In the speech, I told the wives of the men how easy it would be for them to have mink coats instead of rabbit coats and how easy it would be for the men to have Cadillacs instead of Fords. You know what? They had no better sense than to believe me. The wives went to work, and almost every day, we're hearing of some wife of a manager who's bought a new mink coat or a new Cadillac.

Then I was invited to go down to Richmond, Virginia, and tell that story over again to the group down there. They want to learn how to get Cadillacs and mink coats. I told them the same thing that I'm telling you here: that there's no limitation to your mind. If you want a mink coat, don't settle for anything less; see that your husband gets out and earns enough money to buy it. If you want a Cadillac and you make up your mind to have it, put into your work that which will entitle you to the Cadillac. If you don't want a Cadillac, chances are you'll drive a Ford for the rest of your life.

You have to want things. You have to want them with a burning desire, and then you have to do something about the burning desire. What is it?

Action. You've got to start in right where you stand, showing that you do have faith in your ability. Start right where you stand with action.

There are many examples of individuals of achievement, but there is one that I particularly want to call to your attention: Miss Helen Keller, who believed that she would learn to talk despite the fact that she had lost the use of her speech, her sight, and her hearing in her early life. Can you imagine that? She couldn't hear, she couldn't see, and she couldn't speak. And yet Miss Helen Keller became one of the best-educated women in the world. She's more in contact with public affairs and civic affairs and conditions all over the world than nine tenths of the women who have all of their senses. It is an outstanding thing, and all she has to go on is vibration. If you speak to her, she puts her fingers up to your lips; she can tell what you are saying by her fingertips—entirely by vibration. Think of a woman who has a handicap of that kind all the way through life, getting joy out of life, rendering useful service, making speeches. She has learned to talk; she is doing a great work where the majority of people with any one of those afflictions would have settled for a tin cup and a bunch of lead pencils on a street corner.

While I was on the staff of Franklin D. Roosevelt, every day at the corner of Pennsylvania Avenue—the street running by the White House—I passed a man sitting with a tin cup and some pencils. I became acquainted with that man. He had lost the use of his legs; he had exactly the same affliction as Franklin D. Roosevelt, and it happened about the same time. I found out that he had an even better education than Franklin D. Roosevelt had, but there he was, with a tin cup and pencils, trying to eke out a living by begging. Just a block away there was a man with the most important and responsible position in the whole world, running a great nation, who also lost the use of his legs, but this man had lost the use of his brain; he had lost confidence in himself.

These physical losses sometimes turn out to be great blessings. Very often they teach us that we can get along without an eye or without legs or without hands. We can get along without a lot of things if we have the right mental attitude toward what's left of us. That's important.

If you would have faith, keep your mind on that which you want and *not* on that which you do not want. Now how do you go about that?

Look up the word *transmute* in the dictionary and see what it means. You know in a general way, but look it up, because that way it will be more impressed in your subconscious mind.

The way you keep your mind off things you don't want is to transfer your mind over to the things you *do* want and start talking about them, giving thanks for already possessing them. It sounds silly to anybody who doesn't know what you're doing, but it won't sound silly to you, because you know what you're doing. You're talking to your subconscious mind; you're reeducating yourself. You're keeping your mind fixed on things you want and off the things you don't want. In order to do that you have to keep talking. You have to keep thinking. You can't talk without thinking (some people can, but most of them can't). Keep on talking about things you want.

If you ever feel blue or discouraged or lacking in courage, I'll tell you a good remedy. Sit down, take a writing tablet, and start numbering. Number one, write down the thing that you want most in life. Number two, the thing that you want the next most. Number three, the thing you want next most after that. When it gets down to the kind of house you live in, describe the lot that you want it on— whether you want it on a lot of acreage on top of a hill, down below the road, or above the road; how many rooms you want that house to have; how you want each room furnished. You will have a grand time furnishing those rooms. It's better than window shopping because you can go the limit in your mind. In window shopping, you only have two legs and you can only walk so far. Do a little mental window shopping and, believe you me, you will get your mind over that mood. You will get it onto something constructive, and you'll be educating your subconscious mind to keep on the right side of the street.

The assignment I'm giving you now is not foolish. It's not facetious. It's a real assignment, and you'll get real joy out of doing it. Start right in doing something physically. When anything bothers you, write down the things that you want.

I don't know why it is that when a person makes up his mind about what he wants and becomes determined to get it, all the powers of the universe seem to come to his aid to see that he gets it. I don't know why that is, but I know *that* it is, and that's enough for me. There are a lot of things in this world that I can see and a lot of advantages I can use that I don't understand, but I don't need to understand them. I know which button to press to get the result I want. I don't need to know what happens between the pressing of that button and the result. I know that if you can follow the instructions in this philosophy, you will be able to take possession of your own mind, get the things out of life that you want, and make life pay off on your own terms.

How, do you suppose, would I know that a person can actually make life pay off point by point on his own terms instead of accepting the circumstances? There is only one way in this world that I could possibly know that, and that's from my own experience. I can tell you sincerely that there aren't any of the best of things in this world that I want that I don't have or can't get easily. Not anything.

What an astounding statement that is in contrast to what I might have said a few years back, before I'd learned the secret of getting everything that I want. There was a time when I was carrying around in my own pocket the matches with which I was setting my house of opportunity on fire, but I didn't know it. I finally got rid of those matches. I began to build that house of opportunity, and the contents of the house resemble the picture of it that I built in my mind, right down to the finest detail.

There is no such thing as a blanket faith. You must have a definite objective, a purpose, a goal, before you can have faith in anything. Faith is a mental attitude wherein the mind is cleared of all fears and doubts and directed toward the attainment of something definite through the inspiration of infinite intelligence.

Faith is guidance; it is nothing more. It's not going to go out and get you that Cadillac, or that mink coat, or that new house, or that better job, or that better business with all those clients that you need—faith is not going to do that. But faith will guide you as to how you can do it, and you will find that there is always a part you must play. The Creator wisely arranged it so that we can produce our food from the soil of the earth. Everything that we eat, use, or work with comes from the earth—everything. And infinite intelligence has wisely provided a system whereby you can be sure of getting your food out of the soil of the earth. By complying with the laws of nature, you go out and plant the seed. You plant it in soil that you have examined to make sure it has the elements that you want in the plant. You plant it at the right season. You plant it at the right depth in the ground. All of those things you do by way of going the extra mile; you do them in advance. Then what do you do? You go back the next day and start harvesting, do you?

No. You time it properly, you find out what nature requires in order to transmute a seed of wheat into a stalk of wheat with five hundred or a thousand grains. And you comply with nature's law.

It's the same thing identically in connection with faith. You expect guidance, but you have to do your part. You always will find that there is a part that you must do in connection with a demonstration of faith. Faith will do nothing for you if you expect everything to be done for you outside of yourself.

Faith probably works through the subconscious mind. Why do I use the word *probably*? Because nobody knows definitely whether it does or not. It's a theory, and for want of a better theory, I'm using it. Faith appears to work through the subconscious mind, which acts as the gateway between the conscious mind and infinite intelligence. My mental picture of what happens when you pray properly is that you first condition your mind—you know what it is you want—and then you transfer a clear picture over to your subconscious mind. The subconscious is the intermediary, the gatekeeper, between you and infinite intelligence. It's the only thing that could turn on the power of infinite intelligence for you. It is the only way you can reach into infinite intelligence, in my book of rules. If that isn't correct, as far as I'm concerned, it might as well be correct, because that's the way I get it to work.

Steps in Developing Faith

Now let's look at the essential steps in the development of self-reliance based on faith. If there's anything that people need more than anything else, it is self-reliance: belief in yourself.

Here are the most important ones. First of all, adopt a definite major purpose and begin at once to attain it using the instructions described in chapter 1. That's the first step in building self-confidence. When you know what you want, and you start in getting it, you have a measure of self-reliance. You're demonstrating a measure of self-reliance, because if you didn't believe in yourself, you wouldn't even begin, would you? The very fact that you start, even though you're a long way from attaining the thing you're going after, shows that you have a measure of self-reliance. The more you pursue that idea, the stronger that belief will be.

Next: associate as many as possible of the nine basic motives with the object of the definite major purpose. In other words, when you go after anything, inspire yourself with as many of those nine basic motives as possible.

In order to get something that you want very badly—say, extra money—you begin to connive and work out some sort of scheme to earn more money. My little son Blair, when he was about six or seven years old, wanted a nice electric train that cost $50. It was more than we felt we could give him at that time, because we'd have to give the other two children $50 gifts too. I told Blair that, and he said, "Oh, I didn't ask you to buy me anything. I just wanted your approval to buy the train, because I've already got it picked out; I've got the order made out." And he had: Lionel train, $50.

The next day came a big snow. Blair borrowed a shovel from the janitor and went down the street cleaning off the sidewalks. The people all came out and got into a conversation with him. "Oh," he said, "I thought I'd be a nice thing to clean off your sidewalk. I see you haven't started doing it yet. I thought it would be nice, if you'd appreciate it." Invariably they would give him a quarter, a half dollar, sometimes a dollar; one man gave him $5. Long before the end of the month, he had his $50, and $10 more that he earned himself. His mother thought he ought not to be permitted to do that: it kind of disgraced us to let him go out down the street cleaning off sidewalks. "Well," I said, disgrace aside, "they've found out who we are that we can raise a child like this." How did we do it? Motive.

Write out a list of all the advantages of your definite major purpose, and call these into your mind many times daily, thereby making your mind success-conscious. Did you know that in order to be healthy, you have to be health-conscious? No matter what other precautions you take, if your mental attitude is not health-conscious, if you're not thinking in terms of health, if you're not expecting to be healthy, you're not going to be, no matter what else you do.

It's the same thing with success. If you accept any kind of a fear complex or an inferiority complex, if you don't expect success of yourself and develop a success expectation or consciousness, you're not going to be a success. If your major purpose is to achieve some material thing or money, see yourself already in possession of it. It is of vital importance to call it into your consciousness, because, again, your power of faith is coming into play. If your faith isn't great enough that you can see the thing already in your possession even before you start to get it, then you are not making use of applied faith.

Associate with people who are in sympathy with you and your major purpose, and let them encourage you in every way possible. This has reference only to close friends or members of your Master Mind alliance. Don't disclose your aims and purposes to people who are not absolutely dependable, loyal, and close to you. Sometimes people to whom you disclose your ideas—if they're good ideas—go around the corner and beat you to the draw, and they're using your ideas before you use them, or they say something to discourage you.

Let not a single day pass without making at least one definite move towards the attainment of your major purpose, and choose some prosperous, self-reliant person as your pacemaker—someone who paces you, not only to catch up with him, but to accelerate.

I hope and pray with all of my might that every single one of my students that goes into the business of teaching will make up his mind that he's going to surpass Napoleon Hill, and is going to do it pronto. You have my 100 percent cooperation and heartfelt sympathy in helping you do that. A teacher worthy of the name always wants to develop students that surpass the teacher. I'm going to do just that, and I'll tell you why: because you have so many more facilities at your command now than I had when I started. In other words, we have the equipment with which to help you do much more in a much shorter time than I ever did. I can't imagine any intelligent person with a reasonable education not taking the lectures that you're getting here without weaving it into a fine job of teaching. You'll be surprised at how quickly you're going to become able teachers, every one of you that follow the instructions.

Faith is a positive mental attitude in action. Your mental attitude is reflected in every word you speak, and it speaks louder than your words. Your mental attitude is the sum total of your thoughts at a given time. A positive mental attitude has its roots in the spiritual will. Mental attitude is the medium by which adversities may be transmuted into benefits.

Find some suggestions that appeal to you, print them out on a card, or in some form where you can put them up and see them each day and make them your own. Surround yourself with suggestions. Everywhere you look, you'll see something that suggests a positive mental attitude. You'll notice when you go into the office or home of a successful person, you will find that oftentimes he is surrounded with pictures of those whom he considers great. Oftentimes you see mottos on the walls. I've seen hundreds of them.

I walked into my friend Jennings Randolph's office when he was in Congress in Washington, and I found that all of the walls were covered with the pictures of men whom he considered great. He did it to live in the environment of the great, in the environment of things that kept his mind positive.

Start in while you're in your home, in your business, in your office, wherever you stay the most. Maybe it's in your bedroom, where you sleep every night. Put up something that will give you a positive thought just before you go to bed and will remind you of it every time you go in there. You will be surprised how much good it will do you.

5

Going the Extra Mile

The next topic is going the extra mile. That means rendering more and better service than you're paid to render, doing it all the time, and doing it with a pleasant mental attitude.

One reason there are so many failures in the world today is that the majority of people do not even go the first mile, let alone the second. Oftentimes, if they do go the first mile, they gripe as they go along and make themselves a nuisance to people around them.

I don't know of any one quality or trait that can get a person an opportunity more quickly than to go out of his way or her way to do a favor or do something useful for somebody. It's the one thing that you can do in life that you don't have to ask anybody for the privilege of doing. You can always step your services up and go out of your way to do something kind, even when you belong to a labor union, and they don't want you to lay a thousand or twelve hundred bricks when you can easily do it. There is a way of getting around that too. If you belong to a labor union and have to conform to the rules, there's nothing to hinder you from making yourself pleasant and smiling when you work and attracting the attention of somebody who will give you a better job, where you won't have to observe union rules. There's nothing to hinder you from doing that.

As a matter of fact, you might just as well make up your mind that you can never be free, self-determining, and financially independent unless you form the habit of going the extra mile and making yourself as indispensable as you possibly can. I don't know of any way that anybody can make himself or herself indispensable except by going the extra mile, rendering some service that's you're not expected to render, and rendering it with the right mental attitude.

Mental attitude is important. If you gripe about going the extra mile, the chances are that it won't bring you very many returns.

The Example of Nature

Where do I get my authority for emphasizing this principle of going the extra mile? Experience. I get it by looking around and watching the way nature does things. Anytime you can follow the habits of nature, you're not going to go wrong. Conversely, any time that you fail to recognize the way nature does things and fail to go along, you're going to get into trouble sooner or later. There is an overall plan by which this universe operates; no matter what you call it, the first cause or the Creator, there's just one plan. There's just one set of natural laws. It's up to every individual to discover those natural laws and adjust himself to them.

If there is one thing that stands out above all others in nature, it is that nature requires every living thing go the extra mile in order to eat, live, and survive. Man wouldn't survive one season if it were not for this law of going the extra mile. For instance, when the farmer goes out and sows his seed in the ground, he puts out one grain of wheat, let us say, and then he does what? He times it.

That timing is important. Don't render a million dollars' worth of service in a day and expect to go and get a bank check for tomorrow. In other words, if you start off rendering a million dollars' worth of service, you will perhaps have to wait a little bit of time, and you'll have to get yourself recognized. While you're going through that period of recognition, the chances are that you'll not be compensated for going the extra mile. Chances are that you will have to go the extra mile for quite a little while before anybody takes notice of it.

But always be careful. If you go the extra mile too long without somebody taking notice of you, and if the right fellow doesn't take notice, look around until you find the fellow who will. That's equivalent to saying if your present employer doesn't recognize you, fire the employer sooner or later, and let his competitor know what kind of service you're rendering. Have a little competition as you go along.

The Law of Increasing Returns

Nobody ever accepts a rule or does anything without a motive, and I have outlined here a great variety of reasons for going the extra mile.

One of the most adequate reasons that I know of for going the extra mile is that it places the law of increasing returns behind you. The law of increasing returns means that you will get back more than you give out, whether it's good or whether it's bad, whether it's positive or whether it's negative; that's the way the law of nature works. Whatever you give out, whatever you do to or for another person or whatever you give out from yourself comes back to you greatly multiplied in kind. There is no exception to that whatsoever.

Again there is a question of timing. The process of coming back doesn't always occur quickly. Sometimes it takes longer than you expect. But you may be sure that if you send out negative influences, they're going to come back on you sooner or later. You may not recognize what caused them, but they'll come back. They won't overlook you. The law of increasing returns is eternal, it's automatic, it's working all the time, and it's just as inexorable as the law of gravitation. Nobody in the world can circumvent or suspend it for one moment. It is operating all the time.

The law of increasing returns means that when you go out of your way to render more and better service then you are paid to render, it's impossible for you *not* to get back more than you are paid for, because eventually the law of increasing returns takes care of that. If you're working for a salary, for instance, the law takes care of it in additional wages, in greater responsibilities, in promotions, in opportunities, or in going into business for yourself. It'll come back in 1,001 different ways.

Oftentimes your rewards won't come back from the source for which you render the service. Don't be too afraid to render service to a greedy buyer or greedy employer. It makes no difference to whom you render this service. If you render it in good faith and in good spirit and keep on doing it as a matter of habit, it's impossible for you not to be compensated.

That was one thing that puzzled me back in the early years. When I commenced to experiment with these laws, I observed that I would render a lot of service to people who didn't even thank me. I used to let a lot of people into my classes without paying, and I found out that practically every one of them caused me trouble in one way or another and that hardly any of them got any benefit out of the classes. You see, people who are expecting something for nothing have a hard time of getting away with it. That's the law of increasing returns.

When you start applying this principle, you don't have to be too careful about the person to whom you render it. As a matter of fact, you should apply this principle with everybody you come into contact, no matter who it is: strangers, acquaintances, business associates, and relatives alike. Make it your business to render useful service wherever you touch human relations in any shape, form, or fashion.

Quality and Quantity of Service

The only way to increase the space that you occupy in the world will be by the quality and the quantity of the service that you render.

(By the space that you occupy, I don't necessarily mean your physical space, but your mental and spiritual space.) The quality and the quantity of the service, plus the mental attitude in which you render it, will determine how far you will go in life, how much you will get out of life, how much you will enjoy life, and how much peace of mind you will have.

Rendering service also brings one to the favorable attention of those who can and do provide opportunities for promotion. Go into any organization, and if you are alert and take notice, you will quickly find out which people are going the extra mile. You'll also find out that they're the ones that get the promotions. They don't have to ask for them; it's not necessary at all, because employers are naturally looking around for people who will go the extra mile. Doing extra tends makes one indispensable in many different human relationships, and therefore enables one to command more than the average compensation.

The Pleasure of Doing Good

Going the extra mile also does something to your soul inside. It makes you feel better. If there were not another reason in the world for going the extra mile, I'd say that would be adequate. A lot of things in life cause us to have negative feelings and unpleasant experiences. This is one thing that you can do for yourself that will always give you a pleasant feeling. If you go back in your own experiences, I'm sure that you will remember that you never did a kind thing without getting a great deal of joy of it. Maybe the other fellow didn't appreciate it—that's unimportant. It's just like love; to have loved alone is a great privilege. It doesn't make any difference whatsoever whether your love is returned by the other person. You've had the benefit from the emotion of love itself.

So it is with the principle of going the extra mile. It will give you greater courage. Just stepping out and making yourself useful to somebody will enable you to overcome inhibitions and inferiority complexes that you've been storing up through the years.

Don't be too surprised when you do something courteous or useful for somebody who is not expecting it, and they look at you in a quizzical way, as if to say, "I wonder why you're doing that." Some people will be a little bit surprised when you go out of your way to be useful to them.

Going the extra mile also leads to mental growth and physical perfection, thereby developing greater ability and skill in one's chosen vocation. Whatever you do in life, whether it is teaching this course, delivering a lecture, making up your notebook, or filling your job, make up your mind that every time you do it, you will excel all previous efforts on your part. In other words, you're a constant challenge to yourself. You will find how quickly and rapidly you will grow if you'll go at it that way.

I have never delivered a lecture in my life that I didn't intend to deliver better than I did previously. I don't always do it, but that's my intention. It makes no difference what kind of an audience I have. I put just as much into a small class as a big one, not only because I want to be useful to my students, but because I want to grow and develop. Out of effort, out of struggle, out of use of your faculties comes growth.

Profit from the Law of Contrast

The habit of going the extra mile also enables one to profit from the law of contrast. Have you ever thought about that? You won't have to advertise that one very much; it'll advertise itself, because the majority of people around you are not going the extra mile. If everybody did, this would be a grand world to live in, but you couldn't cash in on this principle as definitely as you can now, because you'd have a tremendous amount of competition. Don't worry: you're not going have this competition. I can assure you, you will practically be in a class by yourself.

In some cases, people with whom you're working or with whom you're associated may be shown up for not going the first mile, let alone the second one, and they won't like it. Are you going to cry about that, quit, and go back to your old habits, just because the other fellow doesn't like what you're doing?

Of course not. It's your individual responsibility in this world to succeed. That's your sole responsibility, and you can't afford to let anybody's ideas, idiosyncrasies, or notions get in the way of your success. You should be fair and just with other people. Beyond that, you're under no obligation to let anybody's opinion stop you from going out and being successful. I'd like to see the person that could stop me from being successful, and I want you to feel that way about it too. I want you to make up your mind that you're going to put these laws into operation and that you're not going to let anybody stop you from doing it.

Developing a Positive Attitude

Going the extra mile also leads to the development of a positive, pleasing mental attitude, which is the most important trait of a pleasing personality. As a matter of fact, it's the first trait of a pleasing personality.

You can easily change the chemistry of your brain so that you're positive instead of negative. How? By getting in that frame of mind where you want to do something useful for the other fellow without rendering service with one hand and picking his pocket with the other. Doing it just because of the goodness of doing it, knowing that if you render more and better service than you're paid to render, eventually you will be paid for more than you do, and paid willingly. That's the way the law works. That's the law of compensation, and it's an eternal law. It never forgets. It has a marvelous bookkeeping system. You may be sure that when you're giving out the right kind of service with the right mental attitude, you're piling up credits for yourself somewhere that sooner or later will come back to you multiplied.

The habit of going the extra mile also tends to develop a keen alert imagination, because it keeps one continuously seeking new and more efficient ways of rendering useful service. You begin to look around and see how many places, how many ways and means, there are of helping other people to find themselves. In helping the other fellow to find himself, you find yourself.

The Benefits of Helpfulness

When you have a problem or an unpleasant situation and you don't know how to solve it, even though you've tried everything you know, there is always one thing that you can do. If you will do that one thing, the chances are that you not only will solve your problem, but you will learn a great lesson.

What is the one thing that you can do? Find somebody who has an equal or a greater problem, and start then and there to help that other person. Lo and behold, it unlocks something in you that permits infinite intelligence to come into your brain and give you the answer to your problem.

I don't know why that works, but I know that it does work. Do you know why I can make that statement so positively? From trying it out hundreds and hundreds of times myself and seeing my students try it hundreds and hundreds of times. What a simple thing that is!

I don't know what it does to you. I don't know why it works. There are lot of things in life that you don't know. Then there are some things that you do know but don't do much about. This is one that I don't know anything about, but I do something about. I follow the law because I know that if I need my own mind to open up to receive opportunities, the best way is to see how many other people I can help. I never deviate from that rule; I never have, ever since I assimilated this philosophy. (Previous to that time I did deviate, and I didn't get very far.) Look around, find out somebody who needs your service and start rendering it.

Mr. Stone and I were up at the School of the Ozarks last week. While I was up there, I found a marvelous outlet for some of my energies in going the extra mile. I decided, "I'm going to put on this philosophy up there for those mountain boys and girls. We're going to donate the course to that school, and I'm going to go up there and teach it myself. At least the first class."

The school was elated when they found out that I was going to do that, because they expected it would cost them a lot of money they didn't have. "Well," I thought, "there isn't the money enough in the world to pay me for what I'm going to get from rendering that kind of service for those poor boys and girls up there—Napoleon Hill as he was back in the days when he was even worse off than they are. I know what this philosophy can do for them, and I am going to see that they get it."

It was a joint decision between Mr. Stone and myself, and no one knew that we made that decision. Then a major donor to that school, who supplied many hundreds of thousands of dollars for buildings, came and opened negotiations with Napoleon Hill Associates to have his eight hundred employees take our home study course.

Almost instantaneously my bread cast on the water came back, and it had a lot of butter and jam on it. It paid off handsomely. And that's not the only thing. This man is the majority stockholder in the great J. C. Penney stores. Before we are through, not only will we have this man's eight hundred employees, but we'll have many times that many employees of the J. C. Penney stores.

We didn't go up there looking for contacts; we didn't go up there looking for anything except a chance to deliver a message to those boys and girls. We delivered it with the right mental attitude, and things began to happen immediately. That's how quickly you can change your life when you get into this business of going the extra mile and doing it in the spirit of being helpful to other people.

Developing Initiative

This practice also develops the important factor of personal initiative. It gets you into the habit of looking around for something useful to do and doing it without somebody telling you to do it. Old man procrastination is a sour old bird, and he causes a lot of trouble in this world. People put off until the day after tomorrow things they should have done the day before yesterday. We're all guilty of it, every one of us. I'm not free of it, but I'm freer than I was a few years back.

I can find a lot of things to do now. Why do I find them? Because I get joy out of doing them. Anytime you're going the extra mile, you're going to get joy out of what you're doing; otherwise, you won't be going the extra mile.

Fostering Definiteness of Purpose

The habit of going the extra mile builds the confidence of others in one's integrity and general ability. It also develops definiteness of purpose, without which one cannot hope for success. That alone would be enough to justify it. It gives you an objective, so you don't go round and round in circles like a goldfish in a bowl, always coming back to where you started with nothing that you didn't start out with. Definiteness of purpose comes out of going the extra mile.

This habit also enables you to make your work a joy instead of a burden. You get to the point where you love it. And if you're not engaged in a labor of love in life, you're wasting a lot of your time. I think one of the greatest joys in the world is being permitted to engage in the thing that one would rather do than all other things.

Joy

And surely, when you're going the extra mile, you're doing it exactly because you don't have to do it. Nobody expects you to do it. Nobody asked you to do it. Certainly no employer would ask his employees to go the extra mile. He might ask them to help out once in a while, but he wouldn't do it as a regular thing. So it's something that you do on your own initiative, and it gives a dignity to your labor, even if you're digging a ditch: you're helping somebody. The dignity attached to that takes the fatigue and unpleasantness out of the labor.

Believe me, I've spent a lot of time burning midnight oil and later, and I didn't consider it hard work at all. It was my own idea. I only used my initiative, but I got a lot of joy out of doing it, and I made it pay off.

What application have you ever made of this principle that gave you the greatest amount of joy? Someone might say, being married. When you're courting the girl of your choice or being courted by the man of your choice, it's marvelous how much sleep you can lose. Wouldn't it be wonderful if you could put the same attitude into your relations with people professionally or in business as you put into courtship?

We're going to do just that. We're going to start sparking again. It is going to start at home with our own mates. Believe me, I couldn't begin to tell you the number of married couples that I have started in on a new sparking spree. They've gotten a lot of joy of it. It saves a lot of friction, a lot of argument, and it cuts down expenses.

I don't mean to be facetious about this. I'm very serious when I say that this is one of the finest places in the world to start going the extra mile. Be careful about springing it on your wife too suddenly. One of my students started doing it right away, and his wife became so suspicious that she got the Pinkerton Detective Agency to watch him day and night. He finally caught on to the fact that she was watching him, and he came down to ask me what I could do about it. What happened? He went to the store and bought some nice lingerie—the kind that he hadn't been buying her for years—a nice bottle of French perfume, and a big bouquet of flowers. He bought her too much all at once. She thought he'd been up to something and was trying to pay it off.

Have a Sales Talk

When you start going the extra mile with somebody, sit down and have a little sales talk with them. Tell them you've changed your attitude, and you want a mutual agreement for both partners to change their attitude from here on: "All of us are going the extra mile. We're going to relate on a different basis, and out of it we'll all get more joy, more peace of mind, and more happiness in living." If you went home tonight and had that speech with your mate, it wouldn't hurt, and it might help.

As for that person in business that you haven't been getting along so well with—if you went in tomorrow morning with a smile and walked over to him, took his hand, shook it, and said, "Now, listen, pal, from here on I would like you and me to enjoy working together. What do you say?" It wouldn't work? Oh, yes it will. Try it and see.

One thing that does more damage in this world than anything else is that little thing called pride. Don't be afraid. Don't be afraid to humiliate yourself if it's going to make better relations with the people that you have to associate with all the time.

Earning Obligations from Others

Finally, going the extra mile is the only thing which gives one the right to ask for promotions or more pay. You don't have a leg to stand on in going into the purchaser of your services and asking for more money or promotion unless for some time previously you have been going the extra mile, doing more than you're paid for. Obviously if you're doing no more than you're paid for, then you're being paid for all you're entitled to, aren't you? So you have to first start going the extra mile and putting the other fellow under obligation to you before you can ask any favors from him. If you have enough people whom you have put under obligation to you by going the extra mile, when you need some favor, you can always turn in one direction or another and get it. I don't need to borrow $1,000 or $5,000 or $10,000 or $25,000. But if I did, I know at least a half dozen places where a telephone call would get me the money without even having to ask for it. I would just say that I needed it. Why? Because I have established those contacts: people are under obligations to me for favors that I've done for them. I know at least a dozen multimillionaires who started out from scratch and who owe their fortunes to me. If I want to have $25,000 from them, they couldn't very well refuse me. Of course, I'm not going do it, but if it's a nice thing to know that you have that kind of credit hanging around, isn't it? I want you to have that kind of credit with other people, and I want to teach you the technique by which you can do that.

Nature Goes the Extra Mile

We get our cues to the soundness of the principle of going the extra mile by observing nature. As I've said, nature goes the extra mile by producing enough of everything for her needs together with a surplus for emergencies and waste. Blooms on the trees. Fish in the seas—you don't just produce enough fish to perpetuate the species, you produce enough to feed the snakes and the alligators and to account for those that die of natural causes, with still enough to perpetuate the species. Nature is most bountiful in her business of going the extra mile. In return, she is very demanding in seeing that every living creature goes the extra mile. Bees are provided with honey as compensation for their services in fertilizing the flowers in which the honey is attractively stored, but they have to perform the service to get the honey, and it must be performed in advance.

You've heard it said that the birds of the air and the beasts of the jungle neither weave nor spin, but they always have enough to eat. But if you observe wildlife at all, they don't eat without performing some sort of service, without working, without doing something before they can eat. Pick a flock of common old cornfield crows, for instance. They have to organize. They're traveling flocks. They have sentinels, and they have codes by which they warn one another. They have to do a lot of educating before they can even eat safely.

Nature requires man to go the extra mile. All food comes out of the ground, and if he's going to have food, he's got to plant seed. He can't live entirely on what nature provides. We have to plant our food in the ground. We have to clear the ground first. We have to plow it. We have to harrow it. We have to fence it. We have to protect it against predatory animals, and all of that costs labor and time and money. And all of it has to be done in advance, or you're not going to eat.

I wouldn't have any trouble at all in selling this idea, that nature makes everybody go the extra mile, to a farmer. He knows that beyond any doubt. He knows every minute of his life that if he doesn't go the extra mile, he doesn't eat, and he doesn't have anything to sell. The farmer clears his ground; he plants his seed. He selects the seed with care to make sure that's the right kind of seed and that it's fertile. He plants it at the right depth in the ground, and then he times the entire transaction.

I want to emphasize the importance of timing. Can a new employee going into a new job come right in, start going the extra mile, and then immediately demand top wages or the best job in the place? It just doesn't work that way. You have to establish a record, a reputation. You have to get yourself recognized in this business of going the extra mile before you can put pressure on to get compensation back. As a matter of fact, if you go the extra mile with the right mental attitude, the chances are a thousand to one you'll never have to ask for compensation according to the service you rendered, because it'll be given to you automatically in the way of promotions and increased salary.

The Law of Compensation

Throughout the whole universe, everything has been so arranged through the law of compensation, so adequately described by Emerson, that nature's budget is balanced, so to speak. Everything has its opposite equivalent in something else. Positive and negative in every unit of energy, day and night, hot and cold, success and failure, sweet and sour, happiness and misery, man and woman. Everywhere and in everything, we see the law of action and reaction in operation. Every act causes a reaction of some sort. Everything you do, everything you think, every thought that you release causes a reaction, if not on somebody else, then on the person releasing the thought. As a matter of fact, when you release a thought, you're not through with it. Every thought that you express, silently even, becomes a definite part of the pattern of your subconscious mind. If you store enough negative thoughts in that subconscious mind, you'll be predominantly negative. If you follow the habit of releasing only the positive thoughts, your subconscious pattern will be predominantly positive, and you will attract to you the things you want. If you're negative, you repel the things that you want and attract only the things you don't want. That's a law of nature too.

Going the extra mile is also one of the finest ways that I know of for educating your subconscious mind to attract to you the things you want and to repel the things you don't want. You can put it down as an established fact that if you neglect to develop and apply this principle of going the extra mile, you will never become personally successful, and you will never become financially independent.

I've had the privilege of observing a great many thousands of people, some of whom applied the principle of going the extra mile and some of whom did not, and I have had the privilege of finding out what happened to those who did and to those who didn't. I know beyond any question of a doubt that nobody ever rises above mediocrity or the ordinary station in life without the habit of going the extra mile; it just doesn't happen. If I had discovered just one case where somebody went on to the top without going the extra mile, I would say there are exceptions. But I am in a position to say there are no exceptions, because I have never found that one case. And I can definitely tell you from my own experiences that I have never had a major benefit of any kind in the world that I didn't get as a result of going the extra mile.

When I started with Carnegie, he gave me three hours and then requested that I stay three days and nights in addition. I didn't have to do that; my magazine didn't pay me for those three days and nights. During those three hours, I had all that I went after, which was a story about Mr. Carnegie.

Not only did I stay three days and nights when I was not sure that I would have enough money, but I made myself pleasant. I made myself pleasant enough that I impressed Mr. Carnegie as the one that should give the world his philosophy. I would say that paid off pretty handsomely.

I'm giving you a great variety of illustrations of this principle, but please get up ones of your own. They don't all have to be Andrew Carnegies or Thomas A. Edisons or Henry Fords or even Napoleon Hills. Take the shoeshine boy or anybody that's making himself successful by going the extra mile, and use him as an illustration.

It took me a long time to learn that if you talk too much about these men that I've been associated with, you scare off a lot of people, because they don't aspire to become Henry Fords or Edisons. They just want to be ordinary people with enough to get along on to have independence, good health, and peace of mind. Don't scare those people who don't want to hit the top of the pile, so to speak, by using illustrations that they think they can never equal.

You take this fellow Napoleon Hill. I don't know whether you've heard it or not, but he's the guy that put in twenty years of useful labor working for the richest man in the world without compensation. At least that's what his brothers and his father said. That's what all of his acquaintances said (except his stepmother): he was making a fool of himself to work for the richest man in the world for twenty years without any compensation. The guy had little enough sense to stick by it. He must have been a weak-minded fellow.

The time came finally when this fellow Hill didn't even ask Andrew Carnegie for traveling expenses. He was able to pay his own. He didn't need Mr. Carnegie. That's something, isn't it?

When this fellow first started up, he needed letters of introduction to get him into see these other men, and then came a time when he didn't need Mr. Carnegie for that. He could make his own introductions.

Now that's what I want you to do. I want you to become self-determining, so you can do these things without the help of anybody. That's the time when the payoff will come: when you can go out and do anything in this world that you want to do. Whether anybody wants you to do it or whether they want to help you or whether they don't, you can do it on your own. That's one of the grandest, most glorious feelings that I know. Whatever I want to do, I can do it. I don't have to ask anybody, not even my wife. (But I would, because I'm on good terms with her.) Now there are ways and means of putting yourself in that position.

A Potent Opportunity

As far as I am able to determine, there has never been an author in my field of endeavor who has worked up as definite and as large a following and one in which the relationship is as fine as it is between myself and my followers.

My relationship with my students is out of this world. It does something to them, and it does something to me. That's why I like to see people come into my classes. Even if they've read every book that I have ever written, even if they've memorized the books, I still want them to come in and get a little hunk of Napoleon Hill's sincerity of preparation, his enthusiasm, and his faith, because that takes root and begins to grow, and then it becomes your personality and not mine.

First of all, I have a friendly following of many millions of people who have benefited by the philosophy. I don't honestly know exactly how many millions, but I do know that between thirteen and fourteen million copies of *Think and Grow Rich* have been sold outside of the United States, and we estimate that for every copy that has sold, at least five people read it. That's around seventy million people outside of the United States, and goodness knows how many inside the United States. Out in California, they made a survey and determined that one out of every three people in that state is a follower of Napoleon Hill, has his books, or has read them in the libraries. We made a survey of all the major libraries in the United States, and the consensus was from all of them that *Think and Grow Rich* led all books of all kinds initially, and it's still doing it.

I don't need to apologize for what I'm saying. I don't even need to tell you that I'm not boasting, because whatever I am, you will become. I'm only introducing you to the very potent opportunity that you've got in this philosophy. It will not only be a big help in this world, but it will be of help to yourself too, because when you go out into the world occupying more space in the minds and hearts of people, you're occupying more space in your own mind and your own heart.

My books are in demand. I could contract with any publisher that I choose in my field of publishing for any book that I might write today, even before it's written. Once I was not in an enviable position. When Carnegie gave me this opportunity, I didn't have sense enough to turn it down, as my brother said I should have done. I've always suspected he had a selfish motive in wanting me to turn it down because I had contracted to pay our way through Georgetown University Law School, and that left him on his own. It was two years before he could go ahead with his education, but he did go ahead and earned it. I think it's one of the finest things could have happened to him: that he earned his education instead of depending on me to pay for it. He's never told me, but I've always suspected that it was a good thing for him.

Then there's my radio program. Think about taking a radio program and pitching it onto one of the big stations of the country and having it click from the very first time without a buildup. It just never has been done. Anybody in the radio field will tell you it's an impossibility. And I would have too in the beginning, if I hadn't cut that word *impossibility* out of my dictionary a long time ago. The program went on KFWB, one of the large stations of Los Angeles in 1947 through 1950, three years, summer and winter, with no vacations, as is customary in the radio field, and it led all other programs combined on that station. I had some pretty keen competition, believe you me.

How do I know that happened? You can't tell just from a survey, because they telephone a lot of people and they make averages. We didn't guess at anything, because the mail was the determining factor. There were, I believe, 657 replies on average to every broadcast. They told me at KFWB—and I've since corroborated that in other radio circles—that for everyone who wrote in there were probably a thousand listening who did not write in. This meant that I had over 650,000 people listening every Sunday afternoon.

Why do you suppose that program led all others without a buildup? What were the factors that entered into it?

Number one, I had been building up a tremendous credit account down through life that entitled me to commence getting that kind of results. Number two, my books had been distributed widely in California before I went out there. Number three—and this is probably the most important one—this program was not in competition with any other program. There was nothing else like it, and it was dealing with the listeners' personal success. Anytime you start talking to anybody about increasing his personal success, you don't have to be brilliant, you don't have to be too effective, because he will keep on listening as long as you're giving any information he may be able to use.

That's why that program clicked the way it did. That's why this philosophy is going to click for you when you get out, because it's potent and people want it. There isn't anybody so successful who doesn't want more success.

There's your chance to go the extra mile. I started with a little group of people. Even if it's only two or three in your home or in the place where you work, every time I release a lesson to you, go right back and try it out on somebody else to see how you get along. You'll be surprised at what will happen. Never mind about how much you're going to get out of it. Start by doing it. If you can't find anybody else to try it out on, try it on your wife, your husband, or your children. You may have to reduce it to terms that younger people can understand. But whenever you're interpreting this philosophy for other people, you're doing something for yourself. You'll find that you'll never do a good job of learning and applying this philosophy until you start teaching it to other people. Then you're really going to grow. I've been at it now actively since 1928, and I've been growing all the time and having a grand time doing it. And I should continue to grow as long as I live because of the joy that I get out of growing and seeing other people grow under my influence.

Peace of Mind

Then there's a little item that's not to be sniffed at—the peace of mind that I got out of all those twenty years of going the extra mile.

Do you have any idea how many people in the world are willing to do anything for twenty years in succession without getting something back from it? For that matter, do you have any idea how many people there are who are willing to do something three days in succession without being sure they're going to get something out of it?

You'd be surprised to find out how few there are. It's overlooking one of the grandest opportunities that a human being could possibly have, especially here in this country of ours, where we really can create our own destiny and express ourselves in any way we want. Speeches are free, activities are free, education is free—it's a wonderful opportunity to get right in and go the extra mile in any direction you want to travel. Yet most people are not doing it. That's all to the good for you, because if all people were successful, they wouldn't need you as a teacher.

Incidentally, during my entire career, I have never seen the time when the whole world was so ready and so right for this philosophy as it is today. People all over the world are suffering with fear, frustrations, disappointments, and inferiority complexes. It's due to the unsettled political situation as much as anything else. I've never seen politicians sink so low in attacking one another as they're doing today. I have never seen such a sight in my whole life, which means that there are a lot of sick people in this world. Therefore you, the doctors, will have plenty of patients to look at.

As far as I'm concerned, there's nothing wrong with these times. They're just made to order for this philosophy. I have seen the time when not so many people were interested in their flaws because they were prosperous, they were doing all right, they had no troubles to speak of. Today everybody almost has troubles, or thinks he has. If he reads the Hearst papers, he has one kind of troubles; if he reads the *Daily News*, he has another kind; if he reads the *Tribune*, he has all kinds. If you read the newspapers, you find a lot of things wrong with the world.

Instead of finding out what's wrong with the rest of the world, I try to find out what I can do to correct this guy here. I have to eat with him, I have to sleep with him, I have to wash and shave his face every morning, I have to give him a bath now and then. You have no idea how many things I have to do for him. And I have to live with this guy twenty-four hours a day. So I put in my time trying to improve myself and, through myself, trying to improve my friends and my students by writing books, delivering lectures, teaching, and in other ways. It pays off very much better than if I took any of the papers and read all of the murder stories, the divorce squabbles, and everything else that's blazoned across the pages every day.

For this fellow on the podium, who didn't have sense enough not to decline Andrew Carnegie's offer to work twenty years for nothing, his declining years will be years of happiness because of the seeds of kindness and help he has sown in the hearts of others.

If I had my life to live over again, I'd live it just exactly the way I had. I'd make all the mistakes I had made. I'd make them at the time in life when I made them, early, so I would have time enough to correct some of them. And the period during which I would come into peace of mind and understanding would be in the afternoon of life, not in the forenoon, because when you're young, you can stand trouble; you can take it. But when you pass the noon hour and go into the afternoon, when your energies and mental capacity oftentimes are not as great as they were before, you can't take as much trouble as you used to. You haven't got so many years left to correct the mistakes that you made.

To have the tranquility, the peace of mind that I have today, in the afternoon of life, is one of the great joys that have come out of this philosophy. If you asked me what my greatest compensation has been, I would say that's it, because so many people at my age, and even much younger, haven't found peace of mind. They never will, because they're looking for it in the wrong place. They're not doing anything about it; they're expecting somebody else to do something about it for them. But peace of mind is something that you've got to get for yourself; you've got to earn it.

I think my greatest book has not yet been published. It has been written for three or four years, and I'll release it sooner or later. It tells how to get peace of mind. As a matter of fact, its title is *How to Get Peace of Mind*. Actually I didn't write the book; I lived it; I lived it for forty years. I couldn't have written it until I found myself and I found the clue, the formula, to how anybody can get peace of mind.

You have to start looking for it, not where the average person looks—out there in the joys of what money will buy, in the joys of recognition and fame and fortune—but in the humility of your own heart.

I get peace of mind mostly behind that inner wall that is as high as eternity, where I go in for meditation many times each day. There is where I get my real peace of mind, and I can always withdraw into that inner wall, cut out every earthly influence, and commune with the higher forces of the universe. What a grand thing that is, and anybody can do that: you can do that. When you get through this philosophy, you'll be able to do anything you want to do just as well or better than me.

I'm hoping, incidentally, that every student that I turn out will eventually excel me in every way possible. Maybe you will take up where I left off and write better books than I've written. Why not? I haven't said the last word in my books, in my lectures, or in anything else. As a matter of fact, I'm just a student. I think I am a fairly intelligent student, but I'm just a student on the path, and the only state of perfection I have is that I have actually found peace of mind and how to get it.

Now when you start teaching people this philosophy and you get on to this subject, you need a lot of illustrations, and these things I've been saying about myself for the last few minutes will come in handy. Because you know me and my background, you know that I've been telling you the truth. If anybody questions it, there's always plenty of evidence that I have been telling the truth.

These personal illustrations are very potent from the viewpoint of pedagogy. When you tell a person that a thing works in such and such a way, and you know it works that way because you did it or the other fellow did it, that's impressive. But if you tell a fellow that a thing works and don't give him any illustrations of how it has worked, he's not sure you're right. He's accepting what you say as an opinion, but not necessarily as a fact.

Now the illustrations that I've given you here all are based upon absolute cases that I have observed, and you are at liberty to use as many of them as you choose.

An Assignment

Now I want to give you an assignment: engaging in at least one act of going the extra mile every day. You can choose your own circumstances; if it is nothing more than telephoning an acquaintance and wishing him good fortune, it'll only cost you a dime. You'll be surprised what will happen to you when you begin to call up your friends, whom you have been neglecting for some time, and just say, "Hello, you were on my mind. I was thinking about you and I just wanted to call up and say, how are you doing? I hope you are feeling as good as I am."

You'd be surprised at what that will do to you and what it will do to the friend too. It doesn't have to be a close personal friend. As a matter of fact, it doesn't even have to be anybody you know. It can be somebody you don't know, but want to know. I got a call at my office in Washington one rainy afternoon from one of the most pleasant, million-dollar female voices that I've ever heard. She said, "Mr. Hill, I want to make a date with you, sir, and would you be good enough to tell me yes?"

I said, "Well it just depends on where, when, and why."

"I want you to come over to Woodward & Lothrop department store and come up to the men's clothing department. I have something to show you that I think you will take pleasure in seeing. Would you do that for me?"

I said, "I'll be right over."

I was very curious. Of course, the place where she made the date seemed safe enough. I was quite sure that the other people in the store would protect me if anything happened. When I got over there, there was another man, and she was selling him a raincoat. It was a rainy day, and believe me, she was doing all this business. I not only bought a raincoat, but I bought a suit of clothes before I got out of there. She didn't know me, and I didn't know her, but there was something in her voice that made me want to know her.

Did you know that selling by telephone is becoming one of the most outstanding ways of selling today? In every case, you're talking to somebody you don't know. But you put that something in your voice, and then what you say to that person creates a personal contact.

You see, I wasn't so far wrong after all in saying you could call up somebody you don't even know. Of course, you have to have a motive, and you have to sell the other person the motive satisfactorily, or you won't get very far calling up a stranger.

Another way of going the extra mile is to relieve some friend from duty for half an hour or so, or have some neighbor send over his children while he attends the movies. You might do a little babysitting for one of your neighbors. You're going to be at home anyway. Maybe you've got some children of your own. Maybe you know some neighbor who would like to get off and go down the movies, but she can't get away from her children. I know children are noisy, and they'll probably fight with your children, but if you are a real diplomat, you'll keep them apart. She'll be under obligations to you, and you feel that you've really been kind by helping out somebody who otherwise wouldn't have had a little freedom.

Most housewives don't get any wages. They work twenty-four hours a day. They go through all kinds of trials and tribulations, and it seems to me they oftentimes don't get too much out of life, especially when they're rearing young children. It'd be a nice thing for some of you who don't have any children to say, "Why don't you and your husband go out to a movie or a show and let me come over and babysit for you?" Certainly most of you would have some neighbor that you could approach on some such basis.

It's not so much what you do for the other fellow , it's what you do for yourself by finding ways and means of going the extra mile. Did you know that both the successes and the failures in life are made up of very little things, so little, in fact, that oftentimes they're overlooked? The real reasons for success are overlooked because the things that make success are so small and seemingly insignificant.

I know some people who are so popular that they couldn't have an enemy. They just couldn't have an enemy. One of them is my distinguished business associate, Mr. Stone. I don't believe that Mr. Stone could have a permanent enemy; I just don't think he could. He's too considerate of other people. He goes out of his way. He not only goes the second mile, he goes to the third and the fourth, the fifth, the sixth, and the tenth. Look how prosperous he is. Look at how many people are going the extra mile for him. There are a lot of people who, if they didn't make good money working for Mr. Stone, would pay him a salary to work for him. I heard one say just that, and he's become immensely wealthy himself by working for Mr. Stone. He said, "If I didn't make money out of working for him, I'd pay him if I had to. It'd be just for an association with him."

Mr. Stone's not different from you or me or anybody else, except in his mental attitude towards people and towards himself. He likes to go the extra mile. Sometimes people take advantage of that and don't act fairly with him. I've seen that happen too. He doesn't worry about that too much. Heck, he doesn't worry about anything at all, because he's learned to adjust himself to life in such a way that he gets great joy out of living and gets great joy out of people.

You may write a letter to some acquaintance offering him encouragement. In your job, you may do a little more than you're paid to do—stay a little longer on the job, make some other personnel a little more happy. When you are prepared to teach this philosophy, you may establish a sound basis for yourselves by adding a new student to your complimentary training class each week until your class reaches capacity. That free service might well turn out to be the most profitable service you ever rendered.

Incidentally, this is a training school for teachers because I want to multiply myself by at least a thousand teachers before I stop. I'm not going to do all that training myself, but I hope to get a lot of people here in this class who will train the next class. There's a great opportunity for you to attract and bring into this philosophy people to whom you can give an opportunity that's not to be matched anywhere else in the world.

6

A Pleasing Personality

Now I want to introduce you to the most wonderful person in the world. That's the person sitting in your seat right now. When you commence to break down that person point by point—in accordance with the twenty-five factors that go into making a pleasing personality—you'll find out just exactly where you're wonderful and why.

I'm going to ask you to grade yourself as I set out these twenty-five factors. Give yourself the rating that you think you're entitled to, and it can be anything from 0 to 100 percent. When there's a doubt, don't overrate, don't give yourself the benefit of the doubt. Give the questionnaire the benefit of the doubt and rate yourself down rather than up.

When you get through, add up the total, and divide it by 25. That'll give you your average rating on a pleasing personality, and if you rate all the way through a general rating of 50 percent, you're doing very fine. Some of you will rate much higher than that, I hope.

1. Positive Mental Attitude

The first trait of a pleasing personality always is a *positive mental attitude* because nobody wants to be around a person who's negative. No matter what other traits you may have, if you don't have a positive mental attitude, at least when you're in the presence of people, you're not going to be considered to have a pleasing personality. Rate yourself on that anywhere from 0 to 100. If you can rate 100 on that, you will be up in the class with Franklin D. Roosevelt. That's pretty high.

2. Flexibility

The next one is *flexibility*. By flexibility, I mean the ability to unbend, to adjust yourself to the varying circumstances of life without going down under them. A lot of people in this world are so staid in their habits and their mental attitude that they cannot adjust to anything that's unpleasant or anything that they don't agree with.

Do you know why Franklin D. Roosevelt was one of the most, if not *the* most, popular presidents we've had in our generation? Because he could be all things to all people. I've been in his office when senators and congressmen have come in ready to cut his throat, and they've gone out singing his praises, just because of the mental attitude with which he received them.

In other words, he adjusted himself to their mental attitude, and he didn't get mad at the same time they did. Incidentally, that's a mighty good way of adjusting—to learn to be flexible enough not to get mad when the other fellow's mad. If you want to get mad, do it on your own account, when the other fellow's in a good humor and you'll have a much better chance of not getting hurt.

I've seen presidents of the United States come and go; I've been associated with several of them. I know what this factor of flexibility can mean in the highest office in the world. Herbert Hoover probably was one of the best all-around business executives we've ever had in the White House, yet he couldn't sell himself to the people a second time, because he was inflexible. He could not bend. He was too static, too fixed.

Calvin Coolidge was the same way, and Woodrow Wilson to some extent was the same way. He was too austere, too static, too fixed, too correct. In other words, he wouldn't allow anybody to slap him on the shoulder, call him "Woody" or take any personal liberties with him. Franklin D. Roosevelt allowed you to do all those things and more too if you wanted do. If you slapped him on the back, he would slap you right back. In other words, he was flexible. He could adjust himself.

And listen, boys and girls, there are so many things in this life that you have to adjust yourself to temporarily if you're going to have peace of mind and good health, so you might just well start in now learning to do it. If you're not flexible, you can become flexible.

3. A Pleasing Tone of Voice

Number three is a *pleasing tone of voice.* Here is an important thing to experiment with. A lot of people have harsh, nasal tones, and they put something into their tone of voice that irritates other people. You take any monotonous speaker, for instance: he does not have personal magnetism, does not know how to give pitch and tone to his voice. He'll never get his audience, not in a million years. If you're going to teach, if you're going to lecture, if you're going into public speaking or even good conversation, you've got to learn to get a pleasant, pleasing tone into your tone of voice. You can do it with a little bit of practice. Oftentimes by simply lowering your voice and not talking too loudly, you can make it pleasing to the ear—or you can step it way up, and you'll make everybody want to hit you with a brick. Between those two extremes, there's a happy medium you want to strike in your conversations, in your teaching, and in your public speaking.

I don't think that anybody can teach another person how to make his tone of voice pleasing. I think you have to do that yourself. You have to do it by experimenting. First of all, you have to *feel* pleasing. How could you use a pleasant tone of voice when you felt angry, or when you didn't like the person that you were talking to? You can, but it's not too effective unless you really feel inside the way you're expressing yourself.

Do you have any idea why I can take any audience and within three to five minutes, take that audience over and hold it as long as I choose without walking down the stage or pulling my hair or gesturing or anything of that sort? Do you know how it's done?

First of all, what's inside of my heart? I pour it out in a natural tone of voice. In other words, I speak just exactly as I would speak if I were in ordinary conversation with you, and where enthusiasm is to be turned on, I turn it on.

There's another trick that I think you ought to learn. I can get an audience to applaud anytime I want. You know how I do it?

By asking you a question. Would you like me to tell you how many times have you heard that since we started? Would you like me to tell you? Of course, I get applause. All these things are carefully studied techniques that you have to acquire if you're going to make yourself pleasing. I don't know of anything that will pay off better than to be pleasing in the eyes of other people. It's just one of those things that you can't get along without.

4. Tolerance

Tolerance—what does that mean? A lot of people don't understand the full meaning of tolerance. It means an open mind on all subjects toward all people at all times. In other words, your mind is not closed against anybody or anything. You're always willing to hear an additional word.

You'll be surprised at how few people there are in this world with open minds. Some of them are so closed that you could not open them with a crowbar; you couldn't get a new idea in there if you tried. Did you ever see one of those people who was pleasing? You never did, and you never will.

You've got to have an open mind, because the very minute people find that you have prejudices that involve them and their understanding of religion, politics, economics, or anything else, they're going to back away from you.

Do you have any idea why I can have followers of all religions in my classes and get along well with all of them—Catholics and Protestants, Jews and Gentiles, all races, all the creeds? Because I love them all. To me, they're all of one brand. They're my fellow beings, my brothers and sisters. That's why I get along with them. I never think of anybody in terms of what he believes politically or religiously or economically. I think of him in terms of what he's trying to do to better himself and to better somebody else. Those are the terms in which I think of people, and that's why I get along so well with them.

I didn't use to do that. I used to have some outstanding prejudices; I had a closed mind about a lot of things. You didn't have to ask me what was it was: I'd go out of my way to tell you, which of course made me very popular. I don't volunteer much information anymore, except to my own students, and they have paid me, so I'm under obligation to do it, but so far as outsiders are concerned, I do no more volunteering of information.

An open mind! What a marvelous thing it is to be in possession of yourself so you can keep your mind open. If you don't, you're not going to learn very much. If you have a closed mind, you'll miss out on a lot of information that you need but can't get without an open mind.

Having your mind closed does something to you inside. If you have the last word and you don't want any more information, you've ceased to grow. The very moment you close your mind on any subject—you say, "That's the last word; I want no more information on it"—you've ceased to grow.

5. A Sense of Humor

A keen *sense of humor*—I don't mean that you have to tell lots of jokes. I mean that you have to have a certain disposition. If you don't, you have to cultivate it so that you can adjust yourself to all of the unpleasant things that come along in life without taking them too seriously.

I once saw a motto in the office of Dr. Frank Crane. It impressed me very much, especially finding it in the office of a preacher. It said, "Don't take yourself too damn seriously." He explained to me what the word "damn" means. He said it meant just exactly what it said. If you take yourself too seriously, you go damning yourself. That's obvious, isn't it? It wasn't a profane word after all. I liked it; I still like it. I think it's a good motto for anybody not to take himself too seriously.

After all the recognition that I've had in the world from outstanding people, if I had really taken myself seriously, you couldn't have lived with me at all. I would have been egotistical and vain, and it would have stood out all over me. I'd never have had the confidence of people. Nobody likes a vain or an egotistical person.

Another thing. If you have a keen sense of humor, you'll never have any stomach ulcers. Stomach ulcers only come from one cause; if you get them, they're only cured in one way, and that's to develop a keen sense of humor and work at it all the time.

I read the some of the cartoons in some of the papers because I get a laugh out of them every once in a while. We have a cartoon out on the coast called "Emily and Mabel." They're two elderly spinsters who are constantly gunning for a man and always missing. Their episodes are so much like life that I've really got to laugh. If I don't get a good ha-ha, I always tell my wife that I've been cheated out of a nickel from my paper.

Incidentally, one of the finest tonics that you can take (in addition to vitamins and food supplements, which most of you need) is to have a good laugh at least several times a day. If you don't have anything to laugh at, cook up something. Look at yourself in the glass, for instance. You will always get a laugh out of that. You'd be surprised at how it changes the chemistry of your mind while you're doing it. If you've got troubles, they'll melt away, and they won't seem nearly as big when you're laughing as when you're crying.

I don't know that my sense of humor is keen, but it's alert. I can get some fun out of almost any circumstances in life. I used to get a lot of punishment out of some circumstances that I now get fun out of because I have oiled up my sense of humor and made it a little bit more alert than it used to be.

6. Frankness

Next is *frankness* of manner and speech, with discriminating control of the tongue, based at all times upon the habit of thinking before you speak.

Most people don't do that. They speak first and think, or rather regret, afterwards. Before you utter any expression to anybody, figure out whether it's going to benefit or damage the person that's listening, and whether it's going to benefit you or damage you. If you do a little weighing and a little thinking before you open your mouth, you will never say half of the things that you wish you hadn't said.

There are people who set their mouths going and go off and leave them going. They forget what they said, because they weren't there. They're almost always in difficulty.

Frankness of manner of speech doesn't mean that you have to tell everybody exactly what you think of them, because if you do, you will have no friends. Nor does frankness mean being evasive or engaging in double-talk. Nobody likes a double-talker. Nobody likes a person who's always evasive and has never expressed an opinion about anything.

7. A Pleasing Facial Expression

Number seven is a *pleasing facial expression*. I don't know if you study your facial expression in the mirror. It's a marvelous thing to see how much more pleasing you can make your facial expression when you try. It's a marvelous thing to learn to smile when you're talking to people. You'd be surprised at how much more effective what you are saying is when you are smiling than when you're frowning or looking serious. It makes a tremendous difference to the person that's listening.

I hate to talk to a person who's got a serious expression on, as if the whole world is on his shoulders. It makes me fidgety. I just wish that he'd get through with whatever he's say and go on, but if he limbers up, as Franklin D. Roosevelt used to, and gives you a million-dollar smile, even the most trivial thing that he says sounds like music, like wisdom, because of what it does to you psychologically.

Don't grin at people when you don't mean it, because monkeys can grin. Learn to smile because you feel it. Where does a smile take place first? On your lips, on your face? In your heart, where you feel it—that's where it takes place. You don't have to be pretty. You don't have to be handsome. Put on a smile; it'll decorate you and embellish you no matter who you are. It makes your facial expression look more beautiful.

8. A Keen Sense of Justice

The next quality is a *keen sense of justice* toward all people. In other words, being just to another person even when it's to your disadvantage to do so. It endears you to other people when they know that your being just to them is costing you something. There's no particular virtue in being just to the other fellow when you're benefiting by it.

Many people are fair and just and honest only when they know it's going to come back to them in one way or another. Do you know how quickly they'd be dishonest if it was profitable for them to do it? I wouldn't give you the percentage; I'd hate to tell you what I think it is. It's much too high.

9. Sincerity of Purpose

The next one is *sincerity of purpose*. Nobody likes a person who is obviously insincere in what he says and does, trying to be something that he's not, or saying something that doesn't represent his inner thoughts. It's not as bad as lying out loud, but it's the first cousin to it—a lack of sincerity of purpose.

10. Versatility

Then there is *versatility*: a wide range of knowledge of people and world events outside of one's immediate personal interest.

A person who doesn't know anything except about one subject will become a bore the moment he gets out of that field. You don't have to use your imagination very much to think of somebody you know who's got his nose so closely to the grindstone on one thing that he knows nothing outside of that. He'll not be interesting as a conversationalist or in any other way unless he knows a wide enough range of things to be able to talk to you about what interests you.

You know the best way in the world to make yourself liked by other people? Talk to them about the things that interest them. Incidentally, if you talk to the other fellow about things that interest him, when you get around to talking about things that interest you, he'll be much more of a receptive listener.

11. Tactfulness

Then there's *tactfulness* in speech and manner. You don't have to reflect your mental attitude in your words. If you do that, you'll be an open book, and everybody can read you, sometimes when you wish they hadn't.

You can always be tactful. When you're on the road and the other fellow skins your fenders, you know how tactful they are when they jump out and run around to see how much damage is done. Maybe there's ten cents' worth where the paint's been knocked off, but they do $100 worth of damage cussing one another out.

One of these days, I'm going to have the experience of seeing two fellows collide on the highway and jump out and apologize, each one claiming it was his fault and wanting to pay the bill. I don't know who's going to do it, but I'm going to see that one of these days.

You'll be surprised how much you can do with people if you're just tactful with them. Oftentimes, instead of telling people to do things, it might be helpful if you asked them if they would mind doing something. Even though you're in authority to give them an instruction, it's still better to ask.

One of the most outstanding employers I ever knew never gave any of his employees direct instructions. Andrew Carnegie always asked his associates and his employees if they would mind doing something for him, or he would ask, would it be convenient, or would it be suitable? He never ordered them to do anything; he asked them always. No wonder he got along so well with people; no wonder he was so successful.

12. Promptness of Decision

Next is *promptness of decision*. Nobody can be well-liked or have a very pleasing personality who always puts off making a decision when he has the necessary facts before him. I don't mean that people should go off half-cocked or render snap judgments. But when you have all of the facts and the time has arrived for a decision, get into the habit of making that decision. If you make one that's wrong, you can always reverse it, and don't be too big—or rather, too little—to reverse yourself when you find out that you should. It is a great advantage in being fair with yourself and with the other fellow to reverse yourself if you have made the wrong decision.

13. Faith in Infinite Intelligence

I don't need to make much comment on number thirteen: faith in infinite intelligence. You know what your faith is, and if you are faithfully following your religion, whatever it is, you should rate very high on this one.

You'd be surprised how many people give lip service to faith and infinite intelligence but don't do very much about it. They don't indulge in any outstanding acts backing up their alleged belief in infinite intelligence. I don't know how the Creator feels about it, but I believe that one act is worth a million tons of good intentions or beliefs.

14. Appropriateness of Words

Number fourteen: *appropriateness of words*, free from slang, wise-cracks, and profanity. I never saw an age when people have indulged in so many wisecracks, slang statements, and doubletalk. It may seem smart to the fellow who's doing it, but not to the fellow who's listening. He may laugh, but he's not going to be impressed with anyone who engages too much in wisecracks.

Our English language is not the easiest thing in the world to master, but it is a beautiful language, and it has a wide range of word meanings. It's a wonderful thing to be able to control the English language so that you can convey to the other fellow precisely what you have in your mind (or what you want him to think you have in mind).

15. Controlled Enthusiasm

Then there's *controlled enthusiasm*. You may say, "Why control enthusiasm? Why not turn it loose and let it run wild?" Because you'll get into trouble if you do. Your enthusiasm ought to be handled very much like your electricity. It's a very wonderful thing—washes dishes, washes your clothes, runs the toaster, maybe cooks your food on the stove—but you handle it with care. You turn it on when you want it and turn it off when you don't.

Your enthusiasm should be handled with just as much care. You turn it on when you want to turn it on, and you can just as quickly turn it off. If you're not able to turn it off as quickly as you turn it on, somebody will come along and get you enthused over something that you ought not to be enthused over. Did you ever hear of that happening? And boy, what a sucker you will be.

Do you know what enthusiasm is? It's a mild, and sometimes not too mild, form of hypnotism. You can hypnotize yourself with enthusiasm and you can hypnotize the other fellow as well, but don't do it too much. You can be so enthusiastic with the other fellow that he'll be out pulling down his mental shades. I have had salesmen come around who were so enthusiastic that I wouldn't let them in my place a second time, because I didn't want to go to the trouble of defending myself against them.

I have heard some speakers like that; I've heard some preachers like that too. I wouldn't want to follow them. You know the type I'm talking about. The fellow just turns his enthusiasm battery loose and goes off and leaves it; all you can do is run away from it or try and turn it off.

A man who does that is not going to be popular, but the man who can turn on the right amount of enthusiasm at the right time and turn it off at the right time is the man who's going to be considered to have a pleasing personality.

Incidentally, if you're not able to exude enthusiasm when you want to, you're not going to be considered a pleasing personality, because there are times when you definitely need it. Teaching, lecturing, speaking, or almost anything that you're doing in the area of human relationships requires a certain amount of enthusiasm at times.

Enthusiasm, like all these other qualities, is something you can cultivate. There's only one quality that your attitude can't cultivate. Andrew Carnegie said he could give you every one of the other qualities except this one. It's personal magnetism. If you have just so much of that, even that can be subject to control and transmutation too, but it's something that one person can't give to another.

16. Sportsmanship

The next quality is good, clean *sportsmanship*. You're not going to win all the time in life. Nobody can do that. There are going to be times when you lose. When you do, lose gracefully and graciously. Say, "Well, I lost, but maybe it's best I did, because I'm going to start looking immediately for that seed of an equivalent benefit. Next time I'm going to let somebody else lose. I'm going to wise myself up." Then don't take it too seriously, no matter what it is.

During the Depression, four of my friends committed suicide. Two of them jumped off a tall building. One shot himself in the head, and another took poison. I lost twice as much as they did. I didn't jump off a building; I didn't shoot myself; I didn't poison myself. I said, "It's a blessing, because losing this amount of money now, I'll have to start and earn some more." That was my mental attitude. I said to myself, "If I lose every penny that I have, the last suit I have, even my big BVDs, I can always get a barrel from somebody and start all over again. Wherever I get a bunch of people together to listen, I'll be able to start making money."

How you going to down a person with that attitude? No matter how many times you defeat him, he comes right up again. He's like a cork. You can put him down, but he can bounce up the moment you take your hand off him, and if you don't take your hand off, he will make you take it off.

17. Common Courtesy

Oh, what a marvelous thing that is—just common, ordinary, garden-variety *courtesy*! Especially toward people that are on a lower plane socially, economically, or financially than yourself. It's wonderful to be courteous to a person to whom you don't have to be courteous. It does something for the other fellow, and it does something for you.

I always hate to see anybody lording it over another person. Nothing gets me upset more quickly than to go into a restaurant and see some newly rich somebody come in, order the waiters around, and abuse them. Even if sometimes they deserve it, still, I have never learned to be like that. I've always thought that anybody who would abuse another person in public, with or without a cause, has something wrong with his machinery.

When I was living at the Bellevue-Stratford Hotel in Philadelphia, a waiter spilled some hot soup right on the back of my neck, and it burned me. The headwaiter ran over. In a little while, the manager of the hotel was out there, and he wanted to get a doctor. I said, "It's not that serious. After all, the waiter just spilled a little soup."

"We'll have your suit cleaned."

"No," I said, "just don't get upset. I'm the one to get upset, and I'm not getting upset about it."

When that waiter was off duty, he came up to my room and said, "I want to tell you how much I appreciated what you said. You could have had me fired, since I was just as good as fired. If you hadn't talked the way you did, I'd have been out, and I couldn't afford to be fired."

I don't know how much good it did the waiter, but it did me lot of good. After all, that was a man that I could have humiliated.

As far as I know, I have never, in my whole life, intentionally humiliated anybody for anything whatsoever (although I may have done it unintentionally). I feel good in being able to say that. I feel good to have that attitude toward people. And it comes back to me, because people have that attitude toward me too. They don't want to humiliate me. Why? Because you get back from people what you send out. You're a human magnet, and you're attracting to you the sum and substance of what goes on in your heart and soul.

18. Appropriateness of Personal Adornment

Appropriateness of personal adornment is important to anybody in public life. I don't mean you have to dress yourself up like Mrs. Astor's horse or a clown. You don't have to wear loud clothes, but anybody who's dealing with the public should select personal adornment suited to his personality.

I have never been too fussy about that. I've never used formal clothes except on very few occasions. Some time ago I was delivering a talk for a Chicago sales executives' club, and I was put on notice that I had to be in a tuxedo. I didn't even own a tuxedo; I hadn't owned one for twenty years. I went down and bought a tuxedo just for that occasion.

When I went on the stage, I told the story of one of the local bankers who was talking to me down in the cocktail room just before we sat down to dinner. He said, "Mr. Hill, are you nervous anytime when you go to speak?"

"Well, not anytime except tonight."

"Why tonight?"

"Because of this damn monkey suit that I have to wear."

I told my audience about that, and they really got a kick out of it.

It's perfectly appropriate to wear formal clothes when necessary, but use good taste. Ordinarily, if later on, you were asked to describe what the best-dressed person wore, you wouldn't be able to do it. You'd say, "All I know was he looked nice," or "she looked nice."

19. Showmanship

Showmanship—you've got to be a showman if you're going to sell yourself in any walk of life. Know when to dramatize words, when to dramatize circumstances.

Take the history of the most outstanding man in the world. If you just gave the bare facts about him and didn't dramatize the story as you went along, you'd fall down flat. You've got to dramatize the things that you're talking about to the people that you're doing business with. You've got to learn the art of showmanship as you go along. That's something you can learn.

20. Going the Extra Mile

I don't need to mention that you should have the habit of *going the extra mile*; you've had a whole lesson on that.

21. Temperance

Temperance means not too much, not too little of anything. You can do yourself just as much damage with eating as you can with drinking liquor. The rule that I go by in all these things is that I don't allow anything to take charge of me. When I was smoking, when I got to the point where the cigars were smoking me, I quit. I can take a cocktail; I can take two; I guess I could take three. I don't remember ever having taken more than that socially, but if I ever found them taking me, or if I ever found my being not able to resist them, I would part company with them in a hurry.

I want to be in possession of Napoleon Hill all the time. Not too much, not too little. Temperance is a marvelous thing. Don't you know that there's nothing so very bad in life if you don't overdo it?

There's a wide range of thought there. Right or wrong are relative terms. When you come right down to it, whether it's right or wrong just depends on who's telling it. If it affects you adversely, it's wrong. If it affects you beneficially, it's right. That's the way most people look at it.

22. Patience

Then comes *patience* under all circumstances. You have to have patience in this world we're living in. It's a world of competition. You're constantly being called upon to use your patience; by using patience, you learn to wait for things when the time is more favorable. If you don't have patience and you try to force the hand of other people, you'll get a no or a turndown when you don't want it.

You require patience in order to make time for your relationships with people, and you have to have a lot of patience. You have to be able to control yourself at all times.

Most people don't have much patience. Take the majority of people: you can make them mad in two seconds. All you've got to do is say or do the wrong thing.

I don't need to get angry because somebody says or does the wrong thing. I could if I want to, but it's my choice; I can choose not to get mad. I can be patient and wait my time to strike back at the other fellow, if I want to strike back at all. If a man did me wrong, the only way I would strike back would be by doing him a favor and showing him how little he could be.

23. Gracefulness

Number twenty-three is *gracefulness* of posture and carriage of the body. When I speak, I can stand straight without leaning on anything.

24. Humility

Twenty-four is *humility* of the heart, based upon a keen sense of modesty. I don't know of anything as wonderful as to have true humility of the heart.

Sometimes I do have to criticize the people I'm working with—some, not all, of them—but I always say inside, "But for the grace of God, I'd be the man that I'm over there criticizing, and maybe I've done things ten times as bad as the thing I'm criticizing him for." In other words, I try to maintain that sense of humility in my heart, regardless of what happens to me that's unpleasant.

The more successful I become, the more I observe this feeling of humility of the heart. I recognize that whatever success I have is due entirely to the friendly, marvelous love, affection, and cooperation of other people, because without that I could never have spread myself over the world the way I have. I could never have benefited the people that I have, I could never have grown the way I have grown, had it not been for the love, affection, and marvelous, friendly cooperation of other people. And I couldn't have gotten that cooperation if I hadn't adjusted myself to others in a state of friendliness.

25. Personal Magnetism

Last but not least is *personal magnetism*. That, of course, has reference to sex emotion, to an inborn trait of the owner, one of the personality traits which cannot be cultivated, although it can be controlled and directed to beneficial usage. As a matter of fact, the most outstanding leaders, salesmen, speakers, clergymen, lawyers, lecturers, teachers— the most outstanding individuals in every field of endeavor—are people who have learned to transmute sex emotion: they can convert that great creative energy into doing the thing that they want to do most of the time.

And that word *transmuting*—it's something to conjure with, something to look up in the dictionary; make sure you understand what it means.

You've got a lot of thinking to do about these twenty-five qualities, and you're going to make discoveries about yourself. When you really come down to answering these questions and giving yourself a rating, you're going to find out that you have certain weaknesses that you didn't know you had, and you have certain strengths and good qualities that you perhaps had undervalued.

Let's find out about ourselves to see just where we stand. What it is that makes us tick? Why do people like us, why do people dislike us? I could take any one of you and sit down with you. By asking you—I'll say not over twenty questions—I could lay my finger right on what's keeping you from being popular if you are unpopular.

You can do the same thing. That's what I want you to do. I want you to learn to analyze people, starting with yourself, find out what it is that makes people popular, what makes them tick. When you do that, you have one of the greatest assets that you could possibly imagine.

Now you've got some work to do on this lesson, and I want you to have joy in doing it, I want you to have pleasure in doing it, and I want you to learn a lot about yourself.

7

Leadership and Initiative

I must tell you something that happened last Saturday. I went down to the travel agency to get my ticket changed so I could come back on Monday instead of Sunday. When I walked in, the manager of the travel agency grabbed my hand. He introduced himself and started into selling me *Think and Grow Rich*. In a little while, while he still had hold of my hand, a man came in, a friend of his who was connected with one of the airlines. He heard the name "Napoleon Hill," and he grabbed the other hand and started to sell me *Think and Grow Rich*. He said, "You may be interested in knowing that before I went with the airline, I had a sales organization with approximately one hundred people. And I required every salesman to have all of your books. That was a must."

I felt pretty good. As I started out, there were two very nice-looking young ladies standing on the sidewalk giving out election literature. As I passed by, one of them said, "Aren't you Napoleon Hill?"

I turned around and bowed. I said, "Yes, I am. Who are you?"

"I was at a woman's club about two years ago when you delivered an address, and this is my cousin. Both of our husbands are very successful now due to the fact they have read your books."

I went on over to my car, and the policeman was making out a ticket. I had put a penny in there, thinking that twelve minutes would be all I would be in there, but all of the nice conversations I was getting into made it take much longer.

When I got to my car, this policeman was making out the ticket; he had it about halfway made up.

I walked up to him and said, "Now you wouldn't do that to Napoleon Hill, would you?"

"Who?"

"Napoleon Hill."

"No," he said, "I wouldn't do that Napoleon Hill, but I certainly would do it to you."

I introduced myself, took out my credit card, and handed it to him, along with my driver's license.

The policeman said, "I'll be a monkey's uncle." He took the tab, tore it up, and said, "We'll just forget about that. You may be interested in knowing that I'm on the Glendale police force as a result of reading your book *Think and Grow Rich*."

I got in my car and went home as fast as I could. I was afraid that if I stayed down there any longer, I'd run into somebody else who would start selling me this philosophy.

It makes no difference how successful you become or how much recognition you get: I don't think any normal person ever gets to the point at which he doesn't appreciate honest and sincere commendation. I know I do, and I hope I'll never get to the point when I won't appreciate it.

This is a great lesson because it's the action producing portion of this philosophy. It wouldn't make much difference whether you understood all of the other principles or not if you didn't do something about it; why would it? In other words, the value that you're going to get out of this philosophy will not consist of anything that I will say in these lessons. The important thing is what you will do about all of this—the action you will take to start using this philosophy on your own personal initiative.

There are certain attributes of initiative and leadership, and I want you to start in and grade yourself on them. There are thirty-one of them. The grading may range all the way from 0 to 100 on each of these points. When you finish, add them up and divide by 31, and you will get your general average on personal initiative. Incidentally, this grading of yourself on these qualities will be the first step toward making them your own.

1. Definite Major Purpose

I don't need to make much comment on having a *definite major purpose*, because obviously if you don't have an objective in life, an overall purpose, you haven't very much personal initiative.

That's one of the most important steps to take: to find out what you want to do. If you're not sure what you want to do over a lifetime, let's find out what you're going to do this year, or the remainder of this year. Let's set our goal not too high, perhaps, not too far in the distance.

If you're in a business or a profession or a job, your definite major purpose certainly could be to step up your income from your services, whatever they may be. At the end of the year, you can review your record, reestablish your definite major purpose, and step it up to something bigger, maybe to another one-year plan, or maybe to a five-year plan. But the starting point of personal initiative is to find out where you're going, why you're going there, what you're going to do after you get there, and how much you're going to get out of it financially.

The majority of people in this world could be very successful if they would just make up their minds how much success they want and on what terms they want to evaluate success. There are a lot of people in this world who want a good position and plenty of money, but they're not quite sure just what kind of a position, how much money, or when they want to get it. Let's do a little thinking on that subject and grade ourselves on number one.

2. Adequate Motive

Number two: an *adequate motive* to inspire continuous action in pursuit of the object of one's definite major purpose.

Study yourself carefully and see if you have an adequate motive or motives. It will be much better if you have more than one motive for attaining the object of your major purpose or your immediate purpose.

Again, nobody ever does anything without a motive. Let me restate that: no one outside of the insane asylum ever does anything without an adequate motive. A person who is in an insane asylum or off-balance may do a lot of things without any motive whatsoever, but normal people move only on motive. The stronger the motive is, the more active they become and the more apt they are to act upon their own personal initiative.

You don't have to have a lot of brains in this world; you don't have to be brilliant. You don't have to have a wonderful education in order to be an outstanding success, if you will only take what little you have, whether it's little or much, and start using it, putting it into operation, and doing something about it and with it. And of course that calls for initiative.

3. A Master Mind Alliance

Number three is a *Master Mind alliance*: friendly cooperation through which to acquire the necessary power for noteworthy achievement.

Take the initiative now and find out just how many friends you have that you could call on if you were in need of cooperation. Make a list of the people that you really could turn to if you needed some favor: an endorsement, an introduction, maybe a loan of money.

Unless you have all the money that you need, the time might come when you need a loan. Wouldn't it be nice to know someone that you could turn to and get it? You can always go to a bank: all you have to do is to give four for one security, and you can get all the money you want. But there are times when you want medium-sized sums or other comparable favors, and you need somebody to turn to for favors.

Above all, if you are aiming at anything above mediocrity, you need to have a Master Mind alliance of one or more people besides yourself who not only will cooperate with you, but will go out of their way to help you and also have the ability to do something that will be of benefit to you.

It's up to you to take the initiative to build those Master Mind allies. They don't just come along and join you because you're a good fellow. You have to lay out a plan, you have to have an objective, and you have to find the people suitable for your alliance. Then you have to give them an adequate motive for becoming a Master Mind ally of yours.

Incidentally, I happen to know that the vast majority of people do not have a Master Mind alliance with other people. Don't be afraid to grade yourself zero on this one if you don't have one, but next time you come to grade yourself, grade higher than that. The only way you can do that is to start in and find at least one Master Mind ally that you can attach yourself to right now.

4. Self-Reliance

Number four: *self-reliance* in proportion to your major purpose. Find out just exactly how much self-reliance you have. You may need some help from other people, from your wife, your husband, your closest friend, or somebody who knows you well.

You may think you have self-reliance. How can you tell? Go back up to number one. Carefully evaluate your definite major purpose and see how big it is. If you don't have one, or if it's not above anything that you've attained up to the present, then you don't have much self-reliance, and you should grade yourself low on that. If you have the proper amount of self-reliance, you step your definite major purpose up way beyond anything you have ever achieved before, and you'll become determined to attain it.

5. Self-Discipline

Number five: *self-discipline* sufficient to ensure mastery of the head and the heart and to sustain one's motives until they are realized.

When do you need self-discipline most? When you're on the way up and when things are going well and you're succeeding? No. You need self-discipline when the going is rough, when the outlook is not favorable.

At that point you need a positive mental attitude. You need discipline over your mind to the extent that you know where you're going, you know that you have a right to go there, and you know that you're determined to go there regardless of how hard the going may be or how much opposition you might meet with. You'll need at least enough self-discipline to sustain you through the period when the going is hard instead of quitting or complaining.

6. Persistence

Number six is *persistence* based on the will to win. Do you know how many times the average person has to fail before he quits or decides he wants to do something else? Once? Did you ever hear of the fellow who fails before he starts because he knows that there's no use in starting, because he knows he can't do anything? That cuts it down below one.

The vast majority of people fail before they start. They actually never make a start. They think of things that they might do, but they never do anything about them. The vast majority of those who do start quit at the first opposition or allow themselves to be diverted to something else.

Frankly, my outstanding asset happens to be persistence. I have persistence, the will to win, and the self-discipline to stick to things all the harder when the going is hard. Those are my outstanding qualities; they always have been and always will be. Without those traits, I never would have completed this philosophy, and I never would have been able to have it introduced as widely as it has been.

Is persistence something you're born with, or is it something that you can acquire? Well, if you couldn't acquire it, there'd be no use in talking about this lesson, would there?

Certainly you can acquire it, and it's not very difficult. What is it that causes a person to be persistent, by the way?

Motive, burning desire. Burning desire in back of a motive makes people persistent.

I never think of persistence and a burning desire without thinking of my courtship. I remember that I put more persistence and burning desire into my courtship than anything else in my life.

Don't you think you could transmute that emotion into something else, pulling it back of your business, your profession, or your job and have just as much emotional feeling about attaining success as you could about selling yourself to the one of your choice? Don't you think you could do that?

You know what that word *transmute* means, by the way. If you haven't tried, start trying it. The next time you feel moody or discouraged, try to change that over into an emotion of courage and faith. See what a marvelous thing happens to you. Activate the whole chemistry, the whole brain and your whole body. You'll be much more effective.

7. Imagination

Number seven is a well-developed, controlled, and directed faculty of *imagination*. Imagination that is not controlled and directed might be very dangerous. I wanted to make a survey, an analysis, of all of the men in the federal penitentiary of the United States; I did that for the Department of Justice. The majority of the men in the penitentiary were there because they had too much imagination, but it was not controlled or constructively directed.

Imagination is a marvelous thing, but if you don't have it under control and if you don't direct it to definite and constructive ends, it may be very dangerous to you.

8. Decision Making

Number eight: the habit of *making definite and prompt decisions*. Do you do that? Do you form definite and prompt decisions when you have all of the facts in hand with which to make decisions?

If, when all of the facts are in, you do not have the habit of making clear-cut decisions promptly and definitely, you are loafing on the job, you're procrastinating, and you're destroying this vital thing called personal initiative.

One of the finest places to start practicing personal initiative is to learn to make decisions firmly, definitely, and quickly once you have all of the facts available. Now I'm not talking about snap judgments or opinions based upon half-baked evidence. I'm talking about having all the facts on a given subject, which are in your hands and available. You should then do something with those facts; you should make up your mind exactly what you're going to do and not dillydally around as so many people do. If you do that, the first thing you know, you will be in the habit of dillydallying with everything. In other words, you will not be a person who acts upon his own personal initiative.

9. Basing Opinions on Facts

Next is the habit of *basing opinions on facts* instead of relying on guesswork. Do you recognize how many times you're acting on guesswork in comparison with the number of times you're acting upon facts in forming your opinions? I wonder if you recognize the importance of making it your duty to get facts before you form an opinion about anything. Did you know that you have no right to an opinion about anything at any time, anywhere, unless it's based upon facts, or what you believe to be facts? It's because you don't want to get into trouble; you don't want to fail.

Of course you can have opinions, and we all do—a bunch of them. You can even give them to somebody else without their asking for them, and we do that right along. But before you can really and safely express an opinion, or have one, you must do a certain amount of research and base your opinion upon facts, or what you believe to be facts. If you don't take enough initiative to do that, you are not going to be an expert teacher of this philosophy.

10. Enthusiasm

Now we come to number ten: the capacity to generate *enthusiasm* at will.

Do you know how to generate enthusiasm at will? You can act enthusiastically. But how can you do that? You have to feel the emotion of it. Your mind has to be alerted by some definite objective, purpose, or motive, and then you do something about that motive. You do it with words, with the expression on your face, or by some other form of action. The word *action* is inseparable from the word *enthusiasm*. You can't separate the two.

There are two kinds of enthusiasm. There's passive enthusiasm, which you feel but give no expression of whatsoever. There are times when you need that kind, because if you don't, you will disclose what goes on in your mind when you don't want that to happen.

A great leader, a great executive, may have a tremendous amount of enthusiasm, but he'll display it to whomsoever he pleases and under whatsoever circumstances he pleases. He will not just turn it on and go off and leave it. But that's the way the majority of people do it. When they have enthusiasm, they just turn it on and blubber over it, and they accomplish nothing.

Controlled enthusiasm—enthusiasm turned on at the right time and turned off at the right time—is an important thing, and your initiative is the only thing that can control that. If you took that one subject alone—how to turn enthusiasm on and off—and got the art down fine, you could become a marvelous salesman of anything you might want to sell; you really could.

Did you ever hear of anybody selling anything who didn't have enthusiasm for what he's trying to sell? Did you ever sell anything when you didn't have that feeling of enthusiasm over what you were trying to do for the other fellow? You may have thought you did, but you didn't. If you didn't have that feeling of enthusiasm, and on your own initiative, then you didn't make a sale. Somebody may have bought something from you because he needed it, but you had very little to do with it unless you imparted that feeling to him.

How do you impart the feeling of enthusiasm to another person? How do you do that when you're selling, for instance? You must be sold on it yourself. In other words, it starts inside of your own emotional makeup. You must feel that way.

If you open your mouth to speak, you must speak with enthusiasm. You must put enthusiasm into the expression on your face: you must put on a smile, a good, broad one, because nobody speaks with enthusiasm with a frown on his face. Those two don't go together.

There are a lot of things that you must learn about expressing enthusiasm if you're going to make the most of it, and all of them involve your personal initiative. You've got to do it. Nobody can do it for you. I can't tell you how to be enthusiastic. I can tell you what the parts of enthusiasm are and how to express it, but after all, the job of actually expressing it is up to you.

11. A Sense of Justice

Number eleven: a keen *sense of justice* under all circumstances. I'm not going to comment on that, because I suppose that all of us feel we deal honorably with people and move with a keen sense of justice under all circumstances. If we don't, we should at least feel that way about it.

12. Tolerance

Let's move on to number twelve: *tolerance*. Open-mindedness. We shouldn't have any attitude toward anybody under any circumstances unless it's based upon something to justify that attitude, or at least what we believe to justify it.

Do you have any idea how much value do you deprive yourself of all the way through life just because you close your mind against somebody you don't like, when that person might be the most beneficial person in the world to you?

One of the costliest things in an industrial or business organization is the closed minds of the people. Their minds are closed toward one another, toward opportunities, toward the people they serve, and toward themselves.

When you speak of intolerance, you often think of somebody who doesn't like the other fellow because of his religion or his politics. That doesn't even scratch the surface of the subject. Intolerance extends to almost every human relationship. Unless you form the habit of maintaining an open mind on all subjects, toward all people at all times, you will never be a great thinker, you will never have a great, magnetic personality, and you certainly will never be very well liked.

You can be very frank with people whom you don't like and who do not like you if they know that you're sincere and you're speaking with an open mind. The one thing that people will not tolerate is to recognize that they're talking to somebody whose mind is already closed and that what they're saying has no effect whatsoever, regard-less of how much value or truth there is to it.

Every now and then somebody comes along and wants to get this philosophy into the public schools or universities. Perish the idea. I butted my brains out for a long time, and I finally quit because there are too many closed minds in that field. That's one thing that's wrong with our educational system: too many closed minds and not enough teaching of how to maintain open minds.

13. Doing More than You're Paid For

Number thirteen is always the habit of *doing more than you're paid for*. That's something in connection with which you certainly have to move on your personal initiative. Nobody's going to tell you to do that; nobody's going to expect you to do it. That's entirely within your own prerogative. But it's probably one of the most important and most profitable sources through which you can exercise your own personal initiative. If I had to pick out the circumstance under which you could make your personal initiative most beneficial, undoubtedly it would be in rendering more and better service than you are paid to render, because you don't have to ask anybody for the privilege of doing that.

If you follow that habit—not just doing it once in a while, which is not so effective—sooner or later the law of increasing returns begins to pile up dividends for you, and when the dividends come back, they come back greatly multiplied. In other words, the service that you render in going the extra mile always pays off by giving you back very much more than you gave out.

I served the great R.G. LeTourneau Company for a year and a half, and I indoctrinated their two thousand employees with this phi-losophy. They paid me for that service, and paid me well. But years after I left the service of the company, I received a very substantial check. One half of it was donated by contributions from those two thousand employees, and the other half was matched by the company, mainly because of the value of this principle of going the extra mile. They wanted to emphasize to me the importance of keeping on talking about it in my public classes and otherwise, as I had talked about it there.

In all of my experience, I have never heard of a man getting a bonus check years after he left the service of a company. It was one of the most unexpected things in my whole life.

When you start living by this principle of going the extra mile, you can expect unusual things to happen to you, and they'll all be pleasant, every one of them.

14. Tactfulness

Why is it worth the time it takes to be *tactful*? Because if you are, you get the cooperation of others more easily. If you come in and tell me that I've got to do something, I'll say, "Just a minute. Maybe not. Maybe I have to do something." If you put it to me that way, I'm going to set up some resistance right away. But if you come in and say to me, "I would very greatly appreciate it if you would do something" when you knew in the first place that you had the right to demand on it, you will get very different results.

As I said, one of the most impressive things that I learned from Andrew Carnegie was that he never commanded anybody to do anything. No matter who the man was, he never commanded. He always asked him: "Would you please do a certain thing?"

It's surprising, the amount of loyalty that Mr. Carnegie had from his men. They would go out of their way for him anytime of the day or night because of his tactfulness in dealing with them. When it was necessary for him to discipline one of them, he usually invited him out of the house, gave him a nice, five- or six-course dinner—really put on the dog. After dinner, the showdown came when they went over to the library, and he started asking questions.

One of Mr. Carnegie's chief secretaries was scheduled to become a member of his Master Mind group. This boy found out that he was scheduled for promotion, and it went to his head. He commenced to run around with a bunch of high flyers in Pittsburgh—people who throw cocktail parties and such. In just a little while, he was taking too much liquor and staying out too late. His eyes were hanging out on his cheeks when he came in in the morning.

Mr. Carnegie let this go on for about three months and then invited the young man to dinner one evening. After dinner was over, they went into the library. Mr. Carnegie said, "Now I'm sitting over there in my chair and you're sitting over here in your chair, I want to know what you would do if you were in my place—if you had a man scheduled for an important promotion, and all of a sudden it seemed to have gone to his head. He started running around with fast company, staying out late at night, drinking too much liquor, paying too much attention to everything except his job. What in the world would you do in that case? I'm anxious to know."

This young man said, "Mr. Carnegie, I know you're going to fire me, so you might as well start and get it over with.

Mr. Carnegie said, "Oh, no. If I'd wanted to fire you, I wouldn't have given you a nice dinner, and I wouldn't have brought you out to my house. That could get done in the office. No, I'm not going to fire you. I'm just going to have you ask yourself a question, and see whether or not you're in a position to fire yourself. Maybe you are. Maybe you're closer to it than you realize."

That man turned right around. He became one of Mr. Carnegie's Master Mind group and became a millionaire later on. Mr. Carnegie's tactfulness saved him from himself.

Mr. Carnegie's tactfulness was out of this world. He knew how to handle men. He knew how to get them to examine themselves. It doesn't do much good for me to examine you, but it might do a lot of good if you examined yourself in connection with your faults and your virtues.

Self-analysis is one of the most important forms of personal activity that you can possibly engage in. I never let a day go by when I don't examine myself to see where I have fallen down, where I'm weak, where I can make improvements, what I could do to render more and better service. I examine myself every day. Believe you me, this has been going on for a great number of years, and even today, I can always find someplace where I can improve or I can do something better or something more.

It's a very healthy form of personal initiative, because you finally get down to where you will be honest with yourself. Do you have any idea how many people there are who are dishonest with themselves? It's the worst form of dishonestly that I know: creating alibis in your mind to support your acts and your thoughts instead of examining yourself, finding out where you're weak, and then bridging those weaknesses or getting somebody in your Master Mind alliance to bridge them for you.

Which would you rather have? Would you rather have an outsider criticize you and point out your failures? Or would you rather criticize yourself and find them?

If you do the latter, you can be confidential about it. You don't have to publicize these weaknesses, and you can correct them before anybody else finds out about them. But if you wait until somebody else has to call them to your attention, then they become public property, and they may embarrass you; they may hurt your pride. It may even cause you to build up an inferiority complex if you wait for the other fellow to point out your weaknesses.

That's personal initiative too: finding out your weak spots. What causes you to be disliked by other people? Why aren't you getting ahead as well as some other people when you know you've got just as much brains, or even more, than they have?

Another marvelous place to take personal initiative is to compare yourself with other people who are succeeding beyond your level.

Make comparisons and analyses, and see what they have that you don't have. You'll be surprised to find out how much you can learn from the other fellow, maybe even from the fellow you don't like very well. You can learn something from him, if he's ahead of you, if he's doing better than you are.

Believe you me, you can always learn something from the man who's doing better than you're doing. Sometimes you can learn something from the fellow who's not doing as well as you're doing. It works both ways. You may find out why he's not doing as well.

15. Listening

Do you *listen* more than you talk? Have you ever thought of the importance of taking the initiative on that? Have you ever thought of the importance of learning to ask intelligent questions and let the other fellow do the talking so he reveals what's in his mind and you don't need to necessarily reveal everything that is in your mind? Do you see any value in that?

You learn by listening and observing. I've never yet heard of anybody learning anything while he's talking except that maybe he might learn to not talk so much.

The vast majority of people do a lot more talking than listening, and they seem dead set on telling the other fellow off instead of listening to see what he has to say that they might profit by.

I had the privilege last evening of addressing a very large group of executives in Los Angeles. When my talk was over, I said, "Now I'm going to reverse the rule. I'm going to have an open forum, and I'm going to let you ask me questions and do the talking while I do the listening."

I asked them three questions, one of which brought forth answers that are of vital importance to the Napoleon Hill Associates, to the distribution of this philosophy, and to the future of every teacher that's engaged in or will be engaged in teaching that philosophy.

One of those questions was, if you had the directorship of this philosophy, how would you go about introducing it into the business organizations of this country so that the key men and women of these organizations would have it?

I asked two other questions, and I came away loaded with ideas. And I got myself invited to make the speech that I have been wanting to make for the last ten years. I got myself invited to address the Million Dollar Round Table club next year, which is made up of the big men in insurance from all over the country.

The chairman of the meeting, who had me in mind, is the chairman of the Round Table group next year. He had me in mind, he'd read my books, he'd heard lots of things about me, but he couldn't take a chance on having a dud. He wanted to hear me himself. I was on trial and didn't know it until the speech was over. It's a peculiar thing about life: oftentimes you're under surveillance, and the big opportunities are right there, ready to grab you if you do or say the right thing, or to run away from if you do or say the wrong thing.

The second question I asked that night was, if you were in my place and had the privilege of giving the world its first practical philosophy of individual achievement, what would you do to further the distribution of that philosophy throughout the world? I got around twenty different answers on that one. The third question was not very important. The main one that I wanted to have answered was the first one that I asked.

Let's get back to listening much and talking only when necessary. Next time you start telling somebody off, remember what I said about listening first. Before you start blowing your top, wait till the other fellow blows his. In circumstances where you want to tell somebody off or say something that might offend, let the other fellow have a chance first. Maybe when he gets through, he'll condemn himself; you won't need to say anything to him. Think first and talk less.

16. Observation

Do you feel that you have a keen sense of *observation* of details? Do you feel that you could walk in front of a department store, and after you got at the end of the block, could give an accurate description of everything you saw in the window?

I once belonged to a class in Philadelphia that was directed by a man who was teaching us the importance of observation of small details. He said it was the little details that made up the successes and failures of life. Not the big ones at all, the little ones—the ones we usually pass aside as not being important or that we do not even want to observe.

As a part of our training, he took us out of the hall and down the street one block. We crossed over the street, came up one block, and went back into the hall. In doing so, we passed about ten stores, one of which was a hardware store. In its window, I would say there were easily five hundred articles. He asked each one of us to take a pad, a paper, and a pencil along—mind you, he was giving us a crutch for our memory—and put down the things that we saw as we passed along that we thought were important.

The greatest number of things that anybody had done was fifty-six. When this man came back—he didn't have any paper or pencil—he listed 746. He described each one, what window it was in, and what part of the window it was in.

I didn't accept it. I had to go down after the class was over and backtracked him and checked it. He was 100 percent accurate. He had trained himself to observe details—not just a few of them, but all of them.

A good executive, a good leader, a good anything is a person who observes all things that are happening around him, the good things and the bad, the positives and the negatives. He doesn't just happen to notice those things that interest him; he notices everything that may interest him or may affect his interest. Attention to details.

17. Determination

The best leaders bounce back from defeat, confident that they are now better equipped to achieve victory.

18. The Capacity to Stand Criticism without Resentment

Do you invite criticism—friendly criticism—from other people? If you don't, you're overlooking a big bit. One of the finest things that could possibly happen is to have a regular source of friendly criticism of the thing that you're doing in life—at least the thing that constitutes your major purpose.

Back in the early days, I used to have six, seven, or sometimes eight, nine, or ten secretaries spotted among the audience who would pick up the conversations—everything that people said. As a matter of fact, they'd start conversations with my audience afterwards, and I found out very quickly where I was falling down and where I wasn't.

I want to grow; if I'm making a mistake, I want to find it out. That's why I invite friendly criticism, and if a student or business associate or friend would come up and say, "Dr. Hill, if you just did this one thing a little bit differently, you'd be so much more effective," I'd think it was wonderful. And I have business associates who do just that.

You think the things that you're doing daily are all right, or you wouldn't be doing them, but they may offend other people. Yet you're going to keep on doing them if somebody doesn't call them to your attention.

You need a source of friendly criticism. I'm not talking about people who criticize you because they don't like you. That's no good. I wouldn't let that have any effect on me whatsoever. On the other hand, I wouldn't pay too much attention to the person who gives me friendly criticism just because he loves me. You can do yourself just as much damage that way. I've heard it said out in Hollywood that when those stars begin to believe their press agents (and sometimes they do), they're just about through.

You need to have the privilege of looking at yourself through the eyes of other people. We all need it, because I assure you that when you walk down the street, you don't look the same way to the other fellow as you think you look. When you open your mouth and speak, what registers in the other man's mind is not always what you think is registering.

You need criticism. You need analysis. You need people to point out any changes that you ought to make, because we all have to make changes as we go along; otherwise we wouldn't grow.

Did you know that the majority of people resent any kind of suggestion or criticism whatsoever? They resent anything at all that would change their way of doing things. They do themselves great damage by resenting friendly criticism.

Someone has said that there's no such thing as constructive criticism. I can't buy that. I think there is such a thing as constructive criticism. I think it's absolutely wonderful.

I didn't think so in the beginning. Back in the early days, when anybody criticized what I was doing, I took offense at it, but you know what cured me? One day I was talking to a kindly gentlemen, who was very much older than me, and I had just heard a very vicious criticism that had been made of something that I had done. I don't even remember what it was now; maybe it was an editorial that I'd written in the *Golden Rule* magazine.

I said to this man, "I don't see how in the world anybody could criticize anything that goes in that magazine, because it's designed to help people find themselves. There's nothing negative in it. It's all constructive."

"All of that is true, my friend," he said, "but did you ever hear of a man, a very kindly soul, that passed this way some two thousand years ago? He had a wonderful philosophy, but he didn't get a 100 percent following. Did you ever hear of him? His name was Jesus Christ. If he didn't get a 100 percent following, who are you to think you can get one? Just remember that no matter what you do, who you are, or how well you do it, you'll never get 100 percent approval from the crowd. Don't expect it, and don't be disturbed if you don't get it."

19. Eating, Drinking, and Social Habits

I don't intend to comment on these here.

20. Loyalty

Number twenty is *loyalty* to all to whom loyalty is due. Loyalty comes at the top of the list in my list of qualifications of people that I want to be associated with. If you don't have loyalty to the people who have a right to your loyalty, you don't have anything. In fact, the more brilliant, the more sharp, smart, or well educated you are, the more dangerous you may be if you can't be loyal to the people that have a right to your loyalty.

I have loyalty to people that I like, but I also have a sense of obligation to people if I'm related to them in business, professionally, or in the family circle. There are a few people here that I don't particularly like, but I'm loyal to them because I have their obligation. If they want to be loyal to me, that's all right, and if they don't, that's their misfortune, not mine. I have the privilege of being loyal, and I'm going to live up to that privilege.

I have to live with this fellow—myself. I have to sleep with him. I have to look in the mirror every morning to shave his face. I have to give him a bath every once in a while, and I have to be on good terms with him. You can't live with a fellow that closely and not be on good terms with him. "To thine own self be true, / And it must follow, as the night the day, / Thou canst not then be false to any man." Shakespeare never wrote anything more beautiful and more philosophical than that. To your own self, be true: be loyal to yourself, because you have to live with yourself. If you're loyal to yourself, the chances are you'll be loyal to your friends and your business associates.

21. Frankness

22. Familiarity with the Nine Basic Motives

These are listed in another lesson. Certainly you recognize that they are the ABCs of understanding the motives that move people into action.

23. Attractiveness of Personality

How about this business of an *attractive personality*? Is it something you're born with, or is it something you must bring about on your own initiative?

You can acquire it. There's only one of the twenty-five factors that go to make up an attractive personality that you're born with or not born with, as the case may be: personal magnetism, and you can even do something about that. And certainly you can do something about every one of these other twenty-four factors, because they are subject to cultivation through personal initiative.

Of course, you've got to do it yourself. First of all, you've got to know how you stand on each of these points. You've got to know how you stand, and you can't always take your own word for it. You've got to get your wife, your husband, or somebody else to tell you.

Sometimes you make an enemy, and he'll tell you where you fall down. Did you know that enemies are good things to have once in a while? They don't pull punches. If you will examine what your enemies say about you, the chances are that you might learn something of value. If nothing else, you will learn at least to see to it that they don't tell the truth about you. Whatever they say is not correct, because you are going to be so straight in the road that whatever they derogatorily say about you is not going to be true. That's an advantage, isn't it?

Don't be afraid of enemies. Don't be afraid of people who don't like you, because they may say things that put you on the track of discovering something that you need to know about yourself.

I had a salesman come in and see me some years ago, and he said he'd been with this company about ten years. He had made a wonderful record, had several promotions, and was up in the big ten. Six months previously, his sales began to go down; customers that used to give him the business began to frown on him. I noticed that he had one of these big Texas ten-gallon hats on. I said, "By the way, how long have you had that hat?"

"I got it about six months ago down in Texas."

"Listen, fella," I said, "Are you selling in Texas?"

"No, I don't make Texas very often."

"Listen," I said, "you wear that hat only when you go down in Texas, because I don't like that hat; it doesn't look good on you."

"Well," he said, "would that make any difference?"

"You'd be surprised what a difference your personal appearance will make. If some people don't like the way you look, they won't do business with you."

Yes, you can do something about your personality. You can find out the traits that you have that irritate other people, and you can correct those traits. You have to make the discovery yourself, or you have to get somebody who's frank enough to do it for you.

24. Concentration

Number twenty four is the capacity to *concentrate* your full attention upon one subject at a time. When you start teaching this philosophy and you start to illustrate a point, don't stop in the midst of it and go off into a beautiful field of wildflowers that have nothing to do with the point you're making, only coming back later on. When you start to make a point, exploit it right down to its final analysis, bring it to a climax, and then go on to your next point.

Whether you're selling or speaking in public, don't try to cover too many points at one time. If you do, you'll not cover any points at all. It used to be one of my outstanding weaknesses. I used to do that, and I had a man come to me and call it to my attention. No training in public speaking that I ever had was as valuable as that, and it was for free; he didn't charge me anything. He said, "You have a wonderful command of English, you have a marvelous capacity for enthusiasm, and you have a tremendously big store of interesting illustrations, but you have a bad habit of taking off after something that's not related to the point you're making and then coming back to the point later on. In the meantime, it's gotten cold."

Grade yourself on the capacity to concentrate full attention upon one subject at a time, whether you're speaking, thinking, writing, or teaching. Whatever you do, concentrate on one thing at a time.

25. Learning from Mistakes

On the habit of *learning from your mistakes*: if you don't learn from your mistakes, don't make them. I never see a man duplicating a mistake over and over again without thinking of that old Chinese aphorism: "If a man fools me once, shame on the man, but if you fool me twice, shame on me."

A lot of people should say, "Shame on me," because they don't seem to learn from mistakes at all.

26. Taking Responsibility for Subordinates' Mistakes

If you have subordinates and they make mistakes, it's you who have failed and not the subordinates. You never can be a good leader or a good executive unless you take this responsibility. If someone under your direction is not doing, or can't do, the right thing, it's up to you to take the initiative and do something about it. Either train him to do the thing right or else put him in some other job where you won't have to supervise him; let somebody else do that. But if the person working under you is subordinate to you, the responsibility is yours.

27. Recognizing Others' Merits

Don't try to steal the thunder from the other fellow. If he has done a good job, give him full credit, give him double credit, give him more than he is entitled to rather than less. Another pat on the back has never been known to hurt anybody when you know he has done a good job. Successful people like recognition, and sometimes people work harder for recognition than they will for anything else.

You can overdo that too, you know. However, that depends upon the individual. Some people are incorruptible: you can't overflatter them, because they know their capacity. If you go beyond that, they begin to be suspicious.

Most people, however, are corruptible when it comes to flattery: you can overflatter them to the point where they commence to believe it. That's bad for them and for you too.

There was a book that was widely distributed all over this country. The central theme was that if you want to get along in the world, flatter people. But flattery is as old as the world. It's one of the oldest weapons and also one of the most deadly.

I like approbation. I enjoy it when people happen to know me, compliment me. But if one of them had said, "Oh, Mr. Hill, I appreciate all that you've done for me, but would you mind if I came around the house tonight? I'd like to talk to you about a business proposition." Right away I'd say, "He has flattered me in order that he may get some of my time and get some benefits from it." Too much flattery, too much commendation, is not good either.

28. Applying the Golden Rule

Next is the habit of *applying the Golden Rule* in all human relationships. One of the finest things you can do is to put yourself in the other fellow's position when you go to make any decision or engage in any transaction involving the other fellow. Just put yourself in the other fellow's position before you make a final decision. If you do that, the chances are that you will always do the right thing by the other man.

29. Maintaining a Positive Mental Attitude at All Times

30. Taking Full Responsibility

Number thirty is the habit of assuming *full responsibility* for any task that you've undertaken—not coming back with an alibi. Did you know the one thing at which the majority of people are the most adept in doing? Alibis: creating a reason why they didn't succeed or didn't get the job done. If the majority of people who create alibis would put half as much time into doing the thing right that they put into explaining why they didn't do it, they would get a lot farther in life and be much better off.

Generally speaking, the people who are the most clever at creating an alibi are the most inefficient ones in the whole works. They make a profession of spinning alibis in advance so that when they're called on the carpet, they already have an answer.

There's only one thing that counts, and that's success: results are what count. Success requires no explanations. Failure permits no alibis. If it's a success, you don't need any explanations. And if it's a failure, all the alibis and explanations in the world won't do any good. It's still a failure, isn't it?

31. Keeping the Mind Occupied with What One Desires

Number thirty-one is the habit of *keeping the mind occupied with that which one desires* and not with that which one does not want.

The vast majority of instances in which people engage in personal initiative are in connection with the things they don't want. Here is one place where most people don't have to be taught to take personal initiative. They really work at it; they work at thinking about all the things they don't want. That's precisely what they get out of life: the things that they think about, things that they tune their minds to.

Here's a little place where that word *transmute* can come into play. Instead of thinking about the things you don't want, the things you fear, the things you distrust, the things you dislike, think about all the things you like, all the things you want, and all the things you're determined to get. Train your mind to stay on track in connection with the things that you want. That takes personal ambition.

8

Positive Mental Attitude

Nothing constructive or worthy of man's efforts ever has been or ever will be achieved except that which comes from a positive mental attitude based on definiteness of purpose, activated by a burning desire, and intensified until the burning desire is elevated to the plane of applied faith.

Five Steps toward a Positive Attitude

Here are five steps, five different conditions of the mind, all of which lead up to a positive mental attitude.

Number one is *wishes*. Everybody has a stock of wishes. They wish for this, they wish for that, and they wish for the other thing. We all have wishes. Nothing very much happens when you just wish for things, does it?

Then you go a little bit further and you become *curious*. You put a lot of time into idle curiosity. You can and do consume a lot of time oftentimes with idle curiosity. You put in a lot of time studying what your neighbors do or do not do, what your competitors do or do not do. Do you think anything worthwhile ever happens through curiosity? That doesn't lead to a positive mental attitude.

A step above that, you have *hopes*. Your wishes now have taken on a more concrete form; they become hopes—hopes of achievement, hopes of attainment, hope of accomplishment, hopes of accumulating things that you want.

A hope just by itself is not very effective. We all have a flock of hopes, but not all of us who have hopes have success; we just hope for success. It is, however, better than wishing, because a hope is beginning to take on the nature of faith. You're transmuting a wish into that very desirable state of mind known as *faith*. You step up your mental attitude so that your hopes are transmuted into a burning desire.

The difference between a burning desire and an ordinary desire is this: a burning desire is an intensified desire based upon hope based upon definiteness of purpose.

It is an obsessional desire. And certainly you cannot have a burning desire without a motive or motives back of it, can you? The more motives you can have for a definite thing, the more quickly you will fan your emotions into a burning desire.

But that's not enough. You must have another state of mind before you can be sure of success: *applied faith*. Now you have transmuted wishes, curiosity, hopes, and a burning desire into something still higher.

Applied Faith versus Ordinary Belief

What is the difference between applied faith and ordinary belief? Applied faith is practically synonymous with action. You might call it *active faith*. Applied faith and active faith are exactly the same: faith backed by action. Prayer brings positive results only when it is expressed in a positive mental attitude. And the most effective prayers are those expressed by individuals who have conditioned their minds to habitually think in terms of a positive mental attitude.

Do you have any idea of the amount of your time that you devote each day to thinking of the negative side of things in comparison with the positive side? Wouldn't it be interesting if you kept a tabulation for two or three days of the exact amount of time you put in thinking about the no-can-do side of life and the can-do side, or the positive side and the negative side? Even the most successful people would be astounded to find out how many hours they put in each day in negative thinking. The outstanding successes in the world, the great leaders, are the ones that put in very little if any time thinking on the negative side; they put in all the time thinking on the positive side. I once asked Henry Ford if there was anything in the world that he wanted to do that he couldn't do. He said no; he didn't believe there was. I asked him if there ever had been, he said, "Oh, yes." It was back in the early days, before he had learned how to use his mind.

"Well," I said, "just what do you mean by that?"

"When I want a thing or want to do a thing, I start finding out what I can do about it by starting to do it. I don't bother about what I can't do, because I just left that alone."

That was a homely statement, but there is a world of philosophy wrapped up in it. He put his mind into doing something about the part that he could do something about and thinking about that, and not about the part that he couldn't do anything about.

If you put a difficult problem to the majority of people, they will immediately begin to tell you all the reasons why the problem can't be solved. If there are some things about the problem that are favorable, the majority of people will see the things that are unfavorable first, and oftentimes never see the favorable side.

I don't believe there are any problems about which you can't do something or which are without some favorable sides too. I can't think of a single problem that could confront me that wouldn't have a favorable side to it. If nothing else, the favorable side would consist in the fact that I would say that if it's a problem I can solve, I will solve it, and if it's a problem, I can't solve, I am not worried about it.

But when the majority of people are confronted with difficult problems that they can't solve, they start worrying and go into a negative state of mind. Do you ever accomplish anything worthwhile when you're in that state of mind?

No, you don't. You're only muddying the waters when you make your mind negative; you never accomplish anything worthwhile. You have to learn to keep your mind positive all the time when you want to do things that are worthwhile.

Does a negative mental attitude attract favorable opportunities for you or repel them? It repels them, doesn't it? Does that repelling of opportunities have anything to do with your merit or right to those opportunities? It has nothing to do with it whatsoever. You may have the right to all the good things in life, you may be entitled to them, but if you have a negative mental attitude, you will repel the opportunities leading to the attainment of those things.

So your job is mainly to keep your mind positive so it will attract to you the things that you want, the things that you are going after.

Have you ever wondered why prayer generally doesn't bring anything about except negative results? Oddly, that's the biggest stumbling block for most people in all religions: they don't understand why prayer sometimes brings negative results. You couldn't expect anything else, because there's a law that governs that. The law is that your mind attracts to you the counterpart of the things that the mind is feeding upon. That's a natural law. There are no exceptions for anybody.

So if you want to attract, through prayer or otherwise, the things that you desire, you have to make your mind positive. You not only have to believe, but you have to put actions in back of that belief and transmute it into applied faith. You can't have applied faith in a negative state of mind; the two just don't go together.

Mottos

Constructive mottos are often used by people who recognize the powerful influence of one's daily environment on maintaining a positive mental attitude. The entire industrial plant of the R.G. LeTourneau Company, with two thousand employees, was positivized by placing mottos printed in large letters in all departments and changing them weekly. During the year and a half that I was there, I wrote over four thousand mottos. Those mottos were written for a purpose. Every department in that great sprawling plant had those mottos replaced regularly, sometimes daily, in the cafeteria, and weekly, in the other departments. The mottos were written in the letters half a foot high so that you could read them all the way across the building. Every time they walked into their departments, employees saw that motto.

By the way, we had a funny experience with the mottos. I was standing in the cafeteria one day when the motto was put up. The cafeteria was a place where all the men lined up to get their meals at noontime, and we could catch them all there at one time or another during the day. The motto read, "Just remember that your real boss is the one who walks around under your hat." To anybody that would read it, it would mean that in the final analysis, you're the real boss, but I heard a man let out an Indian yell. He said, "Boy, that's what I've always said! I've always known that my foreman was a louse!"

These mottos are read by people in all walks of life, and sometimes they do make the wrong analysis, but I have heard officials of the LeTourneau Company say that the philosophy, which now is fourteen years old, still holds with the two thousand employees down there. And I have heard officials of the company say that these mottos that went up in these departments had more to do with getting the people to assimilate the philosophy than all the other things that we did. As a rule, the average industrial worker is not very great on reading, but you can always get across a motto that's got meaning in it. So these mottos might be most helpful to you teachers when you teach in industrial plants.

Transmute Failure into Success

Next, there is a method for transmuting failure into success, poverty into riches, sorrow into joy, fear into faith. The transmutation must start with a positive mental attitude, because success, riches, and faith do not make bedfellows with a negative mental attitude.

The transmutation procedure is simple, and you can very well afford to come back to this many times, assimilate it, and make it your own.

Number one, when failure overtakes you, start thinking of it as if it had been a success. In other words, think what would have happened if it had been a success instead of a failure, seeing yourself on the success side of the situation and not on the failure side. Start imagining the failures as a success.

Start also looking for the seed of an equivalent benefit, which comes with every failure. Here you will be able to transmute the failure into success, because every adversity, every failure, and every defeat has the seed of an equivalent benefit. If you go to searching for that seed, you will not take a negative mental attitude toward the circumstance; you will take a positive mental attitude, because you're sure to find that seed. You may not find it the first time you look for it, but if you keep on, eventually you will. That's step number one.

Number two, when poverty threatens to catch up with you (or actually has), start thinking of it as riches. Visualize the riches and all the things that you would do with them. Also start looking for the seed of an equivalent benefit of poverty.

I remember when I was a little boy, sitting on the bank of the river down in Wise County, where I was born, just after my mother had died. Before my stepfather came on, I was hungry. I didn't have enough food. I was sitting on the bank of the river, wondering if I couldn't catch some fish and fry it and have something to eat. As I sat there, I shut my eyes and looked into the future, and I saw myself going away, becoming famous and wealthy, and coming back to that very spot. I was charging up the river on a mechanical horse that was run by steam. I could see the steam pouring out of his nostrils. I could hear his horseshoes clicking on the rocks. It was so vivid to me. In other words, I built myself into a state of ecstasy there in that hour of poverty and want and hunger.

Years passed, and the time came when I drove my Rolls-Royce, for which I had paid $22,500, to that very spot. I went back and again imaged that childhood scene, when I had been there in poverty. And I said, "Well, I don't know whether my imaging this back in the early days had anything to do with it or not; maybe it did."

Maybe I kept alive that hope and eventually translated that hope into faith, and eventually that faith brought me not only a steam horse but something much more valuable and costly.

Look forward and image the things that you want to do, transmuting unfavorable circumstances and adversities into something pleasant. By that I mean switching your mind away from thinking about the unpleasant things over to something pleasant.

Number three, when fear overtakes you, just remember that fear is only faith in reverse gear. Start thinking in terms of faith by seeing yourself translating faith into whatever circumstance or things you desire. I don't suppose anybody ever escapes experiencing the seven basic fears at one time or another, and most people experience them all the way through life. But if you allow fear to take possession of you, it'll become a habit, and it certainly will attract to you all of the things that you don't want. You have to learn to deal with fear by transmuting it in your mind into its opposite. In other words, faith. If you fear poverty, commence thinking of yourselves in terms of opulence and money. Think of ways and means in which you're going to earn that money. There's no end to the daydreaming you do, and it's far better to daydream about the money you're going to have than to use it to fear the poverty that you know you already have. I'll assure you there's no virtue or benefit in sitting down and bemoaning the fact that you are poverty-stricken or that you need money and you don't know how to get it.

I honestly believe that there isn't anything in this world that money can buy that I can't get if I want it. I don't think in terms of what I can't get; I think in terms of what I *can* get. I've been doing that for a long time, and it's a wonderful way to condition your mind to be positive so that when the circumstances arise where you need a positive mental action, you're in the habit of reacting in a positive way at all times rather than in a negative way.

You don't get a positive mental attitude just by wishing for it. You get it by weaving one cord of the rope at a time, day by day, little at a time. You don't just get it overnight.

INVISIBLE GUIDES
- The Guide to Sound Health
- The Guide to Financial Prosperity
- The Guide to Peace of Mind
- The Guides to Hope and Faith
- The Guides to Love and Romance
- The Guide to Wisdom

Invisible Guides

Next, create in your imagination an army of invisible guides who will take care of all your needs and your desires. You've heard me speak of my invisible guides. If you weren't in this philosophy, if you didn't understand metaphysics, you would probably say that I had worked up a fantastic system. But I'll assure you, it's not a fantastic system; it looks after all of my needs and all of my wants.

I will admit that last week, I became a little bit careless, and my guide to physical health let me down for a day or two, but I did something about it. I came to his rescue. I gave him a jab in the rib and woke him up, and I have more energy now than I've had since we started this course. So it's a good thing that I had that little cold, because it made me a little bit more particular to express gratitude to this guide to sound physical health rather than neglecting him.

Now I fully realize that these guys are the creation of my own imagination. I'm not kidding myself or anybody else about that. But for all practical purposes, they represent real entities and real people, and each one is performing the exact duty that I assigned to him and is doing it all the time.

Some students don't know me well enough to know whether I'm telling the truth or not. You have to take me on faith at the present time, but if you stick around me long enough, you'll have an opportunity to know whether I'm telling the truth or not. And I wouldn't be smart enough to fool you if I tried, because you would be able to smell me out.

You will know whether I'm living this philosophy of life. You'll find out. It's your business to find out. If I can't make it work, what right have I to tell you that you can make it work? I am making it work, and it's working well for me. It's doing everything in this world for me that I want done. That's how I know it can do the same for you. That's how I know you can get it to do the same thing for the other fellow. But before you do very much for the other fellow, you have got to do something with it yourself. I don't see how anybody can become an effective teacher of this philosophy who hasn't absolutely demonstrated in his own life that he can make it work.

THE GUIDE TO SOUND HEALTH

The first of these guides is the *guide to sound physical health*. Why do you suppose I put that at number one? What in the world could the mind do going around in a body that has to be supported by crutches all the time? A good, strong physical body is the temple of the mind, and it has to be sound, it has to be healthy, and there has to be plenty of energy there.

When you turn on the old enthusiasm button, if there's no energy there, you can't generate something out of nothing. You've got to have a store of energy, and energy is physical in nature; it's also mental in nature. But I don't know of anybody who can express intense enthusiasm whose body is a series of aches and pains.

Your first duty to yourself is to your physical body—to see that it responds to all of your needs at all times, does the things that it is supposed to do. You need a little bit more help than you can give during the day, because when you lay your body down, nature goes to work on it and gives it a tune-up and working over. You have to have this trained entity called the guide to sound health to supervise that job and to see it's done properly.

Never mind about what anybody else is going to say about this system. You go ahead and work it out to your own satisfaction. Find out that it works, and then, when you start teaching it to other people, you don't need to make any apologies.

I'm explaining this system; I'm not apologizing for it. Why would one apologize for something that serves him day and night, and serves him well? You wouldn't apologize for that.

THE GUIDE TO FINANCIAL PROSPERITY
Number two is the *guide to financial prosperity*. Why do you suppose I put that second?

Do you know of anybody that can be of any great service to others without money? How long can you get along without money? I will tell you how long I can get along without money. I can get along for two weeks without needing anything. I do that twice a year when I fast. But if I had to do it, I'd probably starve to death in three days. I do it because I want to, because it's a tonic to my health.

You've got to have money; you've got to have a money consciousness in this entity that you're building up here. My guide is
controlled, however. I don't permit myself to become greedy, to
want too much money or to pay too much for the money that I get. I
pay enough, but not too much. I know people who pay too much and
die too young, because they put too much effort into accumulating
money that they didn't need and couldn't use. The only purpose it
could serve would be to cause their descendants to fight over it after
they are passed on. Now that's not going to happen to me. I want a
lot, but not too much. It's the business of this money guide to see
that I stop when I get enough, because I don't want too much.

This money-getting business becomes a kind of a vicious circle
with a lot of people. You get in it and you say, well I will make my
first million and then I will quit. I remember the time when Bing
Crosby announced to his brother, who was his manager, that when
they made the first $50,000, that was enough; they were going to
quit. It got down to where they make over a million dollars every year
and are still working harder than they ever did before, struggling in
the rat race. I'm not speaking in a derogatory manner of Bing, you
understand. He is a friend of mine, and I greatly admire him, but I'm
speaking of people in that category who pay too much for trying to
get things that they don't need.

This is a philosophy dealing with economic success. Success
doesn't consist in your destroying your life and dying too young
because you tried to get too much of anything. Stop when you get
enough. Make better use of the things you have right now instead of
trying to get a lot of more things that you're not going to make any
use of at all.

If I could have made this speech to four of my friends prior to
the Depression, two of them wouldn't have jumped off of buildings,
and two of them wouldn't have blown their brains out or poisoned
themselves.

Not too much, not too little—just enough of everything. What a nice trick it is to learn what is enough and not too much! That's one of the blessings of this philosophy: it gives you a balanced life; you learn what is enough and what's too much.

THE GUIDE TO PEACE OF MIND

The next one is the most important: the *guide to peace of mind*. What good would it be to you if you owned everything in the world and could collect royalties from every person living if you didn't have peace of mind?

I've had the privilege of knowing intimately, as friends, the richest and most successful men that this country has ever produced. This means sleeping in their houses, eating with them, knowing their families and their wives and their children, and seeing what happened to their children after they died and passed on. I've seen all of that. I know the importance of learning to live a balanced life so that you can have peace of mind as you go along and make your occupation a game that you're getting joy out of. It's not something to be dreaded, but a game that you play as ardently as a man would play golf or some other game that he loves.

I've always said that one of the sins of civilization consists in the fact that so few people are engaged in a labor of love, in things that they like to do. Most people are doing things because they have to eat and sleep and have some clothes to wear. But when a man or a woman gets in a position when he or she can do the thing that is being done for the sake of love, because they want to do it, they're really fortunate. This philosophy leads to that condition, but you'll never attain that position until you learn to maintain a positive mental attitude at least a major portion of your time.

Out of all the men that collaborated with me in the building of this philosophy—and they represented every outstanding success of that era—there was only one that I could say that even vaguely approached having peace of mind along with his other successes. That was John Burroughs: he was undoubtedly the one that came nearest. The one that came next nearest was Mr. Edison.

I would place Mr. Carnegie at number three, and I'll tell you why. In his latter years, he practically lost his mind trying to find ways and means of disgorging his fortune and giving it away to where it would do no harm. It almost drove him crazy. His major obsession in the latter part of his days was to get this philosophy well organized while he was living and into the hands of the people so it would provide them with the know-how by which they could acquire material things, including money, without violating the rights of other people. That's what he wanted more than anything else in the world.

Mr. Carnegie died in 1919, before I had even translated this into writing, but he had just checked with me and double-checked on fifteen of my seventeen principles.

There are two people that I always regretted didn't live to see me in the day of my triumph after having seen me in the days of my discouragement and opposition: my stepmother and my sponsor, Andrew Carnegie. It would have been a great joy to me and quite enough compensation for a lifetime of effort if I could have displayed to those two wonderful people the results of their handiwork in directing me at the time when I needed direction.

I'm not sure that they are not standing looking over my shoulder now. You know, there are times when I'm sure somebody is standing over my shoulder, because I say and do things that are beyond my reasonable intelligence.

I have noticed, more so in recent years than ever, that the things that I do that might be called brilliant or outstanding are always done by this man who's standing here looking over my shoulder. Always in times of emergency, when I must make important decisions, I can almost feel this man tell me what decision to make. I can almost turn around and imagine he's standing there in person as an influencer.

This is a good time to tell you this: I could never have done what has been done in connection with his philosophy if I had had nothing but the collaboration of those five or six hundred men that helped me; that wouldn't have been enough. I've had more than that. I haven't said anything about it before, because I don't want to have people feel that I have been favored or that I have anything that anybody else can't have. My honest opinion is that I don't have anything that you can't have. I think you can have the same sources of inspiration. It's just as available to you as it is to me; I believe that with all of my heart.

THE GUIDES TO HOPE AND FAITH

The next guides are twins: *hope* and *faith*. How far would you get in life if you didn't have that eternal burning flame of hope and faith working in your soul? There wouldn't be anything worth working or living for. You have to have a system for keeping your mind positive, because there are things that can destroy hope and faith. People, circumstances, things that you can't control, pop up in your life. You've got to have an antidote to those things, something that you can draw upon to offset them. I know of no better system than these guides that I have adopted, because they work for me. I've taught them to a great many other people for whom they work just as well as for me.

THE GUIDES OF LOVE AND ROMANCE

The next two are also twins: the *guides of love and romance*. I don't believe that anything worthwhile can be accomplished unless you romanticize what you're doing. In other words, if you don't put some romance into what you're doing, you don't get any fun out of it.

Certainly if there's no love in your heart, then you're not quite a human being. The main difference between the lower animals and the human being is that the human being is capable of expressing love. It's a wonderful thing. It's a great thing. It's a great builder of geniuses and of leaders, and it's a great builder and maintainer of sound health. To have a great capacity to love has been to have the privilege of rubbing elbows with genius. There's no exception to that. It's absolutely true.

The job of these two guides, love and romance, in my life is to keep me friendly with what I'm doing in life and to keep me young in body and mind. They not only do that but keep me enthusiastic, keep me sold on what I'm doing, and take the drudgery out of it.

In other words, I don't have any such thing as hard work because I don't work at anything; I play at everything I do. Everything I do is a labor of love.

I recognize, of course, that before you get in an economic position where you can forget about earning a living, there is something that you have to think about that may take a little of pleasure out of work, but if you watch yourself, you can develop a system that will make everything that you do, even washing dishes or digging ditches, a labor of love for the time being. When I go home, I help Annie Lou wash the dishes, not because she couldn't do it, but because I want to feel I'm not too good to help wash the dishes, and I get great joy out of doing it.

I also go out and about working in the garden, because if I didn't do it, Annie Lou would do it when I'm gone and deprive me of the pleasure of doing it. It's a great thing to learn to live the simple life, to be a human being instead of a stiff shirt.

Learn to get the habit of love and romance into your life, and learn to have a system whereby it will express itself in everything you do.

THE GUIDE TO WISDOM

The last one is the *guide to overall wisdom*. He controls the other seven. His business is to keep them active and eternally engaged in your service, and also to adjust you to every circumstance of your life, pleasant or unpleasant, so that you benefit by that circumstance.

I can truthfully tell you that nothing comes to my mill of life that isn't grist. I make grist out of everything that comes to my mill. The more unpleasant things that come, the more grist I get out of them, because I grind it doubly to make sure that it won't be anything else but grist. No experience in life is ever lost, whether it's good or bad, if you will adapt yourself to it right. You can always profit by every experience in life if you have a system for doing it. Of course, if you just let your emotions run wild and you go down under these unpleasant experiences, you will attract more unpleasant experiences than you will pleasant ones.

There's a peculiar thing about unpleasant circumstances: they're cowardly. When you say, "Come on, little fellow, I've got a set of harnesses right here, and I'm going to put you to work," somehow they find business around the corner. They don't come your way so often when they know that you're going to put them to work.

If you fear unpleasant circumstances, they'll crawl down on you in flocks. They'll come in through the back door and the front door. They'll come in when you're not expecting them, when you're unprepared to deal with them. I don't particularly invite unpleasant experiences, but if they're foolish enough to come my way, they'll find themselves ground up in my mill of life. I will make grist out of them as sure as anything, but I will not go down under them. Why? Because I have a system for dealing with them. I want you to have a system. I want you to teach other people to have a system.

Manage Negative Influences

Eternal vigilance is the price that one must pay to maintain a positive mental attitude because of certain opposites to positive thinking. First of all, your negative self is constantly maneuvering for power over you. Did you know that there are entities working to gain power over you on the negative side? You have to be eternally on alert to see that those entities don't take you over. You constantly have to deal with your accumulated fears, your doubts, and your self-imposed limitations lest they get the upper hand and become the dominating influence in your mind.

Second are the negative influences near you. People who are negative may include the people that you work with, the people that you live with, maybe some of your own relatives. If you don't watch, you will be just like them, because you will respond in kind. Maybe it's necessary for you to live in the same house as somebody who's negative, but it's not necessary for you to be negative just because you're in the house with somebody who is. I admit that it will be a little bit difficult for you to immunize yourself against that, but you can do it. I have done it. Mahatma Gandhi did it. Look what he did while he was immunizing himself against things he didn't want.

Number three may be some inborn negative traits you brought over with you from birth. These can be transmuted into positive traits as soon as you ferret them out and find out what they are. A lot of people are born with natural traits of a negative nature, for example, a person who's born in an environment of poverty, where all of his relatives are poverty-stricken, all the neighbors are poverty-stricken, where he saw nothing but poverty, felt nothing but poverty, heard nothing but poverty. That was the condition I was born in. It was one of the most difficult things for me to whip—this inborn fear of poverty.

Then there are worries over a lack of money and a lack of progress in your business and professional life. You can put in most of your time worrying over these things, or you can transmute that state of mind into working out ways and means of overcoming them. Think about the positive side instead of the negative side. Worrying over the negative side is not going to do anything except to get you in deeper and deeper. That's all it's going to do.

Then there is unrequited love and unbalanced emotional frustrations in your relationships with the opposite sex. You can waste your time and energy and go to the insane asylum over that, as a lot of people do, but it's not worth it. I never saw a woman who has ever walked that was worth going crazy over. I have a marvelous wife with whom I'm very much in love and who is a great benefit to me, but I wouldn't go crazy over her. If it were necessary for me to unbalance myself in order to have her, I wouldn't.

You don't have to let unrequited love destroy your balance of mind, as so many people do. It's up to you to do something about it, to maintain a positive mental attitude, and to recognize that your first duty is to yourself. Get control of yourself and do not allow anybody to upset your equilibrium, emotionally or otherwise. The Creator didn't intend that, and you shouldn't let it happen.

Next comes unsound health, either real or imaginary. You can worry a lot about the things that you think might happen to you physically, although they never do. In the *materia medica*, we call that *hypochondria*—that's a five-dollar word for it. You can put in an awful lot of time becoming negative if you don't have a positive mental attitude towards your health, if you don't develop and build up a health consciousness. Think in terms of health.

I've often said that if anything of a malignant nature happened to my physical body, I'd go out into the desert, strip my clothes off, and work in the nude in the sunlight, and I'd lick anything. I would run out there and put myself in the arms of nature, and I could lick it. I could lick it with my mind and with the sun that shines down on me. I know I could do it; I just know I could.

Your mental attitude has a tremendous amount to do with what happens to your physical body; there's no doubt about that. You can try that out anytime you please. When you think you're not feeling well, let some good piece of news come along and see how quickly you snap out of it. Haven't you had that experience? You were feeling so bad, but this good news did away with that feeling.

Then there's intolerance: the lack of an open mind on all subjects. How much trouble that gives some people and maintains a negative mental attitude.

Also, there is greed for more material possessions than you need. I've already made extensive comment on that.

Then there's lack of a definite major purpose and the lack of a definite philosophy by which you live and guide your life. The vast majority of people have no philosophy to live by. They live by hook or crook, by chance, by circumstance. They're just like a dry leaf on the bosom of the wind. They go whichever way the wind blows, and there's nothing they can do about it, because they have no philosophy of life, no set of rules to go by. They trust to luck and fortune, but generally misfortune is the one that rules.

You have to have a philosophy that you could live by. There are many fine philosophies that you can die by, but I'm much more interested in one that you can live by, and that's what we are studying here. It's a philosophy that you can live by in such a way that the neighbors around you look upon you as something desirable. They feel happy to have you there, and you feel happy to be there. You not only enjoy prosperity, contentment, and peace of mind, but you reflect that in everybody that comes into contact with you. That's the way that people should live. That's the kind of a mental attitude people should have to live by.

Last, but not least is the habit of allowing others to do your thinking for you. If you're going to do that, you will never have a positive mental attitude, because you won't have your own mind.

Everyone desires to be rich, but not everyone knows what constitutes enduring riches. Below are the twelve great riches: I want you to familiarize yourself with them. Before anybody can become rich, they have to have a fairly well balanced proportion of all of these twelve great riches.

I want you to notice where I place money relative to the others in importance. It's number twelve. Eleven other things are even more important than money for a well-rounded, well-balanced life:

1. A positive mental attitude
2. Sound physical health
3. Harmony in human relations
4. Freedom from fear
5. The hope of future achievement
6. The capacity for applied faith
7. Willingness to share one's blessings
8. Being engaged in a labor of love
9. An open mind on all subjects and toward all people
10. Complete self-discipline
11. The wisdom with which to understand people
12. Money

9

Self-Discipline

I want to call your attention to my essay "A Challenge to Life" because it is my reaction to one of the worst defeats that I've ever had in my entire career. It gives you an idea of how I go about transmuting an unpleasant circumstance into something useful. When this circumstance happened, I had a real reason to go out and fight—and I don't mean fight mentally; I mean fight physically. If I had to settle the business from behind pine trees with six-shooters, it would have been justified under the circumstances, but instead I elected to do something that would damage no one and that would benefit myself. I elected to express myself through this essay:

> Life, you can't subdue me because I refuse to take your discipline too seriously. When you try to hurt me, I laugh—and the laughter knows no pain. I appreciate your joys wherever I find them; your sorrows neither frighten nor discourage me, for there is laughter in my soul.
>
> Temporary defeat does not make me sad. I simply set music to the words of defeat and turn it into a song. Your tears are not for me, for I like laughter much better, and because I like it, I use it as a substitute for grief and sorrow and pain and disappointment.

Life, you are a fickle trickster—don't deny it. You slipped the emotion of love into my heart so that you might use it as a thorn with which to prick my soul—but I learned to dodge your trap with laughter. You tried to lure me with the desire for gold, but I have fooled you by following the trail which leads to knowledge instead. You induced me to build beautiful friendships—then converted my friends to enemies so you may harden my heart, but I sidestepped your figure on this by laughing off your attempts and selecting new friends in my own way.

You caused men to cheat me at trade so I will become distrustful, but I won again because I possess one precious asset which no man can steal—it is the power to think my own thoughts and to be myself. You threaten me with death, but to me death is nothing worse than a long peaceful sleep, and sleep is the sweetest of human experiences—excepting laughter. You build a fire of hope in my heart, then sprinkle water on the flames, but I can go you one better by rekindling the fire—and I laugh at you once more.

You have nothing that can lure me away from laughter, and you are powerless to scare me into submission. To a life of laughter, then, I raise my cup of cheer!

You may think it's easy to have that kind of an emotional reaction to an unpleasant experience, when you've been hurt and injured by those who should have been loyal to you, but I've had that experience so much in life that I have made it a habit always to react in a spirit of kindness.

I want to give you another illustration, which I think will be beneficial to all of you who are studying the finer points of this philosophy.

When *Think and Grow Rich* came out, I took the manuscript down to a well-known publisher in New York and submitted it to him. He said that they liked the title and they probably would be interested in publishing it. Weeks went by; I kept telephoning and writing, and every time I did, they gave me a stall as an excuse for not giving me an answer one way or another.

Six months went by. I went down to the office of this publisher on Madison Avenue, and I said to one of the officials, "Now I came down here to get my manuscript or to get a contract, and I'm not at all particular which it is, but I certainly am going to have one or the other before I go out of this room, and you might just as well know it. I'm tired of this dillydallying. There's shenanigans going on here that I don't know anything about, but I'm going to find out."

The publisher reached down to the bottom of his desk and pulled out my manuscript. With a sheepish, guilty grin on his face, he said, "Mr. Hill, we owe you an apology. When this manuscript came in here, it was read by all of our readers, and every one of them gave us the opinion it was the best manuscript that had ever come into our publishing office. That gave us an idea that we'd write a book of our own, and we've done that. We've been writing it under the name of another gentleman in your field. We paid him $1,000 for the privilege of using his name, but we don't have to pay him any royalties. Now his manuscript that we have written is not as good as yours, but we can sell it just as well because we're going to put $100,000 in advertising behind it. We held on to your manuscript until we got ours written, but we'll probably get ours on the market first."

"Isn't that wonderful?" I said. "What are ethics in publishing to you?" I picked up my manuscript and walked out.

When I went back and told my lawyer what had happened, he was filled with glee. "That's the finest thing that has happened in a long time. I'll collect your royalty on every copy of that book that they sell—every copy."

"Wait just a minute, my friend," I said. "You're not going to collect any royalty on that, and you're not going to sue anybody."

"Oh, yes, I am," he said, "and I can win. I'll guarantee it, so I'll take it without any fee. I'll take a percentage of what I get out of it."

"Oh, I know you want to," I said. "I'm going to try that case in a court that the publisher doesn't know anything about, where they will not be able to present their case. I'm going to try it in that court, and long after this other book has been gone and forgotten, *Think and Grow Rich* will be marching on." That's what's happening all over the world today.

I have a way of striking back at people who injure me. I definitely don't take it lying down; I'm not that kind of a man. Nobody can abuse me without my striking back. I strike back vigorously and effectively by doing the fellow who would injure me a favor instead of trying to injure him in return. Believe you me, it gives you a standing in your own estimation, in the estimation of the world, and maybe in the estimation of your Creator, that you can't get in any other way.

Striking back at people who have injured you or tried to injure you is just a lack of self-discipline. You haven't really become acquainted with your own powers or your own ways and means of benefiting by those powers if you stoop to the low level of trying to strike back at some person who has slandered you, vilified you, cheated you, or even tried to do any of those things. Don't ever do it, because you'll only lower yourself in the estimation of yourself and your Creator.

There's a better way, a better weapon that I'm trying to put into your hands with which you can defend yourself against all who would injure you. Use the self-discipline based upon this lesson and never allow anybody to drag you down to their level. You set the level on which you wish to deal with the people. If they want to come up to your level, all right. If they don't, let them stay down on theirs. There's no sin in that. Set your own high level and stand your ground, come what may. I hope that this attitude will be in your heart, and I hope it will become the same attitude that I have.

I used to strike back. I used to carry a six-shooter. As a matter of fact, I had a couple of them, and I knew how to use them too. I wasn't carrying them as ornaments. I intended to shoot anybody who got in my way. I've long since gotten to the point where a gun or a firearm of any kind would be of no more use to me than anything in the world. I have a better way of defending myself. I have a mind. I know what to do with that mind, and I never am without defense.

Let me go back to my essay "A Challenge to Life." You may be interested in knowing that that essay was largely responsible for the late Mahatma Gandhi becoming interested in my philosophy and having it published throughout India. That essay has already influenced millions of people, and in time, indirectly or directly, will be of beneficial influence to millions of people who have not yet born.

It's not the brilliance of the essay; it's the thought in back of it. You can react to these unpleasant things in life in such a way that life can conquer you, or in such a way that nobody can conquer you. When you've got laughter in your soul, you're sitting very close to the plane on which the Creator acts himself.

I get up every morning. I look at my favorite picture of my wife. I made over a hundred shots before I got the exact expression on her face that I wanted, and it's the exact expression that I saw on her face the day I asked her to marry me. I had never seen anything as heavenly as that. It was the most marvelous expression I had ever seen. I've tried time and again to capture it, and finally got it. I have it now in a picture. She has a smile that can't be described. The moment you walk into that room and take a look at it, you know that there's something in the back of that woman's mind that's very spiritual.

When Mr. Billingsley's family was up here visiting, his two little boys slept over in my apartment. One of them said, "By the way, that's a very beautiful woman—who is she?"

I said, "That's my wife."

"Oh, isn't she beautiful?" he said. "You know, she's beautiful enough to be a moving picture star, isn't she?"

"Yes, I think she is," I said.

Laughter: if you have laughter in the soul, laughter on the face, I want to tell you, you will never be without friends. You will never be without opportunity, and you will never be without a means of defending yourself against people who do not know anything about laughter.

Autosuggestion

Autosuggestion is suggestion to self through which dominating thoughts and deeds are conveyed to the subconscious mind. It is the medium by which self-discipline becomes a habit.

The starting point in the development of self-discipline is definiteness of purpose. You will notice that in every one of these lessons, come what may, approach them from whatever angle you choose, you can't get away from that term *definiteness of purpose*. It stands out like a sore thumb, because it is the starting point of all achievement. Whether it's good or bad, you may be sure that everything that you do starts with definiteness of purpose.

Why should you write out your definite major purpose, memorize it, and go over it as a ritual day in and day out? To get it into the subconscious mind. The subconscious mind gets into the habit of believing that which it hears often. You can tell it a lie over and over again, and you finally get to where you don't know whether it's a lie or not. The subconscious doesn't either. I know of people who have done just that.

Obsessional desire is the dynamo that gives life and action to definiteness of purpose. We've already gone pretty thoroughly into wishes, hopes, desires, burning desires, and faith.

How do you make a desire into an obsession? By living with it in your mind, calling it into your mind, and seeing the physical manifestation of it out there in the circumstances of your life.

Let's say you have an obsessional desire for enough money to buy a new Cadillac, but you're now driving a Ford. You want that nice new Cadillac, but you don't have enough income to pay for it. What do you do?

The first thing you do is go over to the Cadillac agency and get one of those nice, new catalogs with all the models in it. Then you flip through it and pick out the model you want. Every time you get in your Ford, before you start off, kick off the starter, and then shut your eyes for a few moments and see yourself sitting on top of a nice new Cadillac. As she purrs down the street, imagine right now that you already have this Cadillac. For the time being, you're there at the wheel of your Cadillac.

It may sound silly, but it is not silly; I can assure you it's not. I talked myself into my first Rolls-Royce that very way by putting myself out on a limb one evening in the Waldorf Astoria Hotel. I said that I was going to have it, before the week was over, although I didn't have enough money in the bank to get it.

My student sitting in that audience, who had the exactly the same car that I described, even down to the orange-colored wire wheels, called me at my hotel next morning. He said, "Come on down. I have your car, Mr. Hill." I went down there, and he had it. He had the legal transfer made out, and he handed the keys to me. He wanted to show me a little trick or two that you had to know about a Rolls-Royce in order to get the best results out of it. He took me down Riverside Drive, we drove a little bit, and he got out and shook hands with me. He said, "Mr. Hill, I'm very happy to have had the privilege of letting you have this nice car." Was that a wonderful thing for a man to do? He had said nothing about the price. He said, "You need it worse than I do. I don't actually need it all, but you do need it, and I want you to have it."

Can you imagine one man dealing with another man like that? Yes, you can. You've been students of mine, and you know your relationship with me. It doesn't take any stretch of the imagination for you to know that one of my students could do a thing like that, any more than it would take any stretch of your imagination for you to know that if you needed a favor from me and you came to me, you'd get it just as graciously as I got that car.

Be Careful What You Ask For

Be careful what you set your heart upon through obsessional desire, for the subconscious mind goes to work on translating that desire into its material equivalent.

I admonish you to be careful about what you set your heart upon because if you follow the instructions laid down in this lesson, if you set your heart on anything and stand by that decision, you're going to get it. Be sure before you start any obsessional desire about anything that what you're desiring is something that you will be willing to live with after you get it—or her or him.

What a marvelous thing it is to demonstrate in your own mind something that you desire above everything else, something that's hard to get, maybe, and then come to know that you want to live with it the rest of your life. But be careful what you demonstrate before you start demonstrating.

Out of the five hundred or more men that collaborated with me in building this philosophy, every one was immensely wealthy. I didn't pay any attention to any other kind; I was only after the ones that had made a big demonstration financially. I had no time to fool with the little boys. That wouldn't apply today, but it applied then. Every single, solitary one of them had abundance of wealth, but they did not have peace of mind. In demonstrating their wealth, they neglected to demonstrate along with it the circumstances of life through which they would not worship that wealth—through which it would not be a burden to them, through which they would have peace of mind in their relationships with their fellow men. They didn't learn that lesson. If those men could have had that lesson back in the early days, before they became immensely wealthy, they would have learned how to balance themselves with this wealth so it would not have affected them adversely.

To me, the most pitiful sight in the world is an extremely rich man who doesn't have anything else but monetary riches, and there are a lot of them in this world.

The next most pitiful thing is the boy or girl who has come into possession of great riches without having earned them, because I know that that person is doomed to a life of displeasure and unhappiness.

I've known this principle to fail only one time. John D. Rockefeller Jr. inherited a huge fortune, and he has acted in a magnificent way with that fortune, but he's the only one I've ever known.

I know one other person that comes very near it. That's my eldest son. He's now the head of a company that I organized before I was twenty-one years of age. He's a multimillionaire in his own right. The way he's rearing my granddaughters tickles me to death. If they want a diamond necklace, they go over to Woolworth's and get it, not to Tiffany's. They like it; he's taught them to like it. One day one of the girls wanted something a little bit more expensive than they thought she should have at her age. Her mother said, "You go over here to so-and-so and get one just like it, and if you have it on, with your personality nobody will ever know the difference."

In other words, my son is rearing those children as if he didn't have all of his money. In fact, yes, he has inherited it, but he is an exception to the rule because he hasn't allowed it to spoil him. I'm very proud of him, because I believe that maybe a little bit of this philosophy that I got across to him when he was young has stuck with him and always will.

Thought and Will

Your power of thought is the only thing over which you have complete, unchallenged control—control by the power of will. In giving human beings control over that one thing, the Creator must have chosen the most important of all things. This is a stupendous fact that merits your most profound consideration. If you give it this consideration, you will discover for yourself the rich promises available to those who become master of their mind power through self-discipline.

Self-discipline leads to sound physical health, and it leads to peace of mind through development of harmony within one's own mind. I have everything in this world that I need or can possibly use or wish for. I wouldn't have it in abundance if I hadn't learned self-discipline, because that's how I got it.

There was a time when I had much more money in the bank than I have today, but I wasn't as rich then as I am today. I'm very rich today because I have a balanced mind. I have no grudges. I have no worries. I have no fears. I have learned through self-discipline to balance my life. I may not be entirely at peace with the income tax men, but there is a big boy up somewhere, standing and looking over my shoulder, with whom I am at peace all the time. I wouldn't have been at peace with him if I hadn't learned the art of self-discipline, of reacting to the unpleasantnesses of life in a positive instead of a negative way.

I don't know what I would do if somebody came up and slapped my face hard without any provocation. I'm still pretty human, I think—I would double up my fist, and if I was close enough to him, I'd probably hit him right in the solar plexus, and he would go down. But if I had a few seconds to think about it, instead of doing that, I would pity him instead of hating him, pity him for being such a fool.

A lot of things that I used to do the wrong way, I do the right way now. Because I've learned to do them the right way, through self-discipline, I'm in position to be at peace with other people, with the world, and particularly with myself and with my Creator. That's a wonderful thing to have, no matter what other riches you have. If you're not at peace with yourself, your fellow men, and all those you work with, then you're not rich.

You never will be rich until you learn through discipline to be at peace with all people, all races, all creeds. I have sitting here in my audience Catholics and Protestants, Jews and Gentiles—people of different colors, different races. To me, they're all the same color, the same religion. I don't know the difference. I don't want to know the difference, because in my mind there is no difference. There was a time when petty things such as racial differences angered me or caused me to feel, at the least, out of step with my fellow man. Now I just won't let those things happen.

One of the curses of this world we're living in, particularly in this melting pot of America, is that we haven't learned how to live with one another. The Jews and the Gentiles, the Catholics and the Protestants, and the colored and the whites, they just haven't learned how to live with one another. We haven't learned it. We are in the process of learning. When we are all indoctrinated with this philosophy, we'll have a better world here in the United States, and I hope it'll spread over into other countries too.

Self-discipline enables one to keep the mind fixed on that which is wanted and off that which is not wanted. If this lesson didn't do anything else for you except start you on a on a habit or a plan whereby you occupy your mind from here on up with the things you desire and keep your mind off the things you don't desire, all the time and money that you spend on this course would be paid back a thousand times over. You would experience a new birth, a new opportunity, a new life, if you just learned through self-discipline not to let your mind feed upon the things you don't want—upon the miseries, the disappointments, the people who injure you.

Now it's much easier for me to tell you than it is for you to do it. I know what a difficult thing it is to start keeping your mind occupied with the money that you're going to have when you don't have any now. I know all about it, because I tried. I know what it is to be hungry. I know what it is to be without a home. I know what it is to be without friends. I know what it is to be ignorant and illiterate. I know how difficult it is, when you're illiterate and ignorant and poverty-stricken, to think in terms of becoming an outstanding philosopher and spreading this influence throughout the world.

I know all about that, but I did it. If I can conquer the things that I've conquered, I know that you can do an equally good job, but you'll have to be the person in charge. Take possession of your own mind, and keep it so busy occupied with the things that you want, the things you want to do, the people that you like, that you have no time left to think about the things you don't want or the people you don't like.

This philosophy is potent because it deals with the minds and brains and hearts of men in all walks of life and helps some of them have a better understanding of themselves and of other people. It helps people to appreciate why they should have self-discipline, why they shouldn't strike back at people who condescended to injure, slander, or libel them.

I couldn't begin to tell you the number of times I was libeled in newspapers back in the early days. My lawyers have on many occasions wanted me to fight back. I said, "I'm fighting back. I'm going to fight back by becoming so outstanding, by planting my name in so many hearts throughout the world that if newspaper owners are dead, they'll turn over in their graves."

There was an old man by the name of Bob Hicks who was a specialty salesman, and he disliked me because I published *The Golden Rule*. He would have liked to have had that name first, but I beat him to it. He hardly ever missed slandering me in an issue, and some of them were very dangerous slanderings. Mr. Harry S. F. Williams, who was my lawyer in Chicago, wanted me time and again to sue. He said, "I'll take his printing presses, his house, and his riches away from him before I'm through."

"No, you won't." I said.

"Why?"

"I wouldn't have him stop printing because he's calling me to the attention of a lot of people who never heard of me, and when they look into my record and compare me with him, I always come out on top. Why should I worry about stopping him?"

I'm not speaking of these things in order to show how bright or brilliant or successful I am. I think you'll never hear anybody tell you as much about my failures as I tell you myself. I've had plenty of them. I'm calling to your attention some very personal things that I have experienced myself. I was there; I was party to the transaction. I know what was done, and I know what the reaction was, and that's far better than if I told you about something that I'd heard about.

That's why I speak of myself as often as I do: because I've had an experience, a dramatic background, that has never been equaled in the life of any author, as far as I've been able to determine. No author has have ever had as great of variety of experiences as I have, and at least 50 percent of them were failures. Isn't it marvelous to know that you can go through twenty or twenty-five years of defeats and failures and opposition and still come out on top and make them like you? Isn't that an achievement? Whatever I have said or ever will say in the future dealing with the personal pronoun is justified, because I have gone through things that would ordinarily have destroyed me, and I'm teaching you how to do the same.

Three Mental Walls

I want to emphasize the three mental walls of protection against outside forces. I want to make a definite, lasting impression upon you of the necessity of building up a way of immunizing yourself against outside influences that would disturb your mental capacity, anger you, make you unhappy or afraid, or take advantage of you in any way.

I have this system, and it works like a charm.

When you have as many people knowing you all over the world as I do and as many beloved friends clamoring for appointments and so forth as I have, you have to have a system of choosing how many of them you'll see and how of them you won't. You have to have that. Maybe you don't in the beginning; I didn't, but I do now. My friends, my beloved friends, the ones that I love all over the world, would take up all of my time if I didn't have a system of keeping them from doing it. I try to keep most of them confined to dealing with me through my books—then I can reach millions of them—but when they want to deal with me in person, I have to have a system for telling how many I can see in a given length of time.

This system is a series of three imaginary walls—and they're not so imaginary either; they're pretty real. That first one is a rather wide wall. It extends way out from end to end. It's not too high, but it's high enough to stop anybody that wants to get over the wall and get to me with anything unless he gives me a very good reason for wanting to see me. My students—each of them has a stepladder. They can go right over that wall and don't even have to ask me.

Outsiders, who are not privileged as students, would have to go over that wall, and they'd have to make contact in some sort of formal way. They couldn't just come in and ring my doorbell or my telephone, because my line is not listed in a telephone book. They'd have to go through some formality.

Why do I have that wall? Why don't just I leave it down and let everybody come to see and write to me and answer all the letters that I received from all over the world?

You may be interested in knowing that on one occasion I received five mail sacks full of letters. I couldn't even look at the outside of the letters, let alone open them. I didn't have secretaries to open the mail, and thousands of these letters were not even opened. It's not quite so bad today, but the very moment I get a little publicity, letters come to me from all over the country.

Now when people get over that first wall, they immediately come into contact with another. It's much higher, many times as high, and they can't go over it with a stepladder.

For you students, there is a way of getting over it, and I'm going to tip you off on what it is: if you have something I want. You can get over that second wall very easily if I am convinced that the time I devote to you is going to be of mutual benefit to you and me both, but if it's just something that's going to benefit you and not me, the chances are that you won't make it.

There are exceptions, but very, very few, and I do use my judgment as to where the exceptions come, and there's nothing selfish about that. It's of necessity.

When you get over that second wall, you come in contact with one that's very much more narrow and it's as high as eternity. No living person ever gets over that wall, not even my wife. As much as I love her and as close as we are, she doesn't even try to get over it, because she knows that I have a sanctuary of my soul wherein nobody but my Creator and myself commune. There is where I do my best work. When I go to write a book, I retire into my sanctuary, lay out that book, commune with my maker, and get instructions. When I come to an intersection in life where I don't understand which way to go, I go into my sanctuary, I ask for guidance, and I always get it. Always.

Don't you see what a wonderful thing it is to have this system of immunity? Don't you see how unselfish it is? Your first duty is to yourself—Shakespeare's marvelous poetic lines: "To thine own self be true, / And it must follow, as the night the day, / Thou canst not then be false to any man."

I was thrilled through the marrow of my bones when I first read that. I have read it hundreds of times. I've repeated it thousands of times, because how true it is that your first duty is to yourself! Be true to yourself, protect your mind, protect your inner consciousness, your self-discipline in order to take possession of your own mind and direct it to the things you want and keep it off the things you don't want. That's your prerogative. The Creator gave you that as the most precious gift to mankind. You could do nothing less than show your appreciation by respecting that gift and using it.

Five Traits for Improvement

Next, make up a list of five traits of personality in connection with which you need self-discipline or improvement. I don't care how perfect you are; there's not a person who couldn't sit down and find traits that need improvement, if you'll really be honest with yourself. If you don't know the answers, get your wife or husband to tell you. Sometimes you won't have to ask your spouse; he or she will tell you about it. But find out five things in your personality that you need to change, and write them down.

You're not going to do anything about your defects until you take inventory of them, find out what they are, get them on paper where you can see them, and then start doing something about them.

After you discover these five traits in connection with which you need to use self-discipline for improvement, you start in immediately to develop the opposite of those traits. If you're in the habit of not sharing your opportunities or your blessings with other people, start sharing them, no matter how much it hurts. Start in where you are. If you are greedy, start in charity. If you've been in the habit of passing on a little gossip to somebody, stop that for all time to come, and pass on compliments instead.

The government of the United States wanted some information from Al Capone after he was sent down to prison in Atlanta, Georgia. They didn't have this information, and they chose me as the only man who could get it. The attorney general of the United States was responsible for my going down there and getting this information. He knew from his experience with this philosophy, and with me, that I could get it.

I went down there and made a series of three talks, at which all of the prisoners were invited, including Al. In those talks, I laid the foundation for what I wanted to find out from him by condemning those who would look for the bad in people and never look for the good. Then I complimented the men who were there in prison by saying that no matter what other people thought of them, they still had some good qualities, and I would rather center my attention on these rather than the bad ones. I was in the business of publishing and writing, and I was going to spend some time down there to find out as much as I could about some of the good qualities of the men that were there, and I would take volunteers. If anybody wanted to tell me something good about himself, I would see that the public found out about it.

Al Capone was the first one to ask for a permit to come in to the library and interview me. I had it all worked out, how I'd get him, but I didn't have to use my whole plan. He walked right into it.

Do you know that I'm now carrying out my pledge to Al Capone, although he's dead? I've been doing it ever since that time. I've been telling about the good things that I found out about him, although there weren't very many. I found out that he was paying the way of about seven or eight boys and girls through Northwestern University who could not under any circumstances have gone there without his largesse, and they didn't know who was doing it. I know he was telling the truth, because I checked with the man who was handling the funds.

In the process of hearing his story, I asked him a couple of questions indirectly that got the information I wanted for the government. It was in connection with his income tax situation and some other cases that did not involve Al personally, but some of his colleagues. I complimented him and said something good about him. You'll see a man blossom out; he'll be a different person if you start telling him about some of the things that you know are good about him.

I don't rub it on too thick. If you do, he'll wonder what you're after. Be reasonable about it. When anybody walks up to me, shakes my hand and said, "Napoleon, I have always wanted to meet you. I appreciate so much the books that you wrote, and I just wanted to tell you that I have found myself. I've been a success in my professional business now. I owe it all to *Think and Grow Rich* or *The Law of Success*." I know that that man is telling the truth because of the tone of his voice, the look in his eye, and the way he takes hold of my hand, and I appreciate it.

If he stood there and rubbed it on out of proportion to what I deserved, I would know right away that he's getting ready for a touch of some sort.

Next, make up a list of all the traits of personality of those nearest to you that you believe need to be improved by self-discipline. You will have no trouble at all making up that list. Notice the difference in the ease with which you carry out that transaction compared to the one where you're looking into your own traits of character.

Self-examination is a very difficult thing. Why? Because we're biased in our favor. We think that whatever we do, no matter how it turned out, it must be right. If it didn't turn out right, it was always the other fellow's fault, not ours.

One of these days I'm going to have somebody walk in and tell me that they had been at odds with somebody for a long time, only to find out when they got into this philosophy that the trouble was not with the other fellow, it was with themselves.

They started into self-discipline to improve themselves, and lo and behold, when their own house was clean, the other fellow's house was also clean. It's astounding how many motes you can see in the fellow's eye when you're not looking for those in your own eye. I think that everybody, before he condemns anybody, should go before a looking glass and say, "Now look here, fellow. Before you start condemning anybody, before you start passing out gossip about anybody, look yourself in the eye and find out if you have clean hands."

Remember that passage in the Bible? "You among you who is without sin, let him cast the first stone." When you make a practice of that, you'll get to the point at which you can forgive people for almost anything. Instead of hating them for some of the things that you don't like, you start pitying them. Anytime you transmute hatred into pity, you have gone a long way towards being a big person, because that's what all big people do. They learn to translate hatred in this life into pity for those who are making mistakes.

Mr. Stone has done so many things that I have been proud of. We were sitting in a conference some time ago with a couple of gentlemen who had bought a drug from Sweden to America. It was a cure for arthritis. It set a marvelous record in the old country, and they wanted to introduce it over here. Mr. Stone found out from a few questions that the man who brought it over here got it from the chemist who created it, but he created it under the auspices of a firm who had put up thousands of dollars while he was doing it. They had paid him a huge salary for a minimum of twenty years.

Now he had stolen it from them and came over here with it, wanting to sell it. Mr. Stone said, "That's enough. I wouldn't touch it with a pitchfork, because in my book of rules that's nothing but out-and-out thievery, and I will not go into business with a thief."

Oh, boy, did I feel proud of him then, because I was thinking the same thing. I was just waiting for the time when he would show his reaction to it. That's the kind of reaction you'd get from a man whose mind operates the way Mr. Stone's operates.

Control of Thoughts

The most important form of self-discipline, which should be exercised by all who aspire to outstanding success, is, of course, the control of your thoughts, the control of your mind. As a matter of fact, there's nothing else of the importance in the world except the control of your mind. If you control your own mind, you will control everything that you come into contact with. You really will. You will never be the master of circumstances, you will never be the master of the space that you occupy in the world, until you first learn to be the master of your own mind.

Mr. Gandhi, in biding years of time to gain freedom of India, used these five principles.

1. Definiteness of purpose. He knew what he wanted.

2. Applied faith. He began to do something about it by talking to his fellow men, indoctrinating them with the same desire. He didn't do anything vicious. He didn't commit any acts of mayhem or murder.

3. Going the extra mile.

4. Forming a Master Mind the like of which this world probably has never seen before. At least two hundred million of his fellow men, all contributing to that Master Mind alliance, the main object being to free themselves from British rule without violence.

5. Self-discipline on a scale without parallel in modern times.

These are the elements that made Mahatma Gandhi the master of the great British Empire. No doubt about it.

Self-discipline—where in the world would you find a man that would stand all of the things that Gandhi did—all of the insults, all of the incarcerations that he went through while standing his ground, and yet not striking back in kind? He struck back just as I struck back at that publisher that wanted to steal my book. He struck back on his own ground with his own weapons.

That's a very safe thing to do. If you have to go to battle with somebody, select your own battleground, select your own weapons, and then if you don't win, it's your own fault.

In 1942 R.G. LeTourneau called me in. He was in trouble with a vicious communistic outfit operating in the name of a labor union, which by no means represented the higher standard of labor unionism.

They had a three-month start on me and a $100,000 corruption fund with which to carry on their work. They would go in, pick out a key man in each department, and pay him four or five times as much as the company paid to instigate gripes and complaints. When I got down there, there were some thirty-five to fifty complaints, not one of them legitimate.

Here's what I did to combat that. I didn't start in there to fight unionism. In the first place, I believe in unionism, if it is a clean union. I don't believe in racketeers and thugs and ex-convicts taking possession of union men and voting them like they were sheep, but I believe in clean unionism. I started in and I made teachers out of their superintendents and foremen. Through those teachers, I took this philosophy to the rank and file. I indoctrinated them with it. I had the teachers translate the philosophy into the jargon of the man's job so he could understand it.

These racketeers spent their $100,000, and they finally pulled up and went back north. They said that nobody down south had sense enough to join the union. They never did learn, and I suppose don't know today, what licked them. They didn't learn that I was in the plant, or if they did, it didn't mean anything to them. They hadn't the slightest idea, because I chose my own weapons, my own ground, and my own means of fighting. They were helpless to do anything about it because they didn't understand my language.

I want you to remember that, because in one way or another, you're going to have to battle throughout life. You're going to have to plan campaigns, put yourself across, remove opposition from your way. You've got to be smarter than your enemies. The way to do it is not to strike back on battlegrounds of their choice, with weapons of their choice, but to select your own battleground and your own weapon.

Does what I'm saying mean anything to you? The time will come when it will mean something to you, when you've got a problem to solve. Somebody's opposing you and you've got to go around them—then you will think of this lesson wherein I said choose your battleground and choose your own weapons.

Condition yourself first for the battle by making up your mind that you're not under any circumstances going to try to destroy anybody or to do anybody any injury, other than that of defending your own rights.

When you take that attitude, I want to tell you that you've just as good as won before you ever started. I don't care who your adversary is, how strong he is, or how smart he is. If you use those tactics, you're bound to win.

How do you know that I'm telling the truth? I have had almost every conceivable kind of experience wherein I was insulted, defrauded, cheated, lied about, slandered, libeled, and I'm still going stronger than ever. In other words, all of that just contributed to making me popular all over the world. Now why would I back away from the philosophy that I know works better than the average philosophy, whereby the person strikes back in kind?

Create a system whereby you take full possession of your own mind and keep it occupied with all the things, circumstances, and desires of your choice and strictly off the things you do not want.

You may at times find it a little bit difficult to keep your mind fixed on all the money you're going to have from teaching this philosophy when you don't have enough now.

I know you'll be in that position, but if you try hard enough, you're going to look ahead, and you're going to see the time when you're going to occupy space in the hearts of thousands of people. You're going to see the time when you make as much money as I ever made from teaching.

When the money is not coming in as fast as it should, forget about it for the time being. If bills come in that you're not able to pay, there's always one way that you can pay them temporarily: you can put them under the carpet. Don't look at them; don't let them bother you. What's the use of letting them lie around where every time you look, you see them on top of the desk? There's no percentage in that. Hide them; put them away. Of course you will be reminded of them sooner or later, but don't worry about that. Cross that bridge when you come to it.

Commence thinking about the time when you'll have plenty of money. I know that can be done, because I have attained that degree. I was not blessed with anything that you don't have, and maybe not half as much as some of you have. My background was certainly much more difficult than that of most of you. If I made the grade, I know you can make it, but you'll have to take possession. You are an institution and enterprise, each one of you, and you have to be in charge of your institution and your enterprise. You've got to call the shots and see that they're carried off, and you have to have the self-discipline with which to do it.

You go about keeping your mind off the things you don't want by occupying your mind, and seeing in your imagination, the things that you do want. Even though you don't have physical possession, you can always have mental possession. Unless you have mental possession of a thing first, you will never have physical possession of it, unless somebody wishes it upon you or it accidentally falls on you when you're walking by. Anything that you get or acquire by desire must be created and gotten in your mental attitude first, and you must be very sure about it there. You must see yourself in possession of it, and that takes discipline.

Your reward for doing this is mastery of your own destiny through the guidance of infinite intelligence. Isn't that a marvelous reward for taking possession of your own mind? It gives you direct contact with infinite intelligence.

There's a person standing looking over my shoulder and guiding me. When I meet with obstacles, all I have to do is to remember that he's right there. If I come to an intersection and I don't know which way to turn, all I have to do is to remember that that invisible force is looking over my shoulder, and he'll always point the right direction if I pay attention to him and have faith in him. Again, the only way I could make a statement like that and know that it's true is by having practiced it.

Now the penalty for not taking possession of your mind, which is the penalty that the majority of people pay all the way through life, is this: you will become the victim of the stray winds of circumstance, which will remain forever beyond your control.

What are the stray winds of circumstance? You'll become the victim of every influencer you come into contact with—enemies and everyone else alike. All these things that you don't want will sway you like a leaf on the bosom of the wind. Unless you take possession of your own mind, that's the penalty that you must pay. Isn't it a strange thing to contemplate?

Isn't it a profound thing to recognize that you have been given a means by which you can declare and determine your earthly destiny? Along with that comes a tremendous penalty that you must pay if you don't embrace that asset and use it. But there is a tremendous reward that you receive automatically if you accept that asset and use it. If I didn't have any other evidence of a first cause or a Creator, I would know there had to be one, because that's too profound for any human being to think of.

Giving you a great asset and then penalizing you for not accepting it, and rewarding you if you do accept it—that's the sum and substance of what happens when you use self-discipline to take possession of your own mind and direct it to the things you want.

Never mind what you want; that's nobody's business except yours. I don't want you to forget that. Don't let anybody come along and sell you an idea as to what you should want. Who's going to tell me what I want or what I should want? Me. It has not always been that way, but it is that way today. There isn't anybody going to tell me what I want; I'll do that. If I allowed anybody else to tell me, I'd think it was an insult to my Creator, because he intended that I should have the last word about this guy here.

Avoid Harming

I don't hurt anybody else. I would do nothing in this world, under any circumstances, to injure anybody or anything, not even an insect. When I'm driving on the highways, if I see a snake on the road, I carefully steer around it. I don't want to harm anything that's not harming me.

Mrs. Hill and I were out in the mountains of California, in very rugged country on a very steep winding road, and we discovered a rattlesnake. He was a big fellow, coiled on the edge of the road. He was waiting there for a mouse or a bird or some unsuspecting thing to come out so he could get his dinner. I've waited many a time for my dinner, but I didn't get it. I know how troublesome it is to be disturbed when you're working for your dinner. Instead of running over him, I steered immediately around him and made sure I cleared him by three feet or more.

My wife said, "Why didn't you kill that snake?"

"Why kill a snake?" I said. "He's up here in his own domain. We're the interlopers. We're up here in his territory. He wasn't bothering us. He had no chance of damaging us."

"Some children might come along."

"Now listen," I said. "Anybody that would let their children come up here in this rough territory and not protect them—after all, a rattlesnake has his rights too, same as people. He's in his own territory, minding his own business."

Then we both had a laugh about it. Annie Lou put her head on my shoulder, pulled me over, and kissed me, saying, "That's one of the things I love you for, because you don't want to harm anything or anybody."

I walked into a store down in Toccoa, Georgia, while I was working for Mr. LeTourneau. I saw one of these beautiful pump guns—.22 repeating rifles—like I used to have when I was a youngster and with which I killed rabbits and squirrels and anything else that got in my way.

It brought back days of my youth, and I walked into that store and examined the gun. It costs three times as much now as when I bought one a long time ago. I was just about to shell out the cash and take that gun when I said to myself, "What am I going to do with this gun after I get it?"

I became ashamed of myself—I really became ashamed that I even walked in and looked at it. I wouldn't shoot a rabbit: rabbits come up to my place and feed in my backyard. I had quails down in my place in Florida. They would come up for their daily meal, and if they weren't fed on time, they'd squawk about it and call me out to feed them. Would I have gone out there with a shotgun, double-crossed them, and killed two of them? I wouldn't do that. I wouldn't shoot anything; I wouldn't kill anything. If I had a gun, what good would it do to me? There's nothing to shoot at except tin cans, and I've got other things to do better than shooting at tin cans, so I didn't buy the gun.

As I walked out, I heard a remark that the salesman made to the owner of the store. I got a great laugh out of it. It was a very understandable remark, and it was made in words that were very audible.

As I walked out the door, the boss said, "I suppose you asked him why he didn't take the gun?" The boy said. "No. The damn nut."

That was one time I was proud that I was a damn nut. I wouldn't buy a gun to kill something. I don't believe in killing; I don't believe in hurting; I believe in cultivating. I get a tremendous kick out of cultivating wildlife. I can go out into the country and call them right up to me anytime I want to. I've done it time and time again. I talk to them in their own language. I even taught some of the quails down in Florida to sing their song. If there are any country men here, you know that when you flush a covey of quails and they go off, when they want to reassemble, they have a call. I taught them to sing it.

One of my neighbors, who was up there when I was feeding the quail, said, "I never saw anything like this in my life. They act like chickens. They're not afraid of you."

"No, not only that, but I've taught them to sing the song."

"Oh, now. I'm seeing them out there eating your corn, but brother, don't push my credibility, because I'll get to the point where I won't believe I even saw them."

"Just to make sure that you don't put me down as one who, let us say, overstates fact, when they get through eating, they will go back down in there, into the field and they won't all go together. They will be separated and I'll give the assembly call; watch how they reply."

I let out one whistle and the quail picked it right up. I did that a dozen times more than I'd ever done it before, just to show this fellow that he was the doubting Thomas, but I wasn't lying to him.

You can cultivate things that are dumb and don't understand English. There's a way that you can do it, so they love you. They don't fear you. They're a part of you.

You'd be surprised at the conversations I have with my dogs when I go home. I put words in their mouths that they themselves don't understand, don't know about, but they respond. It's a marvelous thing. Everybody that comes to my place marvels at the relationship I have with my dogs, and how much they understand me.

When anybody rings the doorbell, the dogs have to go to the door and be introduced; they will not take no for an answer. They will go up and first smell a man's ankle, see how he smells, and then smell his hands. If he smells right, they treat him civilly, and if he doesn't smell, they bark and put us on notice. We don't have anything to do with it, and they never make a mistake. They always know good people from bad.

The point I'm making is that you've got to have the right kind of discipline over yourself. Understand that everything is put here in this world for a purpose, and it's not your job to go out and annihilate anything else if it's not bothering you, especially your neighbors and the people you work with, and even the people who disagree with you and make it difficult for you. It's not your business to annihilate them. Aren't they doing enough to themselves without you pitching in and helping?

Anybody who would start out to slander me—one of my associates said, "Don't you think he's done himself enough damage without my striking back?" Anybody who wrongs another person does something to himself that I don't want ever to do to myself.

I was talking to a prosecuting attorney, a man with whom I went to school when I was in high school. He was telling me about his marvelous successes—how many people he'd convicted—and he seemed to be boasting about them. Maybe some of them should have been in jail, but when he got through, I said, "Albert, I wouldn't be in your shoes for all of the tea in China."

He said, "Why?"

"Look at the things you've done to people—putting them in jail, taking away their liberty."

"They should have been taken away."

"I'll grant you that, stupid boy. I still stick to my statement. I'd rather you'd have done it than myself."

I told him about old Judas out here at the stockyards. The people had a steer that was trained to go down to the cattle that'd be shipped in there. These cattle instinctively knew that they were there to be murdered, and they didn't want to go up that ramp to where a man was going to knock them in the head with a hammer. But old Judas was trained to go down there and mix with them, tell them a lie or two, and then start back up, and they'd all follow him.

When he got up to the top of the ramp, there was a swinging door. He jumped through that way, and they went on through. They didn't see the swinging door. They would go on through where the man struck them down with a hammer.

That went on for several years, and guess what happened to old Judas? He went crazy, and they had to take him in there and knock him in the head too. That's what happened to him.

Whatever you do to or for another person, you do to or for yourself: it's an eternal law. Nobody can avoid or evade that law.

That's why I wouldn't be a prosecuting attorney. That's why I was proud that I didn't follow my inclination and become a lawyer. I had a long visit with my brother, Vivian. He's a lawyer. He specializes in divorce suits, especially of very wealthy people. I want to tell you the penalty he's paid for knowing too much about the bad side of domestic relations. He got so much of that that he came to the conclusion all women were bad, and he never married. He's never had the pleasure of a wife, as I have had. He thinks that all women are bad because he's judging them by the ones he knows best, which is a common trait of all of us. We judge people by the ones we know best, don't we? It's not always fair to do that, certainly not in this case.

I'm disclosing a lot of my personal experiences. In doing so, I'm calling to your attention some of the vital things in life that you need to deal with. You need to understand yourself, understand people, and understand how to adjust yourself to people that are difficult to get along with. You need to know that, because there are a lot of people in this world that are difficult to get along with, and there are going to be a lot as long as you and I live, and long after that. We can't do away with people that are difficult to get along with, but we can do something about it by doing something with ourselves.

Self-discipline means complete control over both the body and the mind. That doesn't mean changing your mind or your body. It means controlling them. The great emotion of sex gets more people into trouble than all the other emotions combined, and yet it's the most creative, most profound, and most divine of all of the emotions. It's not the emotion that gets people in trouble; it's their lack of controlling it, directing it, and transmuting it, which they would be readily able to do if they had self-discipline. So it is with other faculties of the body and the mind.

It's not that you have to change completely. It's just that you have to be the master. You have to be in control. You have to recognize the things that you must do in order to have sound health and peace of mind.

Maintain the Sewer System

I have a sewer system; each one of us has. You don't like to think of those things, but you might as well, because you know you have one. If you don't give it some attention and adjust it properly, you will have toxic poisoning, and if you have toxic poisoning, you will be in a bad humor when you get up in the morning, and you'll be irritable to get along with.

When I went down to LeTourneau's, I found more bad dispositions than I ever had come in contact with. I found out that men were not getting the right kind of food. I went down to Atlanta and got a food expert to put in a marvelous cafeteria and give them the right kind of food combination. I put it in a battery of detoxifying machines under the direction of a doctor with whom I made arrangements to collaborate with me. Our detoxifying machine was a machine that runs a gallon of water through your intestinal tract every minute—sixty gallons in an hour—water mixed with oxygen and other things that cleanse you inside out. I've had men that were grouchy with headaches; I'd send them over to be detoxified. In one hour, they'd be back on the job full of pep and enthusiasm.

These things are not something that you would want to talk about in your drawing room socially, but here we are professionally. You may just as well know now that if you're going to have a good body and going to be in control of it, you've got to learn to keep this intestinal tract in the right condition.

Self-Control in Speech and Thought

Self-discipline also means the development of daily habits by which the mind is kept busy in connection with the things and the circumstances that one desires and off the circumstances one does not desire. It means that you will not accept or submit to the influence of any circumstance or thing you do not desire—none at all. Don't submit to it. You may have to tolerate it, you may have to recognize it, but you don't have to submit to it. You don't have to admit that it's stronger than you are. Instead you assert that you're stronger than it. You can give your imagination a wide range of operations as to these things that you're going to have to deal with, but you're not going to submit to them.

Self-discipline also means that you will build a three-wall protection around yourself so no one will ever know all about you or what goes on in your mind.

Would you want anybody in this world to know all about you? If you're in your right mind, you won't. Would you want anybody to know all that you think about him? I'm sure you wouldn't.

The average person talks too much for his own good. A lot of people make the mistake of letting anybody know everything that goes on their mind. All you have to do is start them talking. You know these people who start their mouths working and then go off and leave them. They just get started, and you find out everything about them—good and bad.

J. Edgar Hoover, with whom I did some professional work on a great many occasions and still do at times, told me once that the fellow who is being investigated is the best help to him of all, because he gets more information from the guy that he's tracing than from all other sources combined.

"Why?" I said.

"Because he talks too damn much." That was his exact reply.

Tell me what a man fears, and I will tell you how to master him. The minute you find out what anybody fears, you will know exactly how to control them—if you were foolish enough to want to control anybody on that basis. I don't want to control anybody with fear. If I control anybody, I want it to be on the basis of love.

There was a fortune teller in Georgia. There's no doubt about it in this world that she was highly psychic, but she was also an intelligent observer, and the slightest word that you spoke, the tone of your voice, would give her the cues to what your troubles are. She was a whizbanger. People were lined up out there in limousines, Packards, and Cadillacs at $5 per interview, and she was busy all day.

She had a good racket. It wasn't so much of a racket either, because she was doing a lot of those people a lot of good. She didn't pull her punches. If she found something wrong with the person, she'd tell them outright.

They took me out to see her because I was a doubting Thomas. I said there wasn't a person that lived that could penetrate my mind if I didn't want him to. This man said, "Well, you come on out."

I went out. We walked in. She started asking me questions, and I answered as far as I possibly could with a yes or no. Sometimes, I would say, "No comment." I wouldn't give her the satisfaction of it. With some questions, I couldn't answer yes or no without giving her a cue.

She worked on me, and sweat broke out over her face. Beads of sweat dropped as big as the end of my little finger; I never saw anything like it. She was sweating, trying to get some cue to enter my mind, and once she got in there, she would have told me plenty, no doubt.

Finally she turned to the man who brought me and said, "Lee, you take this young man out of here. I don't know anything about him, and I'm not going to know anything about him."

Out we went. I don't know what she thought about it, but I know why she couldn't tell me anything about myself: because I wouldn't let her. You can have that kind of discipline. I know you can, because I've done it.

Mr. Ford once called in one of his most trusted employees. He had been with him for thirty-five years, ever since the beginning of the Ford Motor Company. Mr. Ford paid him, I think, two years' salary in advance and fired him.

The man wanted to know what he fired him for. Mr. Ford said, "To be candid with you, I don't want anybody around me who knows all about me, and you're the only one of my employees that knows all about me."

It seemed a little bit cruel if you didn't understand what he had in mind. He didn't want anybody around him who knew him in the days when he had weaknesses that he perhaps no longer had.

I'm a little bit different from Mr. Ford. A lot of people come in contact with me who knew me when I had my weaknesses and was going through my failures. Far from not wanting them to know all about me, I'm glad to see them again, because they find out how much I've improved.

10

Developing Enthusiasm

We're going to study how one goes about developing enthusiasm. The very first step in creating enthusiasm is based upon a burning desire. As a matter of fact, when you learn how to work yourself up into a state of a burning desire, you won't need the rest of the instructions on enthusiasm, because you've already got the last word in enthusiasm.

When you want something badly, you make up your mind to get it. You have that burning desire. It steps up your thinking processes. It puts your imagination to work on ways and means.

That enthusiasm gives you a brighter mind. It makes you more alert to opportunities. You will see opportunities that you never saw before when your mind is stepped up to that state of enthusiasm, to a burning desire for something definite.

Passive and Active Enthusiasm
Next there is active enthusiasm and passive enthusiasm. What do I mean by *active* and *passive*? I'll give you an illustration of passive enthusiasm. Henry Ford was the most lacking in active enthusiasm of any man I have ever seen. I never heard him laugh but once in his life. When he shook hands, it was like taking hold of a piece of cold

ham. You did all the shaking. He did nothing but stick his hand out and take it back when you let loose of it. In his conversation, there was no magnetism in his voice whatsoever. There was no evidence of any shape, form, or fashion of active enthusiasm.

What kind of enthusiasm did he have? He must have had some to have such an outstanding major purpose and to have achieved it so successfully. It was inward. His enthusiasm was transmuted into his imagination, his power of faith, and his personal initiative. He went ahead on his own initiative. He believed that he could do whatever he wanted to do. He kept himself alert and keen with applied faith through his enthusiasm—his passive enthusiasm—thinking inside his own mind what he was going to do and all the joy he'd get out of doing it.

I once asked him, "How do you go about making sure that whatever you want to do, you know you're going to do it before you start?"

"For a long time," he said, "I have formed the habit of putting my mind on the can-do part of every problem. If I have a problem, there's always something I can do about it. Many things, I can't do, but there's something I can do, and I start where I can do something. As I use up the can-do part of it, the no can do simply just vanishes. When I got to the river, where I expected to have to have a bridge, I didn't need the bridge, because the river was dry."

Isn't that a marvelous statement for a man to make? He started in where he could do something. He said that if he wanted to turn out a new model or increase his production, he immediately put his mind to work on the plans by which he could do that. He never paid any attention to the obstacles, because he knew that his plan was sufficiently strong, definite, and backed with the right kind of faith so that the opposition would melt away when he came to it. He said, "If you take that attitude of putting your mind behind the can-do part of every problem, the no-can-do part takes to its heels and runs." I'm quoting his words.

I can endorse everything that he said because that's been my experience: if you want to do something, you'll work yourself up into a state of white-hot enthusiasm. Go to work where you stand. If it's nothing more than drawing a picture in your mind of the thing you want to do, keep drawing that picture, making it more vivid all the time. Insofar as you make use of the tools that are available to you now, other and better tools will be put in your hands. That's one of the strange things of life, but that's the way it works.

Voice Control

Public speakers and teachers can express enthusiasm by control of the voice. One of my students was riding down to class with me this evening and paid me a very high compliment. She wanted to know if I had had any voice training or voice culture or anything like that.

"Nothing—not a thing." I said. "I had a course in public speaking a long time ago, but I violate everything that teacher ever taught me about it. In other words, I have my own system."

"Well," she said, "you have the most marvelous voice, and I often wondered if you hadn't had carefully trained to impart the enthusiasm."

"No, the answer to the voice I have is this: no matter who hears it, no matter how inexperienced or how much of a cynic that person may be, the person knows one thing: that when I say something, I believe what I'm saying. I'm sincere about it."

That's the grandest voice control that I know anything about: to express enthusiasm through the belief that the thing that you're saying is the thing that you ought to say and that it will do some good for the other fellow and perhaps for you too.

I have seen public speakers march all over the stage, run their fingers through their hair, and stick their hands in their pockets with all kinds of personal gestures. All that does to me is distract my attention.

I have trained myself to stand in one position. I never march around over the stage. I sometimes spread out my hands, but not very often. The effect that I want to have is, first of all, sincerity, and then putting my own enthusiasm back in the tone of my voice. If you learn to do that, you have a marvelous asset.

One must feel enthusiasm before being able to express it. I don't see how in the name of heaven anybody could express enthusiasm when his heart was breaking or he was in distress or in trouble.

The Actor's Discipline

I did sit in a show once in New York where the star came on and gave a marvelous performance. About three minutes before she came on, she had discovered that her father had just dropped dead. You would never have known at all. She gave the performance as perfectly as I could imagine it could be given, with not the slightest indication that anything happened. She trained herself to be an actress once and always, no matter what the circumstances. If she hadn't trained herself, then she wouldn't have been an actress.

An actor who can't fall into the skeleton shape of his character that he's trying to portray and feel as that character ought to feel will not be an actor. He may express the words and lines that are written for him, but he'll never leave the right impression on an audience unless he lives the thing he's trying to put across.

There are really great actors in all walks of life, and they're not all on the stage. There are some in private life. The great actors in life are all people who can put themselves into the role they're trying to portray. They feel it, they believe in it, they have confidence in it, and they have no trouble in conveying a spirit of enthusiasm to the other fellow.

Feeling must be an important part of expressing enthusiasm. Work yourself up into a state of heat, a burning desire. You do that with autosuggestion or self-hypnosis.

Are you afraid of hypnotism? You'd better not be, because you're using it every day, whether you know it or not. You're using hypnotism all the time. Sometimes you use it in a negative way. You hypnotize yourself into believing that you're having hard luck, that your friends are turning against you, that your job is not as it should be. You're probably stricken, maybe you have something wrong with you physically—you're hypnotizing yourself into a belief that's not going to do you any good.

I believe in self-hypnosis with all of my heart, but I believe in hypnotizing myself into getting the things I want and not the things I don't want.

I have never found a successful person in any calling in life that has not learned the art of self-hypnosis, the art of throwing himself or herself into the desired role through hypnotism. In other words, believing in things so definitely that they couldn't be any other way.

That's far from the way the average person uses hypnosis, or allows hypnotism to use him or her. The average person allows the circumstances of life to come along and, through autosuggestion, to hypnotize him into believing in things that are detrimental.

Enthusiasm is a mighty tonic for all of the negative influences that get into your mind. If you want to burn up a negative influence, just turn on the enthusiasm. The two can't stay in the same room at the same time. You start being enthusiastic over anything, and I defy you to let this doubting culture, these thoughts of fear, come into your mind.

Inject Enthusiasm into Conversations

Once you've practiced the development of enthusiasm in daily conversations and learned to turn it on or off at will, there's nothing to hinder you from making a guinea pig out of every person you converse with. You don't need to tell them they're guinea pigs, because they won't like that, but you can immediately start to step up the tone of your voice when you're conversing with other people. You can put a smile in your words and inject a pleasant tone, a pleasant feeling, into it. Sometimes you can do that only when your voice is down, and you're not talking so loud. At other times, you can do it by stepping it up, so that they can't fail to hear you and recognize what you're doing.

In other words, learn to inject enthusiasm into your ordinary daily conversations. You have somebody to practice on in every person you come into contact with. If you don't see anybody around, look for somebody on the street and start talking to him. Why not? Be careful what you say, that's all. I can go up to anybody I want on the street and start talking and get away with it, but I would select my subject, my manner of approach, and tone of voice so as not to create suspicion that I was trying to do something crooked.

This assignment of practicing on people that you come into contact with daily is a marvelous thing. Watch what happens when you start doing it. Naturally, you start changing your tone of voice. You will go out deliberately intending to make the other fellow smile while you're talking to him or her and to make that person like you.

It's not good to put enthusiasm into telling another fellow what you think about him if you don't think something pleasant, because the more enthusiastic you are, the less he likes you. When you start telling another person what you think of him for his own good, you'd better be smiling. Nobody wants anybody to reprimand him, overhaul him, or tell him something for his own good, because he knows very well there's a selfish motive in it somewhere along the line, or at least he's likely to think so.

Speech in a monotone is always boring. If you're not able to get variety, color, and rise and fall in the inflection of your voice, you're going to be monotonous no matter what you're saying or to whom. I can come out here and keep you from going to sleep by arousing you with a question that you weren't prepared for and then letting you answer it, but mostly by getting enthusiasm into my tone of voice—raising my voice, letting it back down again, and keeping you guessing what I'm going to say next. That's a good way to hold an audience: keep them guessing what you're going to say next. If you talk in a monotone and with no enthusiasm in what you're saying, the listener will be way ahead of you. He knows what you're going to say long before you say it. Whatever it is, he doesn't want to hear it in the first place.

Use Facial Expressions

Facial expression should also express enthusiasm with a properly directed smile. I hate to see a person talking to me at close range with a serious expression on his face that never changes. Even though the topic of conversation is one of a serious nature, I like to see the person soften his face with a smile.

If you watch Mr. Stone, he stops quite often through his speeches and smiles. He's got a winning smile. He disarms anybody that he's talking to, even though he's saying something the other person doesn't want to hear. He can disarm the other person by this change of expression on his face. He's a master at that. I'm not a master at it, but I can do it when I want to.

That's a part of self-discipline too—to be able to look at the other person and let him know, by the way you're speaking and the way you look, that you say what you mean and that you mean it for his benefit.

Start now to observe people who express enthusiasm in their conversational relations, also people who do not. You'll get a great lesson in attractiveness of personality. If you see a person that you particularly like, watch that person. Find out what it is about him or her that makes you like him. Chances are that whatever that person says, whatever conversation he engages in, it will be on an enthusiastic basis. You will never be bored, no matter how much he talks or what he says, because he makes it so attractive that you'll never get tired of it.

Practice before a Mirror

Form definite habits by which you learn to express enthusiasm in your ordinary conversations. Practice before a mirror; talk to yourself if you can't find anybody who's willing to listen. You'll be surprised how interesting it is when you start talking to yourself and say the things you want to hear. Don't say the things you don't want to hear when you're looking at yourself in the glass.

I stood before a mirror for years and years, and I told myself, "Look here, Napoleon Hill, you admire Arthur Brisbane's style of writing—that clarity, that simplicity of the language. But Napoleon, you're not only going to catch up with Arthur, but you're going to run rings around him."

Ladies and gentlemen, I did just that by talking to this fellow and convincing him it could be done.

It's not foolish to talk to yourself in the mirror, but be sure to close the bathroom door. Don't leave the door open, and don't talk too loud if there are people around too close, because they will probably call the psychiatric ward.

Use discriminations in all these things, but you've got an overhauling job to do on yourself. We all have at one time or another. You've got to do an overhauling job, and you've got to do it more or less in private, on your own terms, and in your own way, so not to stir up too much opposition from relatives and people who think you're a little bit queer.

If anybody wants to think I'm queer because I've started to rebuild my personality and my character, then I'm queer, because I have done a lot of that, and I'm still at it. I haven't quit yet; I never will. I'm working on myself all the time. In everything that I do in my thinking my talking, my teaching, and my writing, I want to attain to a greater degree of proficiency. My education is never completed. It's wide open all the time.

As long as you're green, you will continue to grow, but when you get to where you're ripe, the next step is to become rotten. I'll never be ripe with knowledge, I'll never learn the last word about anything. I'm always learning from people. I get much more from you than you do from me, because I have several hundreds of you to learn from, and you only have one. But I wouldn't get anything from you if I didn't have an open mind, if I wasn't trying to learn from you all the time.

Write Out a Lecture

To teach the science of success, write out an entire lecture on each of the seventeen principles of success, and practice reading them with enthusiasm. Write it out exactly how you're going to tell it to the other fellow. It won't take you long. Even if it take you an hour, several hours a day, or even two or three days, the time will come when those lectures will be worth a king's ransom. Recognize that the time will come when you can combine those lectures into a book and it can become a best seller.

Write good lectures on the seventeen principles to get ideas and illustrations of your own. You'll be surprised at what those lectures will mean to you in the way of income later on. They'll be helpful to you not only while you're teaching, but in many other ways.

When you start writing out your own lectures, you're going to become really indoctrinated with this philosophy. You will never have the full benefit of the philosophy until you teach it, write it out, and lecture on it.

There was a long time in the beginning when my lectures consisted of my telling the other fellow what to do, although I wasn't doing it myself, but the day came when my self-hypnosis got hold of me and I started believing what I was telling the other fellow. Why? Because I saw it working for him. I discovered my philosophy was good—very good; I could use a little of it too. When I started using it, it made life pay off on my own terms.

When you express enthusiasm in your daily conversations, observe how others pick up your enthusiasm and reflect it back to you as their own. You can change the attitude of anybody that you want to, anybody you're having any sort of mental intercourse with, simply by working yourself up into a state of enthusiasm. It's contagious: they pick it right up and they reflect it back to you as their own. All master salesmen understand that. If they don't, they are not master salesmen. They're not even ordinary salesmen if they don't know how to key up the buyer with their enthusiasm, no matter what they're selling. It works just the same in selling yourself as it does in selling services or commodities or merchandise.

Go into any store and pick out a salesman who knows his business. You'll recognize that that salesman is not only showing you merchandise, but along with it he's giving you some information in a tone of voice that impresses you.

Most salesmen in the stores are not salesmen at all. They're order takers. I've often heard them say, "I sold so much today." I heard a man who sells newspapers tell many papers he'd sold that day. He hadn't sold any at all. He had them out, and people came along, laid their money down, and bought them. He wasn't selling any; he was putting the merchandise where the people could pick it up and buy. But he thought he was a salesman, and a pretty good one.

Now that's an extreme case, but you see a lot of people who wrap up merchandise and take your money who think they've made a sale. They haven't made anything, because you've done the buy. You can't say that about a good salesman. You're going to buy a shirt, and before you get out of there, he'll sell you some underwear, some socks, a tie, and a nice new belt. One did that just a day or two ago. I didn't need a belt, but he showed me a nice one. I bought it mostly because of the personality of the man who was talking about it. I'm not immune to this either.

Transmute Unpleasant Circumstances

When you meet with any unpleasant circumstance, learn to transmute it into a pleasant feeling by repeating your major purpose with great enthusiasm. In other words, when any kind of an unpleasant circumstance comes across your path, instead of brooding over it or allowing it to take up your time in regret or frustration or fear, switch over to thinking about the thing that you're going to accomplish. Start thinking about the thing that you can put enthusiasm into. Use your enthusiasm for the things you want and not for the things that you've just lost through defeats.

A lot of people allow a death in the family or of loved ones to distract them. I've known people lose their minds over that. When my father passed away in 1939, I knew he was going to pass away. We knew what his condition was, and we knew it was only a question of time. I conditioned my mind so it could not possibly upset me or make the slightest impression on me emotionally.

I got a call from my brother one evening down at my estate in Florida. I had some distinguished company there talking about the publishing business. The maid came in and said that my brother wanted to speak with me on the telephone. I went out of the room and talked to him for three or four minutes.

He told me that our father had passed away and that the funeral would be that coming Friday. We chatted a little while about other things. I thanked him for calling me and went back to my company. Nobody, not even many members of my family, knew what happened until the next day. There was no expression of sorrow or anything of that kind. What was the use? I couldn't save him. He was dead. Why grieve myself to death over something I couldn't do anything about?

You'd say that's hard-hearted. No, it's not hard-hearted at all. I knew it was going to happen. I adjusted myself to it so that it could not destroy my confidence or make me afraid. In matters as serious as that, you have to learn to give yourself immunity against being upset emotionally.

When you're upset emotionally, you're not quite sane. You don't digest your food, you're not happy, you are not successful. Things go against you when you're in that frame of mind, and I don't want things to go against me. I don't want to be unhealthy. I want to be successful. I want to be healthy. I want things to come my way, and the only way that I can ensure that is to not let anything upset my emotions.

I don't think anybody can love in a deeper way or more often than I have, but if I had unrequited love (and I've had that circumstance once in life), I could let that upset me badly, but I didn't. Why? Because I have self-control, because I won't let anything destroy my equilibrium.

I didn't want my father to die, but as long as he was dead, there was nothing I could do about it. There was no use of me dying too just because he had. I've seen people do that—go ahead and die because somebody else had died.

I'm giving you an extreme illustration, but it's one that's needed by everybody. We need to learn to adjust ourselves to the unpleasantnesses of life without going down under them. The way to do that is to divert your attention away from the unpleasant over to something that is pleasant and put all of the enthusiasm you've got back of that other something.

When people want to call you queer, let them call you whatever they choose, because after all, your life shouldn't be in the hands of other people. Maybe it is partly, but it shouldn't be. You're entitled to have complete control over your life.

Remember from this day forward that your duty to yourself requires that you do something each day to improve your technique for the expression of enthusiasm, no matter what it is. I've touched upon some of the things that you could do, but I haven't touched upon all of them. Maybe from your circumstances and your relations with other people, you'll know something that you can do to step up your enthusiasm so as to make you more beneficial to some other person.

11

Accurate Thinking

This lesson is on accurate thinking. It's marvelous to be able to analyze facts, think accurately, and make decisions based upon accurate thinking rather than upon emotional feelings. The majority of the decisions that you make—and I and everybody else for that matter—are based upon things that we desire or things that we feel, not necessarily upon the facts at all. When it comes to a showdown between your emotional feelings—the things you feel like doing—and the things that your head tells you have to do, which one do you think wins the most?

The feeling. What's the matter with the head that it doesn't get a better chance, do you suppose? Why isn't it consulted more? Most people do not think. They just think that they think.

There are certain simple rules and regulations that you can apply. This lesson covers every one of them, and they will help you avoid the common mistakes of inaccurate thinking, snap judgments, and being pushed around by your emotions.

The truth of the matter is that your emotions are not reliable at all. Take the emotion of love, for instance: it's the grandest of all of the emotions, and yet by the same token the most dangerous.

Perhaps more difficulty in human relationships grows out of a mis-understanding of love than from all other sources combined.

Reasoning and Logic

Let's see what accurate thinking is. First of all, there are three major fundamentals: *inductive reasoning*, based on assumption of unknown facts or hypotheses. Then there's *deductive reasoning* based on known facts or what are believed to be known facts. There's also *logic*, that is, guidance by past experiences similar to those under consideration.

Inductive reasoning is based on the assumption of unknown facts or hypotheses. You don't know the facts, but you assume that they exist, and you base your judgment on that. When you do, you must keep your fingers crossed and be ready to change your decision readily: your reasoning may not prove to be accurate, because you're basing it upon assumed facts.

Deductive reasoning is based on known facts or what is believed to be known facts. You have all the facts before you, and from those facts you can deduce certain things that you ought to do for your benefit or to carry out your desires. That's supposed to be the type of thinking that the majority of people engage in, only they don't do a very good job of it.

Fact versus Fiction

There are two major steps in accurate thinking. First of all, separate facts from fiction or hearsay. Before you do any thinking at all, you must find out whether you're dealing with facts or fiction, real evidence or hearsay evidence. If you're dealing with hearsay, it behooves you to be exceptionally careful to keep an open mind and not reach a final decision until you have examined those facts very carefully.

Second, separate facts into two classes: important and unimportant. You'll be surprised when I tell you that the vast majority of facts that we deal with day in and day out—I'm talking about facts now, not hearsay evidence, not hypotheses—are relatively unimportant.

Let's see what an important fact is. An important fact may be assumed to be any fact that can be used to advantage in the attainment of one's major purpose or any subordinate desire leading toward the attainment of one's major purpose. That's what an important fact is.

I wouldn't miss by very much, I suspect, if I said that the vast majority of people spend more time on irrelevant facts, which have nothing whatsoever to do with their advancement, than they do on facts that would benefit them. Curious people, people that meddle in other people's affairs, and gossipers put in a lot of time thinking and talking about other people's affairs, dealing with small talk and petty facts. If you consider these in the right light, they are of no benefit to you, no matter how you use them.

If you doubt what I've just said, take inventory of the facts you deal with for one whole day. At the end of the day, sum it up and see how many really important facts you have been dealing with. It'd be better to do this on a Sunday or on an off day, when you're not on your occupation or any business, because that's where an idle mind usually goes to work on unimportant facts.

Valueless Opinions

Opinions are usually without value, because they are based on bias, prejudice, intolerance, guesswork, or hearsay evidence. Practically everybody has a flock of opinions about practically everything in the world. They have an opinion about the atomic bomb, its future, and so forth. Most people know practically nothing about the atomic bomb or what may happen in the future; I'm sure I don't. You and I have an opinion in reference to it. I have an opinion that it should never have been invented. It's nothing but an evil in my book of rules. Beyond that, I have no opinion because I have nothing on which to base it.

It's surprising to find out how many people have opinions that have no basis whatsoever, except from the way they feel, what somebody said to them, what they read in the newspaper, or whatever other influence they've come under. Most of our opinions come as a result of influences that we don't have any control over.

Free advice volunteered by friends and acquaintances is usually not worthy of consideration, because it's not based upon facts, or too much small talk is mixed up in it. The most desirable kind of advice is from someone who's a specialist in the problem at hand and is paid for this service.

Don't go after any for free advice. Speaking of free advice, I want to tell you what happened to a student of mine—a friend of mine first and then a student—out in California. For three years, he used to come over to my house every weekend and spend three or four hours, for which I ordinarily would get $50 an hour, although I didn't get anything from him because he was a friend and acquaintance. He comes over there to get three or four hours of free counsel, and I gave it to him. I gave it to him every time he came, but he didn't hear a single word that I said.

That went on for three years. Finally he came over one afternoon. I said, "Now look here, Elmer. I have been giving you free counsel for three years, and you haven't heard a darn thing I've been saying. You will never get any value out of this counsel that I'm giving until you start paying for it. Now we're starting our Master Course right away. Why don't you go ahead and join that course like everybody else, and then you'll commit to getting some value."

He took out his checkbook and gave me a check for the Master Course. He entered the course and went through it. I want to tell you that his business affairs began to thrive from that moment on. I had never seen a man grow and develop so fast. After he paid a substantial sum for some counsel, he commenced listening to it and putting it into action.

That's human nature. Free advice is just about worth what it costs; everything in this world is worth just about what it costs. Love and friendship—do they have any price? Try to get love and friendship without paying the price, and see how far you go. Those are two things that you can only get by giving. You can only get the real McCoy by giving the real McCoy. If you try to mooch and get friendship and love without giving in return, your source of supply will soon play out.

Our Most Valuable Asset

Accurate thinkers permit no one to do their thinking for them. How many people permit circumstances, influences, radio, television, newspapers, relatives, and other people to do the thinking for them? The percentage is way up there.

If I have one asset that I feel proudest of, and I do, it has nothing to do with money, bank accounts, bonds, stocks, or anything of that kind. It's something more precious than that: I've learned to hear all evidence, get all of the facts I can from all of the sources, and then put them together in my own way and have the last word in making my own thinking.

That doesn't mean that I'm a know-it-all, that I am a doubting Thomas, or that I don't seek counsel. I certainly do seek counsel, but when I have gotten that counsel, I determine how much of it I will accept and how much of it I will reject. When I make a decision, nobody could ever say that isn't the decision of Napoleon Hill. Albeit it might be a decision based upon a mistake, it's still mine. I did it, and nobody influenced me.

That doesn't mean that I'm hard-hearted or that my friends have no influence on me. They do. But I determine how much influence they have on me and what reaction I will have to their influence. Certainly I would never permit a friend to have such influence on me as to cause me to damage some other person just because that friend wanted it done. That's been tried many times. I would never permit that.

Why, I want to tell you that I think the angels in heaven cry out when they discover a man or woman that does his or her own thinking and doesn't allow relatives and friends and enemies and other people to discourage their accurate thinking.

I'm emphasizing this because the majority of people never take possession of their own minds. It's the most valuable asset that anybody has, the only thing that the Creator gave you that you have complete control over, but it's the one thing that you generally never discover or use. Instead you allow other people to kick it around like a football.

I don't know why our educational system hasn't informed people that they have the greatest asset in the world, an asset sufficient unto all of their needs, and that asset consists in their privilege of using their own mind and thinking their own thoughts and directing those own thoughts to whatever objective they choose.

People don't know they have it. There has not been the proper system of education. I want to tell you that wherever this philosophy touches, you see people blossom out as they never blossomed out before. It makes a difference, because they begin to sneak in and find out that they have a mind, that they can use that mind, and that they can make it do whatever they want it to do. I don't say that they all run in immediately and take possession of their own minds; rather they sneak in a little at a time. But eventually the affairs of their lives begin to change, because the people discover this great mind power and start using it.

"I See by the Papers"

It's not safe to form opinions based upon newspaper reports. "I see by the papers" is a preparatory remark that usually brands the speaker as a snap judgment thinker. "I see by the papers" or "I hear tell" or "they say"—how often have you heard those terms? "They say so-and-so": when I hear anybody start off with that, immediately I pull down my earmuffs and don't hear a doggone thing that they say, because I know it's not worth hearing. If anybody starts to give me information and identifies this source by saying, "I see by the papers" or "they say" or "I hear tell," I don't pay the slightest attention to what is said. Not that what they are saying might not be accurate, but I know that the source is faulty and therefore the chances are that the statement is faulty also. The scandalmongers and the gossip cruisers are not reliable sources from which to procure information on any subject whatsoever. They're not reliable, and they're biased. When you hear anybody speak in a derogatory way of anybody else—whether you know them or not—the very fact that one speaks in a derogatory way of another person puts you on guard. It gives you the responsibility of studying and analyzing very closely everything that's said, because you know you're listening to a biased person.

The human brain is a wonderful thing. I marvel at how smart the Creator was in giving a human being all of the equipment and machinery with which to detect lies and falsehood from truth.

There is something ever present in the falsehood that alerts the listener to it. It's there. You can tell it, you can feel it. The same is true when someone is speaking the truth. The most finished actor in the world couldn't deceive you if you used your innate intelligence in reference to statements that are made.

By the same token, you should study the remarks of a complimentary nature just as closely as you study the others. For instance, if I send somebody to you for a job with a very laudatory letter, or get you on the telephone and give you a sales pitch about what a marvelous person this is, if you are an accurate thinker, you're going to know that I'm rubbing it on pretty thick, and you'd better be careful how much of it you accept. You'd better do a little outside investigating.

I'm not trying to make doubting Thomases or cynics out of you, but I am trying to bring to your attention the necessity of using your God-given brain to think accurately and search for the facts, even though they may not be what you're looking for.

Confidence Games

A lot of people fool themselves, and there is no worse fooling in this world than the fooling that one does to himself. As the Chinese proverb says, "Fool me once, shame on the man. Fool me twice, shame on me."

I know people that have been fooled over and over again—by the same trick, so old that it has whiskers on it. Confidence games, for instance: somebody rushes up to a woman in a department store and says, "Here, I've got $500; I've just found this. Now you put up $500. Show me that you've got that much, and I'll give you half of it." By some hocus-pocus, the woman gets her $500, and they put it in the package, and she thinks she's got the two amounts of money. When she gets home, she found she has two packages of paper. The other person, the gyp artist, has gone with the money. That's been going on for years.

You'd think that bankers, for instance, would be so shrewd that a confidence man couldn't come in and take them. I heard one of the most outstanding con men in the world, Barney Birch—I don't know whatever happened to him, but he used to operate in Chicago. I got acquainted with him once and interviewed him on several occasions. I asked him what type of men were the easiest victims. "Why," he said, "bankers, because they think they're so damn smart."

Wishes often are furthest from facts, and most people have a bad habit of assuming that facts harmonize with their desires. Therefore you have to look in the looking glass when you're searching for the person who can do accurate thinking. You've got to put yourself under suspicion, haven't you? Because if you wish a thing to be true, oftentimes you will assume it is true and you will act as if it were.

We all like to meet and associate with people who agree with us. That's human nature. Oftentimes people you associate with and who agree with you and are very nice and lovely come to the point where they can take advantage of you, and they do.

If you love a person, you will overlook his faults. We need to watch ourselves in connection with those we admire most until they have proved themselves entirely, because I have admired a great many people who turned out to be very dangerous indeed.

As a matter of fact, I think most of my troubles back in my early days came from trusting people too much and letting them use my name, and sometimes they wouldn't use it wisely. That's happened five or six times in my life. I trusted them because I knew them, and they were nice people, and they said and did the things that I liked. Be careful of the fellow that says and does the things you like, because you're going to overlook his faults.

Don't be too hard on the man who steps on your corns and causes you to reexamine yourself. He may be the most important friend you've ever had—the person who may irritate you, but causes you to examine yourself carefully.

Information is abundant. Most of it is free, but facts have a habit of being elusive, and generally there is a price attached to them: the price of painstaking labor in examining them for accuracy. That's the least of the prices that you have to pay for facts.

"How Do You Know?"

This question, "How do you know?" is the favorite question of the thinker. When a thinker hears a statement that he can't accept, immediately he says to the speaker, "How do you know? What is your source of information?"

If you have the slightest doubt and ask someone to identify his source of knowledge, you will put the person out on a limb; he won't be able to do it. If you ask him how he knows, he'll tell you, "Well, I believe so." What right have you to believe anything unless you have based it upon something, unless you can give some background for it?

I believe there's a God. A lot of people do, but a lot of people who say they believe in a God couldn't give you the slightest evidence of it if you backed them into a corner. I can give you evidence. When I say that I believe in a God and you say, "How do you even know?" I can give you all of the evidence. I don't have as much evidence in connection with anything else in this world as I do with the existence of a Creator, because the orderliness of this universe couldn't go on and on to the end of time without a first cause, without a plan in back of it. You know that's absolutely true. Yet a lot of people undertake to prove the presence of God in devious ways that in my book of rules wouldn't be evidence at all. Anything that exists, including God, is capable of proof, and where there is no such proof available, it is safe to assume that nothing exists.

Logic is a wonderful thing. When no facts are available for the basis of an opinion or a judgment or a plan, turn to logic for guidance. No one has ever seen God, but logic says that he exists: of necessity he has to exist, or we wouldn't be here. We couldn't be here without a first cause, a higher intelligence than ourselves.

There are times when you have a hunch; you have a feeling that certain things are true or not true. You'd better be careful to pay respect to that hunch, because that's probably infinite intelligence trying to break through the outer shell.

If one of you got up and said, "My definite major aim is to make a million dollars this coming year," what would I say if you did that? What would be the first question I would ask you, do you think?

How are you going to do it? I want to hear your plan, and then what you are going to do about it. First of all, I'm going to weigh your ability to get a million dollars and to find out what you're going to give for it. Then my logic will tell me whether or not your plan for doing it is provable, workable, and practical. It doesn't take an awful lot of intelligent thinking, but it's a very important thing to do.

I believe in my students, I love them, I have great respect for them. If one of them got up and told me that he was going to make a million dollars next year, would I say, "Atta boy. Now you're talking. Now you can do it"? You'd know right away I was a liar. If I said that, you'd know that I didn't know what I was talking about, or I was not telling the truth.

Let's say I said, "Well, now, fine. I hope you're right. Now let's see how you're going to do it. Sit down and tell me your plan." I'd go over your plan, I'd analyze it, I'd analyze you, I'd analyze your capabilities, I'd analyze your past experience, your past achievements. I'd analyze the people that you're going to get to help you make those million dollars. When we got through analyzing, I would be able to tell you, "Well, probably you can do it," or I'd be able to point out to you that probably it'd take longer than the year that you said—maybe two years, maybe three.

Then again, I might tell you that you wouldn't be able to do it all. If my reasoning taught me that that was the answer, I'd give it to you just that way. I've had some of my students put propositions before me which I've had to turn down; I had to tell them just to forget about it because they were wasting their time. I've also had some come out with ideas that were marvelous; one of them is sitting right in this audience tonight. I was able to send him over to one of the most distinguished consulting engineers in the country, and that engineer's giving him the answers. I didn't just pass haphazard judgment on his ideas. I sent him to an expert where he'd get the real lowdown and who could possibly help in carrying out his ideas.

That's the way an accurate thinker perceives. He doesn't allow his emotions to run away with him. If I allowed my emotions to do my thinking for me, anything that one of my students undertook to do, I'd tell him he could do it.

Now let me jump to this famous motto or epigram that you've seen quoted a lot of times. You've heard it in my lessons: "Whatever your mind can conceive and believe, your mind can achieve."

I don't want anybody to misread that statement by reading into it whatever your mind can conceive and believe, your mind *will* achieve. I said, "It *can* achieve." Do you get the difference there between the two? It *can*, but I don't know that it *will*. That's up to you. Only you know that. The extent to which you own your own mind, the extent to which you intensity your faith, the soundness of your judgments and your plans—all of these factors, everything translates into how well you fulfill that epigram, "Whatever your mind can conceive and believe, your mind can achieve."

Separating Fact from Fiction

Now for my acid test in separating facts from information. Let's see how we go about it. First of all, scrutinize with unusual care everything you read in the newspapers or hear over the radio, and form the habit of never accepting any statement as a fact merely because you read it or heard it expressed by someone. Statements containing some proportion of fact often are, carelessly or intentionally, colored to give them an erroneous meaning. A half-truth is more dangerous than an out-and-out lie, because the half-truth part is likely to deceive somebody who thinks the whole of it is true.

Scrutinize carefully everything you read in books, regardless of who wrote them, and never accept the works of any writer without asking the following questions and satisfying yourself as to the answers. These rules also apply to lectures, statements, speeches, conversations, or anything else.

First of all, is the writer, speaker, teacher, or the one making the statement a recognized authority on the subject on which he's speaking or writing?

That's the first question that you ask. Suppose you apply that to me. You're taking the course, you're paying a substantial sum for it, and you're putting in a substantial amount of time in taking it, which is worth money. It would be too bad if, after you had taken the course, you were to find that I was not an authority, wouldn't it? It would be too bad if you found that this philosophy was not sound and wouldn't work. It'd be a big disappointment to you, wouldn't it? It would be a mighty big disappointment to me too if you found that out.

Let's put myself under the microscope and see how would you go about testing whether or not my science of success is sound and you can depend upon it. What proof has been given that it does work?

In the first place, it's very easy to determine if this philosophy has spread all over the world. It's published and distributed widely in practically every civilized country on earth, and it has been accepted and passed upon as sound by the shrewdest brains that this world has ever created—not just a few hundred but a few thousand of them. No one at anytime, anywhere, has ever found any weakness in connection with it.

You know very well that, people being what they are, if there had been any weakness in this philosophy, they would have found it. They found a lot of weaknesses in Napoleon Hill, and they didn't hesitate to point them out, but they didn't find any in the philosophy. Therefore Napoleon Hill is an authority, because going on forty years now, he's devoted his time to presenting the know-how gained by five hundred or more of the outstanding men of the world. That's where the information came from. It came from men who got it by experience, by the trial and error method.

The very fact that it has been accepted and the fact that it has made thousands and thousands of successful people—both money-wise and otherwise—all over the world is evidence that Napoleon Hill, as an author of *The Science of Success*, is an authority.

That's how you would determine it. You wouldn't determine it by how well you think of me, by whether you like me or don't like me, because that has very little to do with it. You determine it by examining the works themselves and the effects they've had on people.

Ulterior Motives

Next, did the writer or the speaker have an ulterior motive or a motive of self-interest other than that of imparting accurate information? The motive that prompts a man to write a book, make a speech, or to make a statement, in public or in private, is very important. If you can get at a man's motive when he's talking, you can tell pretty well how truthful he is in what he's saying.

For instance, last week I allowed a man to talk to me for two hours, mostly about himself. He was giving himself a very good recommendation. I don't think he thought I suspected that he was trying to sell himself into our organization, but that's exactly what he was trying to do. He had the hook pretty cleverly baited. He started off by telling me that he had all the books I'd ever written, he had memorized some of them, and he was one of my great admirers. That didn't hurt his case at the start. As time went on, he began to rub it on thicker and thicker, and he swung over into what I suspected he was going to say all the time, for he began to tell me how clever he was at applying this philosophy and how clever he would be at teaching it.

Then I put on the brakes. I asked him a few questions. I asked him if he'd ever taught the philosophy. No, he hadn't taught it, but he knew very well he could, because he knew so much about it. He had an ulterior motive, and therefore I discounted a lot of the things that he said about himself. At least I held them in abeyance. I didn't accept them hook, line, bait, and sinker, because he was a biased witness; he was selling himself.

Propaganda

Next, is the writer a paid propagandist whose profession is that of organizing public opinion? In these days it behooves us to be eternally on the outlook for propaganda. With these organizations, especially those with big-sounding names like "the organization of who and what's-it for America," it behooves us to look into them, because many have proved to be propagandists, not to support the American way of life, but to undermine it. The Russians have turned loose in the world a clever set of fifth columnists and propagandists; the world has never known anything equal. That's why they've taken one country after another under submission until they control probably two-thirds of this world without firing a gun, and the rest of the world seems paralyzed to do anything about it.

You can see the effect of allowing propaganda to spread unchecked. Has the writer an interest, of profit or any other kind, in the subject on which he writes or speaks? When you find out about a man's motive, whatever he's doing, it'll be impossible for him to fool you in the least, because you'll be able to smell him out. Is the writer a person of sound judgment and not a fanatic on the subject of which he writes? I have seen a lot of people who are overzealous about to the point of fanaticism, like Karl Marx, or Lenin or Trotsky or any of that group in back of communism. They're overzealous. I have no doubt that they think that we're wrong and they're right; I have no doubt that they believe supremely in what they're doing. They would have to, to carry on the way they do. Before I'm going to believe in their doctrines, I'm going to reserve my own judgment, and I'm going to examine them, not by what they say, but by what they do to people who come under their subjection.

You wouldn't judge me on account of the kind of tie I wear, the kind of suit I wear, how I cut my hair, or how well I speak. You'd judge me by how much influence I'm having for good or evil on people.

That's the way you judge me. That's the way you would judge anybody else.

You might not like a man's brand of religion or politics, but if he's doing a good job in his field and helping a lot of people and doing no damage, never mind about his brand. Don't condemn him if he's doing preponderantly more good than harm.

Before accepting statements by others as facts, ascertain the motive which prompted the statements. Ascertain also the writer's reputation for truth and veracity, and scrutinize with unusual care all statements made by people who have strong motives or objectives they desire to attain through their statements. Be equally careful about accepting as facts the statements of overzealous people who have the habit of allowing their imaginations to run wild. Learn to be cautious and to use your own judgment, no matter who is trying to influence you. Use your own judgment in the final analysis.

Expert Advice

What do you do if you can't trust your own judgment? Is there an answer in this philosophy for that?

There certainly is. A lot of times an individual can't trust his own judgment, because he doesn't know enough about the circumstances that he's faced with. He's got to turn to somebody with broader experience or a different education or a keener mind for analysis.

For instance, can you imagine a business succeeding that is all made up of master salesmen? Can you imagine that? Did you ever know such a business? You need a wet blanket man in every organization: a man who controls the assets of the company and keeps them from getting away at the wrong time and the wrong way. You also need a hatchet man—a man who will cut through the red tape and everything else that gets in his way and let the chips fall wherever they may. I wouldn't want to be a hatchet man. I wouldn't want to be a wet blanket man, but certainly I'd want those two in my organization if it was very extensive.

In seeking facts from others, do not disclose to them the facts you expect to find. If I say to you, "By the way, you used to employ a John Brown, and he's applied to me for a position. I think he's a wonderful man. What do you think?"

If John Brown has any faults, I'll certainly not get them with that kind of question, will I? If I really wanted to find out about someone who used to work for you, I wouldn't get it from you at all in the first place. I'd have a commercial credit company get an unbiased report on him from you. You'd probably give out facts to the credit rating company that you wouldn't give out to me or anybody else. It's surprising how much information you can get if you know the right commercial agencies through which to get it. Oftentimes when you go directly for information about a man, the chances are you won't get the real facts; you'll get a varnished or watered-down set of facts.

Most people are lazy: they don't want to go to too much trouble in explaining. If you ask a man a question and you give him the slightest idea of what you expect the answer to be, he'll just give you the answer he knows you want. You're tickled to death, you go on with it, and then fall on it later on.

Smart people have ways and means of getting information from others very cleverly without disclosing to the others exactly how they get it.

Science is the art of organizing and classifying facts. That's what science means. When you wish to make sure you're dealing with facts, seek scientific sources for testing where possible. A man of science has neither the reason nor the inclination to modify or to change facts in order to misrepresent. If they had that inclination, they would not be scientists, would they? They'd be pseudoscientists or fakes, and there are a lot of pseudoscientists and fakes in this world who assume they know things that they don't know.

Balance Head and Heart

Your emotions are not always reliable; as a matter of fact, most of the time they're not reliable. Before being influenced too far by your feelings, give your head a chance to pass judgment on the business at hand. The head is more dependable than the heart, but balancing them so both have an equal say makes the best combination. If you do that, you'll come up with the right answer. The person who forgets this generally regrets his neglect.

Of the major enemies of sound thinking, the emotion of love stands at the head of the list. How in the world could love interfere with anybody's thinking? If you said that, I'd know right away you hadn't had very many love experiences. If you've ever had an experience with love at all, you know very well how dangerous it is, like playing around TNT with a match in your hand. When it starts to explode, it doesn't give any notice.

Hatred, anger, jealousy, fear, revenge, greed, vanity, egotism, the desire for something for nothing, and procrastination—all of these are enemies of thinking. You have to be constantly on the lookout to be free of them, provided that the thinking at hand is of importance to you. Maybe your whole future destiny depends upon your thinking accurately, and in fact it does. If that were not true, then what would be the use of giving you complete control of your mind?

The answer is that mind is absolutely sufficient to fulfill all of your needs, at least in this lifespan. I don't know about the preceding plane, where you came from, or the succeeding plane, where you're going. I don't know about those planes, because I don't remember where I came from, and I don't yet know where I'm going—I wish I did—but I know a great deal about where I am right now. I've found out a great deal about how to influence my destiny here. I also get a lot of pleasure out of it, so I can give joy, make myself useful, and justify my having passed this way.

I have discovered how to manipulate my own mind and keep it under control, make it do the things I want it to do, throw out the circumstances I don't want, and accept the ones that I do want. If I don't find the circumstances I want, what do I do? Create them, of course. That's what definiteness of purpose and imagination are for.

The Dangers of Fanaticism

There's also religious and political fanaticism. My, oh my, the useless time and energy that's wasted on those two forms of fanaticism—fighting over what's going to happen hereafter, when as a matter fact none of us know what's going to happen hereafter. We may think we do, but we don't actually know. (It's just as well that some of us don't know where we're going hereafter; it might be very unhappy.)

Fighting over politics—do you know what the difference between a Republican and a Democrat is? The difference depends on who's in and who's out. That's all. I mean that seriously, not facetiously. If I asked you to describe the difference between a Democrat and a Republican, you'd be hard put to it to give me a real, practical, intelligent sense of that difference. The only difference I've ever found is that sometimes the Democrats are in, and they misuse their power, and sometimes the Republicans are in, and they misuse their power. Yet look at the furor and hatred that they stir.

You hardly believe anything that's coming out of Washington, because you wonder whether it isn't some political trick to tear somebody down or build somebody up politically. It's a difficult matter to get at the truth, because you know how dangerous, tricky, and dishonest politics are. It used to be an honor to call a man a congressman or a senator. Nowadays you're likely to be sued for damages if you do. To call a man a politician—you'd better be ready to fight when you do that. In certain circles today, a man doesn't want to be called a politician, because politicians have sunk to an all-time low of disgrace and dishonesty.

I'm not talking politics, you understand. I'm just giving you a little information on accurate thinking, but we happen to know that's true. That's one reason we're in such a mess in the United States: we don't have honesty at the source of our government. I don't mean that we don't have some honest individuals, but the preponderance of power at the source is dishonest and has been ever since—well, I won't tell you how long.

The Eternal Question Mark

Now your mind should be an eternal question mark. Question everything and everyone until you satisfy yourself that you are dealing with facts. Do this quietly, in the silence of your own mind, and avoid being known as a doubting Thomas. Don't come out and question people orally—that's not going to get you anywhere—but question them silently.

If you're too outspoken in your questioning, it puts people on notice, they'll cover up, and you won't get the information you want. Quietly go about seeking for information and doing some accurate thinking, and you'll probably come up with it.

Be a good listener, but also be an accurate thinker as you listen. Which is most profitable, to be a good speaker or a good listener? I don't know of any quality that would help an individual to get along in the world better than to be an effective, enthusiastic speaker. Yet I would follow that statement immediately by saying that it's far more profitable to be a good, analytical listener, because when you're listening, you're getting information, but when you're speaking, you're only expressing what's in your mind. You're not acquiring anything at all, unless it's self-confidence or something of that sort.

Let your mind be an eternal question mark. I don't mean that you should become a cynic or a doubting Thomas, but rather that no matter whom you're dealing with, in every relationship you have, deal with them on the basis of thinking accurately. You'll get a lot of satisfaction out of that. You'll also be more successful.

If you're tactful and diplomatic as you go along, you'll have a lot more substantial friends than you would by the old method of snap judgment. If you're an accurate thinker, most of your friends will be friends worth having.

Your thinking habits are the results of social heredity and physical heredity. Watch both of these sources, particularly social heredity. Through physical heredity, you get everything that you are physically: the stature of your body, the texture of your skin, the color of your eyes and hair. You're the sum total of all of your ancestors back further than you can ever remember, and you've inherited a few of their good qualities and a few of their bad. There's nothing you can do about that. That's static; it's fixed at birth.

By far the most important part of what you are is the result of your social heredity—your environmental influences, the things that you have allowed to go into your mind and that you've accepted as a part of character.

I had an experience once that made me very angry, but I got a great lesson out of it. The man who employed me to write stories about successful men, which led to my meeting Mr. Carnegie, was Robert Love Taylor, the former governor and senator for Tennessee.

When I was talking to him, he was a senator in Washington, and I was dining with him in the Senate dining room. We were talking about politics. He being from Tennessee and I being from the adjoining State of Virginia, both of us were Democrats. We were building ourselves up big. I was selling democracy, and he was selling me the same thing. Finally he said, "By the way, Hill, how did you come to be a Democrat?"

"Because my grandfather was a Democrat, my father was a Democrat, my uncles are all Democrats, and my great-grandfather was a Democrat."

He said, "Now isn't that grand. Wouldn't it have been unhappy for you if your ancestors had been horse thieves?"

I got mad. I didn't see the point. I wasn't old enough, and I didn't have enough experience at that time, but he put me to thinking. In asking that question, he told me that you have no right to be anything just because your dad or your uncle or somebody else is.

I learned a great lesson from that. Later on, I wasn't a Democrat anymore. I'm not a Republican either. I'm an accurate thinker. I take a little of the good out of both the Republican idea and out of the Democrats' idea. When voting, I've never voted a straight ticket in my whole life. I'd think it'd be an insult to my intelligence to vote a straight ticket. I study the men that are on that ticket and try to pick out the man that I think will do the best job, and I don't give a continental whether he's a Republican or a Democrat. I've always voted for the man that I think will do a good job for the people, and I believe any accurate thinker would do it that way.

Conscience as a Guide

Your conscience was given to you as a guide when all other sources of knowledge and facts have been exhausted. Be careful to use it as a guide and not as a conspirator. A lot of people use their conscience as a conspirator instead of as a guide. In other words, they sell their conscience on the idea that what they're doing is right. Eventually the conscience falls in line and becomes a conspirator.

When I first interviewed Al Capone, I was astounded to know what a mean deal he'd gotten from the people of the United States through their government and what a mean, nasty long-nosed man it was that had persecuted—not prosecuted, but persecuted—him for carrying on a perfectly legitimate business. He was supplying people a service that they wanted and paid for. What business did Uncle Sam have sticking his long nose into a legitimate business like that?

Now that was Al's story. That's the way he told it to me, and he believed it, because he had long since choked off his conscience or converted it to aiding and abetting. You can do that if you don't listen to your conscience in the beginning. It will become a conspirator, and it'll back you up in everything that you're doing.

The Price You Must Pay

If you sincerely wish to think accurately, there's a price that you must pay, a price that is not measurable in money. First, you must learn to examine carefully all of your emotional feelings by submitting them to your sense of reason. That's step number one in accurate thinking. In other words, the things that you like to do best are the things that you should examine most and first to make sure they lead you to the attainment of the object that you want.

I knew a fellow once who wanted to marry a certain girl more than anything else in the world. It became his obsession, his definite major purpose. She turned him down time after time. Finally he was so persistent that in order to get rid of him, she married him. They both lived to regret it afterward, especially the man, because she never ceased throwing it up to him. Don't get any false notions: I was not the man; I was just the observer.

Be careful about the thing that you set your heart upon, because when you get it, sometimes you find out it's not what you wanted at all. I've already told you about Bing Crosby, who set his heart on making his first $50,000. When he and his brother, who was his manager, got it, they found out they wanted another $50,000. When they got up to $100,000, they said, "Gosh, it's come so easy. Let's make it a million and then stop." He first got the million, and the million got him. A lovely character, but he got ensnared in his own desires, and now he doesn't know when to stop.

I can multiply that by a thousand illustrations: the men who paid too much for what they got, who wanted something too badly, who tried to get too much out of it and did get too much of it, but didn't get peace of mind and balancing of their lives along with it.

I think the saddest thing that ever came out of my research in building this philosophy was what I learned about the wealthy men that collaborated in the building of this philosophy. They didn't get success along with their money, because they became too obsessed with the importance of money and the power that money would give them. I don't know why anybody would want a million dollars—so help me, I don't—unless it'd be somebody like myself, who wants it to spread this philosophy all over the world so that a lot of other people can get it. I want many millions of dollars, and I'm going to have them in quick order. Not for myself; I don't need that kind of money. It's all going to be plowed back into this business of helping people all over this world. I don't think that's going to hurt me or anybody else; I don't see how anybody can be hurt that way.

Avoid Expressing Opinions

You must curb the habit of expressing opinions which are not based upon facts or what you believe to be facts. Did you know that you didn't have a right to an opinion about anything, not anything at all, unless you base it upon facts or what you believe to be facts? I bet you wouldn't admit that that's true. I bet you won't admit that you have no right whatsoever to have an opinion about anything at any time unless it's based upon what you believe to be facts or actual provable facts.

Why do I say you don't have a right to this? You have a right, of course, but you have the responsibility of assuming what happens to you if you express an opinion that's not based upon facts or what you believe to be facts. You can fool yourself that way.

A lot of people go all the way through life fooling themselves by opinions that have no basis for existence. You must master the habit of being influenced by people in any manner whatsoever merely

because you like them or they are related to you or they may have
done you a favor.

When you've gone the extra mile, you're going to put a lot of people under obligations to you, and I want you to do that. Nobody can
find any fault with that, but be careful. Be careful about being influenced by people just because they have done you a favor. I'm talking
now about the people for whom you've gone the extra mile. And you
may be in that position sometimes too, where somebody puts you
under obligations to an extent that you don't want.

I have one friend, Ed Barnes, who is the only partner that Thomas
Edison ever had. I've been going out to lunch with Ed for the last
forty years everywhere from the Waldorf Astoria down to restaurants
where we'd have a cup of coffee and a sandwich.

I never was able to pick up the check but once in my life. Last
time when he was up here, he, Mike Ritt, and I and went out for the
ball game. I'd sent Mike ahead to buy the tickets, and we already had
them and there's nothing he could do about it.

One day I asked him, "Why won't you let me pick up the check?"

"Well, to be candid with you," he said, "I'll tell you the truth. I
want you to always be under obligations to me, because I am under
obligations to you from a way back, and I want to pay that off a little
over time, so you won't be throwing it up to me that you helped me
make my first million."

There was a whole lot of logic to what he was saying. He didn't
want to be under too much obligation to me, so just to show me that
he was independent himself, he insisted on always picking up the
check. Of course, I could have reached faster if I had wanted to. On
one occasion when he and I had a dinner together, if I had reached
for the check and gotten it, I would have been wrecked, because it was
more money than I had in my pocket.

You must form the habit of examining the motives of people who
seek some benefit from or through your influence. You must control

both your emotion of love and your emotion of hate in making decisions for any purpose, because either of these can unbalance your thinking.

Don't Make Decisions When Angry

No man ought to make an important decision while he's angry. For instance, it's a bad mistake to discipline children when you're angry, because nine times out of ten, you'll do and say the wrong thing and do more harm than good. That applies to a lot of grownups too. If you're really angry, don't make decisions. Don't make statements to people while you're mad, because they can come back on you and do you a lot of injury.

You can see why we have a lesson on self-discipline. It plays right along with this lesson. A lot of times, if you're going to be an accurate thinker, you've got to have a lot of self-discipline, and you've got to refrain from saying and doing a lot of things you'd like to say and do. Bide your time. There's always a time for you to say and do every-thing properly.

Accurate thinkers don't fly off the handle, start their mouths going and leave them going, unlike some people. They carefully study the effect on the listener of every word they utter even before they utter it.

Recently I made a statement over at the Club Success Unlimited. I told about an incident in our organization when Mr. Stone had to discipline somebody we considered disloyal. I did not tell about it because I was in any malicious spirit that night; I was putting this class on notice that there was fifth-column activity going on, and I want to put you on notice so that if it showed up, you would be able to defend yourself against it. That's why I did it, and the only rea-son why. I'm pleased to tell you now that the circumstance has been entirely corrected, and there's no more fifth-column activity.

The thing was handled the way it should have been handled. There was no maliciousness in it, there was no mentioning of names, and the only one that heard it that could possibly have been hurt would have been the guilty person. The innocent ones, who didn't know anything about it, certainly couldn't have been hurt one way or another.

That was my way of taking care of a situation that might well have torn asunder this marvelous organization. It's just one of those things that had to be handled, yet I handled it in such a way that it got the right results. Everybody was satisfied, and there's no more trouble.

I could have called names. I could have engaged in personalities. I could have done what any person who is not engaged in accurate thinking would have done, but I didn't.

When you get this philosophy down properly and apply it, it makes no difference how disagreeable the circumstances are that come up in your life; you'll always be able to handle them right. By handling them right, I mean with justice to yourself and to everybody else that your decisions or actions may influence. I wouldn't want under any circumstance to engage in any transactions that would offend or hurt anybody if I could possibly get out of it. I would never hurt anybody except in self-defense or in defense of my profession, which I know benefits millions of people.

If they threatened my organization, this philosophy, and my ability to take it to the people, I would be in there fighting like a demon if necessary. This philosophy we're engaged in is bigger than me, it's bigger than you, it's bigger than all of us combined.

In Sum

In appropriating the habits and characteristics of other people, you must learn to adopt only those which fit into the pattern of your major purpose in life. Don't take over the pattern of another person just because you admire that person. Take only so much out of the other fellow's pattern as will fit into your purpose in life. You must learn to make decisions promptly, but never make them until you have carefully weighed their possible effects on your future plans and on other people.

I can think of a lot of things I could do that would benefit me but wouldn't benefit you; they might even injure you. I can think of a lot of things I could do to someone, but I wouldn't engage in them, because eventually I'd have to pay the price, because whatever you do to or for another person, you do to or for yourself. It comes back to you greatly multiplied.

That's another thing that comes under the heading of accurate thinking. After you've become thoroughly indoctrinated with this philosophy, you learn not to do anything that you don't want to come back and affect you—not to say anything, not to do anything that you don't want to come back to you later on in life.

Before accepting as facts the statements of other people, it may be beneficial if you ask them how they came by the so-called facts. When they express opinions, ask them how they know their opinion is sound. For someone to come along and say, "It's my opinion," would not influence me in the slightest, because I don't want an opinion. I want some facts; then I'll form my own opinion. "You give me the facts, and I'll put them together in my own way," says the accurate thinker.

You must learn to examine with extraordinary care all statements of a derogatory nature made by one person against others, because the very nature of those statements brand them as being not without bias (and that's putting it very politely).

You must overcome the habit of trying to justify a decision you have made that turns out to have been unsound. Accurate thinkers don't do that. If they find they're wrong, they reverse themselves just as quickly as they made the decisions.

Excuses and alibis and accurate thinking are never friendly bedfellows. Most people are very adept at creating alibis for their faults and omissions, but they don't amount to a thing unless there's something back of them that's sound, that you can depend upon.

If you are an accurate thinker, you will never use the expressions, "They say" or "I heard." Accurate thinkers, in repeating things they have heard, identify the source and attempt to establish its dependability. If I told you that I knew that God exists and why I know he exists, I would proceed to give you the source of my information and lay it out in terms that you could understand. If I told you that I was a Democrat or a Republican, and it was important that you know why, I'd give you sound reasons. (I'm not either one, because I don't have any sound reasons for being either one.)

It's not an easy matter to be an accurate thinker. Have you reached that conclusion already? There's quite a little bit you have to pay in order to have it but it's worth it. If you're not an accurate thinker, people are going to take advantage of you. You're not going to get as much out of life as you'd like to. You're not going to be satisfied. You'll never be a well-balanced person without accurate thinking.

In order to think accurately, you've got to have a set of rules to go by, and you will find them in this lesson. Go over this lesson and study it carefully, add some notes to it of your own, and start now to do some thinking. Start putting into practice some of these principles of separating facts from information and separating the facts themselves into two classes, important and unimportant.

This lesson will very much more than have justified itself, and could well be worth a thousand times as much as you have put into the entire course, if it teaches you to do those simple things. Start separating fact from information. Be sure that you're dealing with facts. Then take the facts and break them down. Throw off the unimportant facts on which you've been wasting so much time.

12

Concentration

This lesson is devoted to controlled attention or concentration of effort. I've never known of a successful person in any calling who hasn't acquired great powers of concentration upon one thing at a time.

You've heard people derogatorily speak of others by calling them people with one-track minds. Have you ever heard that term? Anytime anybody says I have a one-track mind, I want to thank him for it, because a lot of people have multitrack minds. They try to run on all of them at the same time and don't do a good job on any. I have observed that the outstanding successes are people who have developed a high capacity to keep their minds fixed upon one thing at a time.

You may be interested in knowing that I have what I call my silent hour. One hour out of every twenty-four, I withdraw to myself behind that third, very high, mental wall and devote my entire time to developing a consciousness that can contact and commune with infinite intelligence.

I devote that time also to expressing gratitude for the service my eight guiding princes have rendered me during the day, for the service they rendered the day before, the service they're rendering now, and the service they will render tomorrow.

You might think that that silent hour isn't profitable, but to me it's the most profitable of my twenty-four hours, no matter what else I may do. That silent hour of meditation enables me to think in connection with the higher achievements of life, with the things that I want to do with self-improvement.

It's a marvelous thing to go off to yourself. If you go there in the right sort of a mental attitude, you will find your marvelous company—but you do have to go with the right mental attitude. You do have to go with purpose and forethought.

Let me go through the principles of this philosophy that blend into and become a part of this lesson on concentration of effort. Just as each strand, though very small, makes up the total of our rope, so these principles blend into and become a part of this principle of concentration of effort.

Autosuggestion or Self-Hypnosis

First of all, autosuggestion or self-hypnosis is the basis of all concentration. Self-hypnosis is a wonderful thing if you hypnotize yourself on behalf of the right objective, but it's not such a wonderful thing if you allow the circumstances of life to hypnotize you on behalf of the wrong circumstances and the wrong objectives. A lot of people become self-hypnotized in connection with fear, self-limitations, desires, unbelief, and lack of faith. When you have learned to concentrate on one thing at a time, you have learned to see yourself already in possession of the thing that you're concentrating on.

Don't be afraid of autosuggestion or self-hypnosis. Be afraid if you don't deliberately embrace it and make use of it for the development of the things that you want to represent your life and your success.

The nine basic motives are the starting point of all concentration. In other words, don't concentrate unless you have a motive for doing it.

Let's say you want to make enough money to buy an estate or a farm. If you concentrated on that, you'd be surprised at how that concentration would change your habits and attract to you opportunities for making money that you never thought of before. I know that's the way it worked out, because some years ago, I wanted a 1,000-acre estate. At the time I didn't know just how much 1,000 acres were, but I was concentrating on 1,000 acres. It cost approximately $250,000 to get the land that I was looking for, and that was a lot more money than I had at that time. But almost from the very day that I fixed in my mind the size of the estate that I wanted, opportunities began to open up and develop for me to get that money in the larger blocks that I had never gotten before. The royalties on my books commenced to increase, demand for my lectures commenced to increase, demand for my business counsel commenced to increase, all in conformity to the pattern that I had set up through self-hypnosis. I just sold myself on the idea that I had to have the money, I was going to get it, and I was going to render service for it.

When I got the estate, I didn't get 1,000 acres; I got 600 acres. I told the man from whom I bought it that I wanted 1,000 acres. He said, "I have 600. By the way, do you know how much 600 acres are?"

"I have a rough idea," I said.

"Would you mind walking around this estate with me?"

We started out one morning with a couple of golf sticks to knock the rattlesnakes in the head with. We started around the outer edge, and we walked until noontime. We went more than halfway around, up, down, and over the Catskill Mountains. At noontime, he said, "We're just about halfway around."

"Well," I said, "instead of going all over around, let's just turn and go back. I've seen enough." Six hundred acres is a planet.

I bought the place. Then the Depression came on—1929, '30, and '31. It was tough going, but I had accumulated enough money to buy the place. I wouldn't have had it if I hadn't concentrated on that idea.

Concentration and Definite Purpose

Definiteness of purpose with obsessional desire is the moving spirit back of the motive. There's no use of having a motive unless you put obsessional desire or obsessional purpose back of it.

What's the difference between an ordinary purpose or desire and an obsessional desire? Intensity. In other words, the wish for a thing or the hope for a thing doesn't cause anything to happen, but when you put a burning or obsessional desire in back of a thing, it moves you into action. It attracts to you others and things that you need in order to fulfill that desire.

How do you go about developing obsessional desire? By thinking about a lot of things, changing from one thing to another? No. You select one thing: you eat it, you sleep it, you drink it, you breathe it, you talk about it as long as you can find anybody to listen. If you can't find anybody, you talk to yourself. Repetition. Keep on telling your subconscious mind exactly what you want. Make it clear, make it plain, make it evident, but above everything else, let your subconscious mind know that you expect results and no fooling.

An organized endeavor of personal initiative starts the action with concentration, and applied faith is the sustaining force that keeps action going.

In other words, without that applied faith, when the going gets hard—and it will, no matter what you're doing—you would either slow down or quit. You could see that you need applied faith to keep your action keyed up to a high degree, even when the going is hard and when the results are not coming in as you would like them to come.

By the way, have you ever heard of anybody starting out to do anything and achieving an outstanding permanent success right from the start without any opposition?

No. Nobody ever did that and probably nobody ever will. The going is always hard with everyone, no matter what you're doing. It's not going to be as hard for you in starting out as teachers of this philosophy as it was for me, because I had to create the philosophy first. Then I had to learn how to teach it. Then I had to go ahead and do it for about ten years before I got to where I could do it properly.

You won't have to work as hard as I did, because you've got more information to go on. You've got a tremendous amount of information in back of every one of these lessons that you can concentrate on. The work's already been done, just as if I had chewed your food for you so you wouldn't have to. (I don't know if that's a good simile or not, but in other words it's predigested; we'll put it that way.)

This information is put out there; the skeleton of each one of those principles is outlined. All you've got to do is to add your own notes to the notes that I've made up, and you'll have a wonderful lecture on each one of these principles. You'll have to concentrate on every one of these lessons when you come to it, but concentrate on that lesson, and add to your notes. You'll have to come back to each lesson many times. You have to keep thinking about each one, but while you're concentrating on a given lesson, don't let your mind run over all the other lessons. Stick straight to that one lesson while you're at it.

The Master Mind and Concentration

The Master Mind is the source of allied power necessary to ensure success. Can you imagine anybody concentrating on the attainment of something of an outstanding nature without making use of the Master Mind and the brains, influence, and education of other people? Did you ever hear of anybody achieving outstanding success without the cooperation of other people?

I never have. I have been around quite a bit in this success field about as much as the average—maybe more—and I have never found anybody yet in the upper brackets of achievement in any line that didn't owe success largely to the friendly, harmonious cooperation of other people, to the use of other people's brains and sometimes other people's money.

If your undertaking is very large and you don't have the money with which to carry it out, you may have to share your opportunity with the other fellow, who in return for that sharing will put up some of the money necessary to get you going. That's the way big business operates. I don't know of a single corporation, except perhaps the Ford Motor Company, that's owned outright by one group of people. Most of these big corporations, like the American Telephone & Telegraph Company and all of the railroad companies, are owned by tens of thousands of individuals, who put the money in to operate them. Without that kind of financial cooperation, Master Minding, these big corporations would not be able to carry on.

You need the Master Mind alliance in your concentration if you're aiming for anything above mediocrity. Of course, you can do your own concentrating on failure: you won't need any help on that, you won't need any Master Mind, in fact you'll have a lot of volunteer help.

If you're going to succeed, you've got to follow these regulations as I'm laying them down for you. You can't escape them. You can't neglect any one of them.

Self-discipline is the watchman that keeps action moving in the right direction, even when the going is difficult. You need self-discipline in regard to desires, and when you meet with opposition, or when you've got to cut through difficult conditions and circumstances.

You need your self-discipline to keep your faith going and keep yourself determined that you're not going to quit just because the going is hard. You couldn't possibly get along in concentrating without self-discipline. Of course, if everything went your way and you didn't meet any difficult circumstances, it'd be no trouble at all; you could concentrate on anything.

The Creative Vision

The creative vision or imagination is the architect that fashions practical plans for your action in back of your concentrating. Before you can concentrate intelligently, you've got to have plans, you've got to have an architect. That architect is your imagination and the imaginations of your Master Mind allies, if you have them.

Did you ever hear of anybody who's had a very fine objective, but it failed because it didn't have the right kind of plan for putting it over? It's a common pattern, as a matter of fact. People have ideas, but their plans for carrying them out are not sound.

Going the extra mile is the principle that ensures harmonious cooperation from others. Going the extra mile—you'll need that in the business of concentrating. If you're going to get other people to help you, you got to do something to put them under obligation, so you've got to give them a motive. Even your Master Mind allies won't serve as allies without a motive.

Of course, the most outstanding motive is the desire for financial gain. In all business and professional undertakings, I would say the desire for financial gain is the outstanding motive. If you're going into a business—that's where the main object is to make money—if you don't allow your allies or key people to get sufficient returns, you're not going to have them very long. They'll be going into business for themselves. They'll be going over to your competitors and whatnot.

I was astounded once to hear Mr. Andrew Carnegie tell me that he paid Charles Schwab a salary of $75,000 a year, and in some years a bonus of $1 million. I wanted to know why a man of this great intelligence would pay one man a bonus of more than ten times as much as his salary. I said, "Mr. Carnegie, did you have to do that?"

"Why, no," he said. "Certainly I didn't have to. I could have let him go out and go into competition with me."

There's quite a bit of meaning behind that statement. He had gotten a good man that was very valuable to him. He wanted to keep him, and he knew that the way to keep him was to let him know that he was making more money with Mr. Carnegie than he would without him.

Right here is the proper place to say to you who are going to become teachers in this philosophy that you'll make a lot more money with our organization than you will with others. You can get along without us. After you pass your final examinations, you can go out as a freelance. I would be very happy to have you do that if you want to, but it wouldn't be good judgment on your part. Good judgment and sound, accurate thinking will prompt you to get under the wing of Napoleon Hill Associates, because we have the equipment, facilities, mechanism, influence, and know-how to keep you from making some of the mistakes that otherwise you would inevitably make. You'll do some Master Minding and you'll do some concentrating if you are as smart as I hope you will be when you get through this course. Then the applied Golden Rule gives one moral guidance to the effect of what you are concentrating on.

Accurate thinking saves one from daydreaming in creating plans. Most so-called thinking is nothing but daydreaming or hoping or wishing. A lot of people spend the vast majority of the time daydreaming, hoping, wishing, thinking about things, but never taking any concrete action in carrying out their plans.

A long time ago, when I was lecturing over in Des Moines, Iowa, on this philosophy, after the lecture an elderly man tottered up to the stage—he was decrepit and not very strong. He fished around in his pocket and came up with a great bundle of papers that had dog-ears on them. He fished around and came up with one yellow paper. He said, "Nothing new, Mr. Hill, in what you just said. I had those ideas twenty years ago. There they are, on paper." Sure, he did. Millions of other people had them too. But did he do anything about them?

There's nothing new in this philosophy, not a thing, except the law of cosmic habit force. Even that, strictly speaking, is not new. It's a proper interpretation of Emerson's essay on compensation, but stated in terms that people can understand the first time they read it.

Yes, there he was, the old man. He carried those ideas around in his pocket, and he could have been Napoleon Hill instead of me if he'd only gotten busy back before I started.

One of these days, some smart fellow will come along, and he'll take up right where I stopped. He'll create a philosophy based on what I have done that may be far superior to this. Maybe that person sits right in this room now.

A Good Teacher

You know what makes a good teacher? It's his mental attitude toward his students: he wants every one of them not only to catch up with him but to excel. I hope and pray, with all my heart and soul, that every student in this class will see the day when he or she will excel me in every way in connection with the teaching in this philosophy. I mean that with all of my heart. You can, if you make up your mind today, because you have so much better opportunity now than I had when I started. You have all of the answers. They're written out, they're spelled out for you, they're pinpointed, they're blueprinted. You've got a skeleton to go by. I know you can do it if you want to.

What will enable you to do the job better than I do? An obsessional desire to do it. It doesn't make a difference what you look like, what your age may be, or what your sex may be; it doesn't make any difference at all. The mental attitude that you take towards it will be the determining factor, because you have everything else available. You all can surpass me, and it won't take you very long to do it.

The Power of Adversity

Learning from defeat insures against quitting when the going is harder. Isn't it a marvelous thing to know that in this philosophy you have learned, beyond any question of a doubt, that failure, defeat, and adversity needn't stop you, that there's a benefit in every such experience?

Can you see any benefit in a man going through a Depression and losing all of his money, right down to the last penny, having to start all over again?

If you can't, take a good look now, because you're looking at a man who did just that. It was one of the greatest blessings that ever came along, because I was getting to be a smarty-pants. I was making too much money and making it too easily. I had to get taken back a notch.

I came out fighting, and I have done more good work since that time than I ever did before. Without that experience, I probably would be up there on my estate in the Catskill Mountains instead of down here teaching.

Sometimes adversity is a blessing in disguise. Oftentimes it is not so disguised if you take the right attitude towards it. You can't be whipped, you can't be defeated, until you have accepted defeat in your own mind. Just remember that, and remember that no matter what the nature of your adversity is, there is always the seed of an equivalent benefit if you will concentrate on the circumstance, and look for all the good that came out of it instead of the bad. Don't spend any time brooding over the things that are lost or gone or the mistakes that you have made, except to put in some time analyzing them and learning by them so that you won't make the same mistake twice.

Controlled attention involves the blending and application of many of the other principles of the philosophy. Persistence should be the watchword behind all of these principles. Controlled attention is the twin brother of definiteness of purpose.

Just think what you could do with those two principles: definiteness of purpose—knowing exactly what you want—and concentrating everything you've got on carrying out that purpose. Do you know what would happen to your mind, to your brain, and to your whole personality if you would concentrate on one definite thing?

By concentrating, I mean putting all of the time that you can possibly spare in seeing yourself in possession of the thing that represents your definiteness of purpose. Seeing yourself in possession of it, seeing yourself building plans for attaining it, working out the first step that you can take, and then the second and the third and so on, concentrating on it day in and day out. In a little while, you'll get to the point at which every way you turn, you will find an opportunity that will lead you a little closer to the thing that represents your definiteness of purpose. When you know what you want, it's astounding how many things you will find that are related to exactly what you want.

I was living in Florida some years ago, and I had a very important letter coming to the Tampa post office. I knew the letter came, because I talked on long distance to the National City Bank in New York. I knew that letter was in the mail, and it was not dropped at the post office. I had to have it before twelve o'clock. I lived out in the country, ten miles off.

I called the postmaster, who was a friend of mine, and he said that the mail was somewhere between there and Temple Terrace, on route number one. "I don't know of any way for you to get that letter before twelve o'clock, except to run that postman down," he said. "I'll tell you which station is and where to start, because he's already passed station number nine. You pick him up there. I'll give you instructions on how to follow his route."

Route number one came over the same highway that I use in traveling from Tampa out to my home at Temple Terrace. I travel it every day. I didn't know there were any mailboxes on it, but it began to be important for me to observe mailboxes. I want to tell you, I'd never seen some of the mailboxes in all my life. It looked as if there was one every hundred feet. They were all numbered, and I was looking for the number that the postmaster gave me as the one where he would probably be at that very hour.

I finally caught up with the postman, and he had it. It was on a Monday, and he had an enormous load of mail. "Why, man," he said, "I can't do anything about that. I don't know where your letter is. I won't know until I get rid of it all."

I said, "Listen, fellow. I have got to have that letter. It's in there. I have got to have it. The postmaster told me to run you down and not to take no for an answer, to tell you to get out and sort that mail and let me have that letter. That's what he told me, and if you don't think so, come out over to this farmhouse and you can call him."

"It's unlawful. I can't do that."

"Unlawful or not, I've got to have that letter." Now I saw where he stood. I said, "Now listen, fellow. Be a good sport. You've got a job to do, and I've got a job to do. Yours is important, and mine is important too. It's not going to hurt you to look for that mail. You can do it in a little while."

"Oh, hell," he said. "All right."

So he went to work. The third letter that he picked out was mine. It's just one of those things. When you know what you want, and somehow or another you're determined to get it, it's not nearly as difficult to get as you thought it was.

I've often thought how indicative that is of the experiences of people who know what they want and are successful in getting it. They don't let anything stop them at all. Opposition—why, they just don't pay any attention to opposition.

I've often watched Mr. Stone, my distinguished business associate, talk to his salesmen. I get a thrill every time I hear him speak, because I don't believe he knows what the word *no* means. I think that for a long time he's believed it means yes, and the results he gets shows that he believes it means yes. He can be the most definite about the things he wants of anybody I've ever known and the most definite in refusing to accept a turndown. In other words, when objects get in his way, he goes right over them or around them, or he blows them out of the way, but he never lets them stop him. Now that's concentration. That's definiteness of purpose put into action.

Illustrious Persons

Let's study some of these people who are illustrative of achievement through concentration. Take Henry Ford, for instance. Everybody knows what his obsession or definite purpose was. Most people have been riding a part of his major purpose around every day of their lives. It was a dependable, low-priced automobile. He didn't allow anybody to talk him out of it. I have heard promoters approach Mr. Ford with opportunities that seemed to me glittering. His reply always was that he was engaged in the thing that consumed all of his time and effort. He was not interested in anything outside of his definite major purpose, which was to make and distribute low-priced, dependable automobiles all over the world.

Sticking to that job made him fabulously rich. I saw hundreds of people come into the field and spend more money, infinitely more, than Mr. Ford had to start off with. They went into the graveyard of failure, and I couldn't find a dozen people in the world today who would know what their names were.

These men were better educated than Mr. Ford, had better personalities, had everything that he had and a lot more, except one thing. They didn't stick to the last. They didn't stick to the one definite purpose the way that he did when the going was hard.

In the field of invention, Mr. Edison was a marvelous illustration of what concentration could do. If Mr. Edison was a genius in any sense, it was because when the going was hard, he turned on the most steam rather than quit.

Think of a man standing by and keeping on through ten thousand different failures, as he did when he was working on the incandescent electric lamp. Can you imagine yourself going through ten thousand failures in the same field without wondering if you shouldn't have your head examined? I was astounded when I heard about that. I saw his logbooks. There were two stacks of them. Each book had about 250 pages. On every page there was a different plan that he had tried, and it had failed.

"Mr. Edison," I said, "suppose that you hadn't found the answer. What would you be doing right now?"

"I would be in my laboratory working instead of out here fooling away my time with you." I will say on his behalf that he grinned when he said it, but believe you me, he meant exactly what he was saying.

Another example is William Wrigley Jr. Mr. Wrigley, by the way, was the first man that ever paid me money for teaching him this philosophy. The first hundred dollars that I ever made came from Mr. Wrigley. I never ride down Michigan Boulevard and see that white building on the river, lighted at night, without thinking of what concentration can do even in connection with a five-cent package of chewing gum.

Aid from Infinite Intelligence

Infinite intelligence will throw itself on your side when it finds out that you're not going to quit until it does. If you don't get anything else in your notebook, get that down. If you do not give up when the going is hard, infinite intelligence will throw itself on your side. Remember that when the going is hard.

You have your faith tested, you have your initiative tested, you have your enthusiasm tested, you have your endurance tested. When nature finds out that you can stand the test and you're not going to take no for an answer, it says, "All right. You pass. Come on in. You're in." Infinite intelligence throws itself on your side if you don't give up when the going is hard.

I know this the only way anybody could know: because I've seen it happen to me. There have been times when I had no right to succeed except that I didn't quit just because I hadn't yet found the answer.

Think of devoting twenty years of research in the field that I'm engaged in without any compensation. All the money I made from other sources went out into the research for twenty years. Think of that. How many people in the world do you think would be that foolish?

One. I don't know of another person that ever put that much research into any field of endeavor without any monetary compensation. But look what's happened—benefits extending to millions of people not yet born and the potentials of this philosophy. What may happen throughout this troubled world that we're living in no man can say. If I may judge by what's happened so far to individuals who have been indoctrinated by this philosophy, I might conjecture that this might be the antidote for communism and all the other isms that are inimical to the interest of mankind. Because in the final analysis, I think that nature—or infinite intelligence or God or whatever you choose to call it—likes to convey information to people in simple terms and through things they can understand. Surely this philosophy comes within that category. It wouldn't send high-school boys or girls to the dictionary or the encyclopedia. You can read it or hear about it, and you can understand it; your own intelligence tells you the moment you come across one of these principles that it is bound to be sound. You just know that it is; you don't need any proof. It wouldn't have been in existence today if I hadn't concentrated through twenty years of adversity and defeat.

You see, it does pay to concentrate, and my own experience corroborates what I've said: if you stand by when the going is hard and you have failed, infinite intelligence will throw itself on your side.

I don't think that would be true in a case like that of Hitler. No doubt he had definiteness of purpose and an obsessional desire, but they ran counter to the plans of infinite intelligence, to the laws of nature, to the laws of right and wrong. If whatever you're doing works hardship or injustice upon one single individual, you may be sure that it will come to naught and come to failure, and you'll come to grief.

If you hope to have infinite intelligence throw itself on your side, you have to be right, and you can only be right when everything that you do benefits everybody whom it affects, including yourself.

Christ's whole life was concentrated upon developing a system of living for the brotherhood of men. He didn't fare too well while he lived. On the other hand, he must have been doing the right thing, because even after he passed on, he only had twelve people to start out with.

I have lots more than that now, but I have a lot of people criticizing me too from time to time. When I think of what happened to Christ, how badly he got treated, how few followers he had, I can see that I have been blessed beyond my greatest imagination. Because there is no single force in this world today that's as extensive and as far reaching as the force that Christ let loose when he was here with those twelve disciples.

That's why I believe that what Christ was doing and preaching must have been right. If it hadn't been, it would have been gone long before this, because there is something in nature, in infinite intelligence, which brings forth with every evil the virus of its own destruction. There's no exception. Every evil, everything that's not in conjunction with the overall plan of nature, of the natural laws of the universe, brings with it the virus of its own destruction.

The Objective of Freedom

The object of concentration of George Washington, Thomas Jefferson, Abraham Lincoln, and the signers of the Declaration of Independence was to give personal liberties to all of the American people and eventually to the people of the world. It may well be that this is the cradle for the birth of the freedom of mankind, because I know of no other nation on the face of this earth that is concentrating upon the freedom of the individual as we're doing here in the United States. And I know of no other people whose objective is to free so many as those who are studying this philosophy.

Your objective, first of all, is to give yourself freedom, and the next, to give freedom to the people that come under your influence, indoctrinating them with this philosophy.

13

Learning from Adversity

If there is one thing in the world that people do not like, it's adversity, unpleasant circumstances, and defeat. Yet if I have taken inventory of the laws of nature properly, it was intended that we all should undergo adversities, defeat, failure, opposition—and for a very definite reason.

Had it not been for the adversities that I went through during my early life, I wouldn't be standing here talking to you tonight, I wouldn't have completed this philosophy, and I wouldn't be reaching millions of people all over the world. It was out of the opposition I met with that I grew the strength, wisdom, and ability to complete this philosophy and to take it to people. Yet if I were to go back over the past and had my choice, I have no doubt that I'd make it easier for myself, just as you would.

We're all inclined to do that, to find the line of least resistance. Taking the line of least resistance is what makes all rivers and some men crooked, yet it's very common for us to do that. We don't want to pay the price of intense effort, no matter what we're doing. We like to have things come the easy way.

The mind is just like any other part of the physical body: it becomes weak and atrophies through disuse. When you meet with problems and incidents that force you to think, it is probably the finest thing that could happen to you, because without a motive, you're not going to do very much thinking anyway.

There are seventeen principles of success, but at least thirty-five major causes of failure. That is not all of them; these are just the major causes.

Self-examination is one of the most profitable things that you can indulge in. Sometimes you don't want to do it, but it's very necessary for us to know ourselves as we are, especially our weaknesses.

In putting out a philosophy of success, it is necessary to tell you the things that you should do in order to succeed and also the things you should *not* do.

At this point, we're dealing with the things that you should not do and the weaknesses you should or must conquer if you're going to be successful. Write the thirty-five major causes of failure below, and grade yourself in the right-hand column as I go along. Grade yourself from 0 to 100, meaning if you're 100 percent free of any one of them, grade yourself 100 percent. If you're only 50 percent free, grade yourself 50 percent. If you aren't free at all, grade yourself 0.

When you get through, add the total up, divide it by 35, and you'll get your general average on the control of the things that cause men and women to fail.

1. Drifting

First of all is the habit of *drifting* with circumstances without definite aims or plans. If you don't follow the habit of drifting, if you make decisions quickly, if you lay out plans and follow them, if you know exactly where you're going and are on the way, you can grade yourself 100 percent on that.

Be careful before you put down the grade, because it's rare for anybody to be able to grade himself 100 percent on that one. You really have to be organized, and you really have to be prepared if you're going to do that.

2. Unfavorable Physical Heredity

Number two is an *unfavorable physical hereditary* foundation at birth. Although it can be a cause of failure, it can also be a cause of success. Some of the most successful people I have ever known were handicapped by bad afflictions at birth. The late Dr. Charles P. Steinmetz was crippled. He had a hunchback and a misshapen body at birth. Yet he was one of the most useful men of his time. He had a wonderful brain, he used it, and he didn't allow that affliction to give him an inferiority complex.

I've always been very proud of the job that I did with my son Blair, who was born without ears. At first we let him go to school with his hair down around his neck. The children commenced making fun of him, calling him a sissy. One day he took the matter in hand in the usual Napoleon Hill way. He went by the barbershop on his way home and had the barber cut all of his hair off. When he came home, his mother was badly upset about it. He said, "From here on out, they won't need to tease me about having long hair, and they'll know now why it was long."

From that day until this, he's not the slightest bit self-conscious. He walks along the street. People will turn and gaze and gape at him, and he's not even conscious of it, because I told him not to be. I told him that affliction was a blessing, and it has been because it has caused people to be more kind to him. You can take an affliction of that kind and convert it into an asset if you take the right attitude toward it.

3. Meddlesome Curiosity

Number three is *meddlesome curiosity* in connection with other people's business and affairs. Now curiosity is a wonderful thing. If we weren't curious, we'd never learn anything, we'd never investigate. Notice the wording: "meddlesome curiosity with other people's affairs"—with something that doesn't really concern you.

Now remember, as you grade yourself, go back in your past experiences and determine to what extent you have control of these weaknesses.

4. Lack of a Definite Major Purpose

Number four: lack of a definite major purpose as a lifetime goal. We've been talking about that for a long time. Now we're putting down the lack of it. If you lack it, here's a mighty good place to rate yourself zero.

5. Inadequate Schooling

There is very little relationship between *schooling* and success. Some of the most successful people I have ever known have been those with the least amount of formal education. A lot of people go through life as failures, and they alibi themselves out of it. They kid themselves into believing that they're failures because they don't have a college education. In a lot of cases, a college education puts a man or a woman in a position where they have a lot to unlearn and have to reeducate themselves.

If you come out of college feeling that you should be paid for what you know instead of what you do, that college education hasn't done you much good. When you meet old man destiny standing around the corner with a stuffed club (and it's not stuffed with cotton), you'll find out that you're not going to be paid for what you know. You're going to be paid for what you do with what you know, or what you can get other people to do.

6. Lack of Self-Discipline

Lack of self-discipline generally manifests itself in excesses in eating and drinking and in indifference toward opportunities for self-advancement and improvement. I hope you can grade yourself very high on that one.

7. Lack of Ambition

Lack of ambition to aim above mediocrity—there's a humdinger. Just how much ambition do you have anyway? Where are you going in life? What do you want out of life? What are you going to settle for?

A young soldier came in to see me just after World War I. He wanted to settle for a sandwich and the place to sleep that night. I wouldn't let him do it. I talked him into settling for a higher aim than that, with the result that he became a multimillionaire within the following four years. I hope I'll have as much success with you in stepping your ambition up to the point where you're not willing to settle with life for a penny.

Aim high. It's not going to cost you anything. You may not get as far as you aim, but you will certainly get farther than you would if you don't aim at all. Raise your sights, be ambitious, be determined that you're going to become in the future what you have failed to become in the past.

8. Ill-Health

Number eight is *ill-health*, often due to wrong thinking and improper diet. There's a lot of alibis on the count of ill-health too, I can assure you, and a lot of imaginary ailments. They call it hypochondria. I

don't know to what extent you've been coddling or babying yourselves with imaginary ailments, but if you have been doing that,
grade yourself low on that one.

9. Unfavorable Childhood Influences

Once in a great while, you will find that the influences upon a person
during childhood are of such a negative nature that the individual
goes all the way through life with those negative influences.

I'm quite convinced that if I had been permitted to continue in
my childhood as I started out before my stepmother came into the
picture, I would have become a second Jesse James (only I would have
been able to shoot faster and straighter than he did). Everything in
my environment had caused me to build myself into a hero patterned
after Jesse James.

Until this wonderful, marvelous mom came into my life. She took
that same bad boy, with all of his badness, and she transmuted those
negative qualities into positives and lived to see the time when that
bad boy had an influence on millions of people. It's too bad she hasn't
lived up until the present.

10. Lack of Persistence

There's a honey: *lack of persistence* in following through with one's
duty. What causes people to fail to follow through when they start
something? What's the main reason people do not follow through
and do things right?

Lack of motive. They don't want to do it badly enough. Believe
you me, I'll follow through on anything that I want to follow through
on, but if I don't want to follow through, I can find a lot of alibis to
keep from doing it.

Is it profitable for you to get into the habit of following through
when you undertake something, or is it profitable for you to permit

yourself to be sidetracked? Do you follow through, or are you easily sidetracked? Are you easily dissuaded from doing the thing when somebody criticizes you?

If I had been afraid of criticism, I never would have gotten anywhere in life. I eventually got to the point where I embraced criticism because it would put the fight in me. When I found out that when the fight was in me, I did a much better job; I carried through better.

A lot of people fail because they lack the driving force to carry through, especially when the going is hard. No matter what you're doing, you're going to run into a period when the going is hard. If it's a new business, you'll probably need finances that you don't have in the beginning. If it's a profession, you will need clients that you don't have in the beginning. If it's a new job, you'll need a recognition with your employer that you don't have. You have to earn that recognition. The going is always hard in the beginning, and that's why you need to follow through.

11. A Negative Mental Attitude

Which are you: preponderantly negative most of the time, or preponderantly positive? When you see a doughnut, what do you see first? Do you see the hole first or the doughnut? When you go to eat a doughnut, you don't eat the hole, do you? You eat the doughnut.

A lot of people, when they come across a problem, are like the fellow who sees the hole in the doughnut and growls about it because it took so much of the nice cake out, but does not see the doughnut itself.

What is the result for a person who has the habit of allowing his mind to become negative and remain negative? A negative mind repels people. A positive mind attracts people who harmonize with your mental attitude, your character. You know the saying, "Birds of a feather flock together"? Negative birds flock to the negative mind, and positive birds flock to the positive mind.

Who has control over your mind? Who determines whether it's positive or negative? You. Grade yourself on the extent to which you exercise that prerogative. It's the most precious thing you have on the face of this earth or ever will have. It's the only thing that you have complete unchallenged and unchallengeable control over: the right to make your mind positive and keep it that way, or to allow the circumstances of life to make it negative.

You have to work at it if you're going to keep your mind positive, because there are so many negative influences around you. So many people, so many circumstances are negative that if you are going to become a part of them instead of creating your own circumstances in your mind, then most of the time, you'll be negative.

Do you have a clear concept of what the difference is between a negative mind and a positive mind? Can you picture what happens in the chemistry of the brain when your mind is positive and when it's negative? Have you ever demonstrated or experienced in your own life the differences between your achievements when you are afraid and achievements when you're not afraid?

When I first wrote *Think and Grow Rich*, I was working for President Roosevelt during the bad Depression during his first term. I wrote it in the same negative mental attitude that everybody else was in; it was forced upon me unconsciously. Several years later, when I got that book out and read it, I recognized it was not a salable book, because its tempo was negative, and you could pick that up. A reader will pick up exactly the mental attitude that a writer is in when he writes a book, no matter what language or terminology he uses.

I didn't change a lesson in that book, but I sat down to my typewriter when I was in a new frame of mind—up on the beam, as we say, 100 percent positive—and I typed that book over again. That's what made the book click. When you're negative, you can't afford to do anything that you expect to benefit you or influence other people. If you are to get people to cooperate with you, if you want to sell people something, or if you want to make a good impression upon people, don't come near them until you're in a positive frame of mind.

I have emphasized this so much because I want to give you a chance to grade yourself accurately on that one. Grade yourself on the average state of mind that you maintain, not just on your state of mind at any given time for a short time.

I'll tell you a good rule for determining whether or not you are more positive than you are negative: observe how you feel when you wake up in the morning and get up out of bed. If you're not in a good frame of mind then, it's because a lot of the preceding thought habits, perhaps from the day before, have been negative. You can make yourself very ill by allowing your mind to become negative, and it will be reflected in the next morning in particular. You see, when you come out of sleep, you're just fresh from coming out of the influence of your subconscious mind. Your conscious mind has been off duty. When it goes back on duty, it finds the mess that the subconscious mind has been stirring up all night long, which the conscious mind has to clean up.

If you wake up full of joy and you want to get out of bed and do what you're going to do today, chances are that you've been pretty positive the day before, and maybe several days before.

12. Lack of Emotional Control

Had you ever thought that it's just as necessary to control your positive emotions as it is your negative ones? Why would you want to control the emotion of love, for instance? Because it not only can get you in hot water, it can scald you.

Let's take another emotion: desire for financial gain. Do you need to control that? Yes, because you may be working it up to where you want to get too much. I've met a lot of people who had too much money for their own good, especially people who got it without earning it, like people who inherited it.

Do you know why I'm called Napoleon? My father named me after my great-uncle, Napoleon Hill of Memphis, Tennessee, who was a multimillionaire cotton broker, hoping that when Uncle Napoleon died, I would get some of the money.

He died, and I didn't get any of the money. When I found out that I was not going to get any of it, I felt very bad. Later on, as I swapped some of my youth for wisdom and observed what happened to the ones who did get it, I was eternally grateful that I didn't get a dime, because I learned a better way of getting it for myself without having it given to me.

13. The Desire to Get Something for Nothing

Are you ever troubled with *the desire to get something for nothing,* or for less than its value? Are you ever troubled with the desire for something without giving adequate compensation for it? Which of us hasn't been at one time or another?

You can have a lot of faults, but you want to find out what they are and start getting rid of them. That's why we're making this analysis. We're giving you a chance to be a trial judge, a defendant, and a prosecutor all at one time, and you make the final decision. It'd be far better for you to find your faults than it would be for me to find them for you, because if you find them, you're not going to try any alibis. You're going to try to get rid of these faults.

14. Failing to Reach Prompt Decisions

Do you reach decisions promptly and firmly? Or do you reach decisions very slowly, and after you reach them, do you allow the first person that comes along to reverse you? Do you allow circumstances to reverse your decisions without a sound reason? To what extent do you stand by your decisions after you make them? Under what circumstances would you reverse a decision that you've made?

You should hold an open mind on that subject at all times. You should never make a decision and say, "That's it, and I'm going to stand by it forever," because something might develop later on that would prompt you to reverse that decision.

Some people are known as stubborn, and once they've made a decision, right or wrong, they die by it. I've seen a lot of people like that, who would rather die than reverse themselves or have somebody reverse them on a decision.

Of course, you're not like that. That is, if you're really indoctrinated with this philosophy. You may have been like that once, but you're not like that now, or you're not going to like the results you get out of this survey.

15. The Seven Basic Fears

Number fifteen is one or more of the *seven basic fears*:

1. Fear of poverty
2. Fear of criticism
3. Fear of ill-health
4. Fear of the loss of love
5. Fear of the loss of liberty
6. Fear of old age
7. Fear of death

Every person suffers from practically all of these at one time or another. I can remember the time when I had all of them. Now I don't have any of them.

I have no fears of any nature whatsoever, not even the fear of death—least of all of that, because to me, death is just one more marvelous interlude that I'll have to go through, and when I get there, I'll be equal to it. I'll probably have a lot of fun with it.

This is a wonderful world we're living in. I am glad I'm here. I'm glad I'm doing just what I am. If unpleasant circumstances cross my path, I'm glad for them too, because I'll find out whether I'm stronger than the circumstances or not. As long as I can conquer them, I'm not going to worry about circumstances—things that oppose me, people that don't like me, people that say mean things about me. Why would I worry about that?

If people say mean things about me, I'll examine myself and find out whether they were telling the truth. As long as they're not, I can stand back and laugh at them, at how foolish they are, and at how much damage they're doing themselves.

16. The Wrong Selection of a Mate

Don't be too quick to grade yourself on this one. If you made a 100 percent mistake on it, look around before you grade yourself and see if you can't do something about correcting that mistake.

I've often wondered how many marriages I have helped to save. Some, which I separated, should have been separated before they were married, but they didn't have the courage to recognize that they made a mistake. But I have helped to save far more marriages than I ever helped to undo, because it's my contention that people who don't belong together—they don't find harmony; they do not complement each other—ought to live in separate houses at least.

Some people believe that all marriages are made in heaven. It'd be a wonderful thing if they were, but I have seen some that were not. I don't know where else they might have been made, but they certainly weren't made in heaven.

I've also seen some business relationships that were not made in heaven. I've helped to correct a lot of those—business associates that were not working together in a spirit of harmony. There's no business on the face of this earth that can succeed unless the people, at least at the top level, are working in harmony.

There is no household or home that can be a joy, a place that you want to go to, unless there is harmony at the top.

Harmony starts with loyalty and dependability, then would come ability. As I've pointed out, that's the way I evaluate people. If I want to select a man or woman for a high position, the first thing I look for is whether that person was loyal to the people to whom he owed loyalty. If he wasn't, I wouldn't want him or her on any terms whatsoever.

The next thing I would look for would be dependability: whether or not you can depend upon him to be at the right place at the right time and do the right thing. After that would come ability. I've seen a lot of people who had great ability but were not dependable. They were not loyal and therefore were very dangerous.

17. Overcaution

Number seventeen: *overcaution* in business and professional relationships. Have you seen people so cautious that they wouldn't trust their own mother-in-law?

I once knew a man who was so cautious that he had a special wallet made with a little lock on it. He hid the key in a different place every night so that his wife couldn't go through his trousers and take money out of his wallet. Wasn't he a honey? I bet his wife loved him.

I knew another man. He was a farmer whose wife had to steal the egg money a little at a time in order to buy herself a few ribbons for the bonnet now and then. That's the only way she could get any money. He carried the money and spent it all; he looked after the family budget. There must also have been some wrong selection of mates there.

18. Lack of Caution

Then there's lack of all forms of caution in human relationships. Have you seen people like that, who just didn't have any caution? People who start their mouths to going and leave them going; never mind what the effects are going to be on other people.

You've seen people like that, haven't you? No caution whatsoever, no discrimination, no diplomacy, no consideration of what they're going to do to other people through their words. I've seen people with tongues that were sharper than a double-edged Gillette blade that never has been used. They start them to cutting and just walk away. No caution whatsoever.

I've also seen people who would sign anything the salesmen put in front of them without even reading it. They wouldn't read the big title, let alone a little dot. Have you seen people like that?

You can be overcautious, and you can be undercautious. What is the happy medium? It's found in the lesson on accurate thinking: you carefully examine the things that you're going to do before you do them, not afterward, and you evaluate your words before you express them, not afterward.

It's got to be a little bit difficult to grade yourselves accurately on this one. To be perfectly candid, it would be a little bit difficult for me to grade myself accurately on these two—seventeen and eighteen— because there have been a lot of times in my life when I wasn't cautious at all. I think most of my troubles in my early days came through my trusting too many people. I let somebody come along and flatter me into using the name Napoleon Hill, and he'd go out and flimflam a lot of people in the name of Napoleon Hill. That happened several times in my life before I tightened up and became cautious.

On the other hand, I wouldn't want to become so cautious that I didn't trust anybody for anything. You get no joy out of living if you do that.

Incidentally, this is one of the most valuable lessons in this whole course, because this is a lesson in self-examination. You're really on the spot, and you're doing the judging. You're going to find out things; if you don't find them out tonight, you're going to find them out when you go over this lesson again, when you check over the grading that you've given yourself.

I'll bet you any amount of money up to—well, up to a dime—that when you go over this grading, you'll make at least half a dozen changes when you sit down and really think the thing through properly.

19. Wrong Choice of Associates

Next is the *wrong choice of associates* in one's occupation or calling. How many times have you heard of people getting into trouble because they were associated with the wrong kind of people?

I've never seen a youngster in my life that became bad or went wrong where it couldn't be traced back to the influence of some other person. Not once have I ever known a youngster to go wrong or get into bad habits unless that person had been influenced by somebody else.

20. Wrong Selection of Vocation

Number twenty: wrong selection of a vocation, or a total neglect to make a choice of a vocation. About 98 people out of every 100 would grade 0 on that one. Of course, you students of this philosophy, who have had a chance to become indoctrinated with lesson number one on definiteness of purpose, would grade much higher.

You either grade 0 or 100 percent; there's no halfway point. You either have a definite major purpose, or you don't. You can't grade 50 or 60 percent or any other amount on that one, or on definiteness of purpose. You either have one, or you don't.

21. Lack of Concentration of Effort

This means divided interests. You split your interest, and divide it over a lot of different things. One person is not strong enough and life is too short to ensure your success unless you learn the art of concentrating everything you've got on one thing at a time and following through on that one thing and doing a good job.

22. Lack of a Budget

Here's one that may be difficult to grade yourself on: *lack of a budget*, lack of a systematic way of taking care of your income and your expenditures.

Do you know how the average person manages a budget? His expenditures are somewhat controlled by the amount of credit that he can get from other people. That's about the only thing. When the credit shuts down, he more or less slacks off, but until that happens, he runs wild with spending.

A business firm would go bankrupt in a little while if it didn't have a system of control over its income and expenditures. That's what a controller and an organization is for. They usually call them wet blankets. Every successful business of any size has to have a wet blanket: a man who controls the assets of the company and keeps them from getting away at the wrong time and the wrong way.

23. Failure to Budget Time

Next is *failure to budget time* to best advantage. Time is the most precious thing you have. You have twenty-four hours every day. You must devote eight hours, or at least an average of that, to sleep if you're going to have health. You have another eight hours to make a living, and then you have another eight hours of free time. In America, you're a free citizen; you can do anything you want to with those other eight hours: you can sin, you can spend, you can establish good habits, you can establish bad habits, you can educate yourself.

What are you doing with those eight hours? That's the determining factor in how you grade yourself on this question. Are you budgeting the use of your time to best advantage? Do you have a system of making all of your time count?

Of course, you have the first sixteen hours practically taken care of automatically, but the other eight hours are not: you can do pretty much do as you want with them. There's a whole lesson in this course on budgeting time and money, and some definite suggestions for using those eight hours of free time.

24. Lack of Controlled Enthusiasm

Here's a honey too. Enthusiasm is beyond doubt among the most valuable of all the emotions, provided that you can turn it on and off as you would a water spigot or an electric light. If you can turn your enthusiasm on when you want to and turn it off when you want to, you can grade yourself 100 percent on this. Lack of the ability to do that would grade you somewhere down toward that little zero.

Have you ever thought about your willpower? What it was placed there for? You have a power of will, and what is its purpose?

It's discipline. That power of will is for discipline over your mind, so you can make your mind wherever you want it to be. You can form whatever kind of habits you want.

I have never been able to determine which is worse: no enthusiasm at all, a cold fish, or red-hot enthusiasm that's out of control. If you're going to be able teachers, you will have to learn to turn on your enthusiasm when you're teaching, because if you don't, your words are going to be flat; they're going to be monotonous; they're going to be lacking in magnetism. You're not going to get the attention of the people who are listening unless you put enthusiasm into your words, and you can't put enthusiasm into your words unless you feel it inside of you.

If somebody made me mad right now, I could turn off my enthusiasm just like that and turn on something else. That would be much more appropriate, maybe (provided I didn't use the wrong language). There has been a time when I could turn on anger much more quickly than I could turn on enthusiasm, and I couldn't turn it off nearly as easily. That's something you'll have to overcome too. You have to gain the ability to turn on any of your emotions or to turn them off.

25. Intolerance

Intolerance is a closed mind based on ignorance or prejudice in connection with religious, racial, political, or economic ideas. How do you rate on that one?

It would be marvelous if you could grade 100 percent on that and say that you have an open mind on all subjects toward all people at all times. If you could say that, you'd probably not be human, you'd be a saint.

However, there are times, I suppose, when if you made up your mind to be open-minded on all these things, you could for a little while. I know I can for a little while.

Suppose you can't grade 100 percent on that; suppose you can't be open-minded toward all people at all times on all subjects. What is the next best thing to do?

You can be tolerant some of the time. The more you try it out, the more you'll find that *sometime* will take on more and more time, and eventually tolerance will be a habit with you instead of intolerance.

There are people in this world—and I regret to say that they're in the vast majority—who, when they meet others, immediately begin to look for things they don't like, and they always find things they don't like.

Then there is another type of person. I've noticed that this other type of person is always much more successful, much more happy, and much more welcome when he comes around: when he meets a person, whether it's an acquaintance or a stranger, he immediately begins not only to look for the things that he likes in that person, but to compliment them or indicate that he recognizes good qualities instead of bad things.

I get a great feeling when somebody walks up to me and says, "Aren't you Napoleon Hill?"

I say, "Yes, I'm guilty."

"Well, I want to tell you, Mr. Hill, how much good I got out of your book."

I thrive on that; I love it. It does me a lot of good, unless they rub it on too thick (and you can do that too).

I've never seen the person that wouldn't respond in kind to a compliment. If you stroke even a bad-natured pussycat on the back, its will curl up its tail and begin to purr. Cats are not very friendly, but you can make them friendly if you do the things they like.

26. Failure to Cooperate

Twenty-sixth is *failure to cooperate* with others in the spirit of harmony. There are circumstances in life, I suppose, where a failure to cooperate would be justified. I very often come into contact with people who want me to do things that I can't possibly do for them. They want my influence. They want me to write letters or recommendation. They want me to make telephone calls—well, I can't do it. I can't cooperate unless I'm sold on whom and what I'm cooperating with.

27. Possession of Unearned Power or Wealth

Next is possession of power that is not based on merit or earned. I hope you won't have any trouble grading yourself on that one.

28. Lack of Loyalty

Next is *lack of loyalty* to those to whom it is due. If you have loyalty in your heart to those to whom loyalty is due, you can grade 100 percent on that. Unless you practice that all the time, you wouldn't grade 100 percent; you'd grade somewhat lower.

Incidentally, when you grade yourself lower than 50 percent on any of these, put a cross mark on it, and go back to study it later. You should have all of these causes of failure at least 50 percent under control. If it falls below that, you've reached the danger point.

29. Forming Opinions Not Based on Facts

Number twenty-nine is the habit of *forming opinions not based upon known facts*. If you grade below 50 percent on that, begin to work on yourself right away. Stop having opinions that are not based on facts or what you believe to be facts.

When I hear anybody expressing an opinion on something he knows nothing about, I always think of that story about two men who were discussing Einstein's theory of relativity. They got into a hot argument about it, and one of them said, "Oh, hell. What does Einstein know about politics anyway?"

There are people like that, who have opinions about everything in the world. They can run their country better than Eisenhower is running it. They can tell J. Edgar Hoover a few things about his job, and they could always work their friends over and improve them. Generally if you examine them very carefully, they're not doing too well themselves.

30. Egotism and Vanity

Number thirty is egotism and vanity that are not under control. Egotism is a wonderful thing, and vanity is a wonderful thing. If you didn't have a little vanity, you wouldn't wash your neck or your face or have your hair curled or whatever women do.

You have to have a little vanity, a little pride, but you can't have too much. I think lipstick is wonderful f it doesn't get on my shirt. Rouge on the face is a wonderful thing, but you know, nature has a pretty good old hand at painting faces just right. When I see a sixty or seventy-year-old woman painting her face up to look like a sixteen-year-old, I know she's fooling herself and nobody else, because she's certainly not fooling me.

A lot of people need to build up their egos. They have allowed the circumstances of life to whip them down until they've got no fight left in them—no initiative, no imagination, no faith. Your ego, your human ego, is a wonderful thing if you have it under control and don't allow it to become objectionable to other people.

I have never seen a successful person yet that didn't have great confidence in his ability to do anything he started out to do. One purpose of this philosophy is to enable you to build your ego up to where it will do for you anything you want to do, no matter what it is. There are some people whose egos need to be trimmed down a little bit, but I'd say there are very many more that need a buildup.

31. Lack of Vision and Imagination

I have never been able to determine exactly whether this great capacity for vision and imagination is an inherited quality or an acquired quality. I think perhaps in my case, it was inherited, because I have a lot of imagination right back to the earliest days that I can remember. That got me in difficulty in the early days. I had too much imagination and didn't direct it in the right direction.

32. Unwillingness to Go the Extra Mile

If you have the habit of going the mile and have learned to get joy out of it, the chances are that you're going to put a lot of people under obligation to you—willing obligation. They don't mind being under obligation to you on that basis. If you have enough people obligated to you, there's no reason why you couldn't make legitimate use of those people, their influence, their education, their ability, and whatnot to help you succeed.

Do you know how to get anybody to do whatever you want them to do? Do something for them first. Look at how easy it is to do something nice for another person. You don't even have to ask, do you?

How do you grade on that? How many times will there be when you want to have a long list of people who are standing ready as an army to help you when you need help? What are you doing to cultivate that army in advance of the time of need? You can't just go the extra mile this minute and turn around the next minute and ask the person to whom you rendered that service to render you twice as much service. It won't work that way. You've got to build up goodwill in advance.

The timing has got to be right. For instance, when I was working for Mr. LeTourneau, I lectured one day on going the extra mile. One employee got the wrong impression. He was a toolmaker, and toolmakers were very scarce: it was during the war. He conceived of going the extra mile by coming back each night and working a couple of hours extra. He told Mr. LeTourneau the idea, but didn't tell Mr. LeTourneau that he was going to expect time and a half for overtime. On the weekend, when he turned in his bill for time and overtime, he made Mr. LeTourneau angry. Instead of benefiting himself, he lost an opportunity to get the confidence of Mr. LeTourneau.

A lot of people will go the extra mile only if for the sake of expediency. They do it just to put you under obligations, and they don't time it sufficiently. They do not allow you to forget about it. They turn right around after having done you a favor and ask you for two or three favors. Have you had that experience? Have you seen other people make that mistake? Or have you made it?

If I had to select one principle with which you can do the most, I'd say it's this principle of going the extra mile, because that's the one thing that anybody can control. You don't have to ask anybody for the privilege of going out of your way to be nice and to be of help. The moment you start doing it, you probably will feel a little contrast, because most people are not doing that.

As a matter of fact, if you've got an enemy or somebody you don't like, one of the best things you can do is to start rendering him favors, doing things for him that make him ashamed.

Some two years ago, I went up to Paris, Missouri, to teach class. The people up there became suspicious of me. They investigated me through the Better Business Bureau, through the FBI, Dun & Bradstreet, the Securities and Exchange Commission, the Post Office. They just knew that I was up there to steal a bank or do something. Why would the great Napoleon Hill come up to a wide place in the road like Paris, Missouri, if he wasn't up here for some mischief?

I did something about it. There isn't anybody who can do that to me without my doing much more to them than they can do to me. When anybody starts doing me an injury, you may be sure that I'm going to take notice of it.

I'll tell you what notice I took. When I had delivered the preliminary course and collected the money, I started in and I gave my students the Master Course that you're paying $500 for. In addition, I took all the money that I had collected from the preliminary course and spent it for radio time to broadcast over the length of the whole neighborhood, five or six counties.

That's what I did. If you want to strike back at somebody who has injured you or tried to injure you, that's the way to do it—going out of your way to swamp them, drown them, with good service and good mental attitude.

You know what came out of it, what the seed of an equivalent benefit was? I made a discovery second to none that I've made during my whole career. I discovered that there is a great thirst for this philosophy in the grassroots of the people out in the country, in farming communities like Paris, Missouri. I would never have discovered that if I had struck back at the people who were suspicious of me.

You students of this philosophy are going to be on a higher plane than the majority of people. You're going to settle your differences in a different court from that used by the average person. If you must strike back at another person, you are going to make him feel ashamed by being good to him instead of making him afraid.

I could have struck back at some of those people up at Paris legally with a slander suit, maybe libel. What would been the use? As you see, I would have fallen to their level.

In a fistfight, there are plenty of men that I wouldn't stand toe to toe with at all, because they're stronger and bigger and more adept at using their fists. I'd be quite foolish to try to settle my differences with anyone on the basis of a fistfight, wouldn't I?

I like to settle my differences in a court where I control the judge, the jury, the defendants, and the prosecution. That's the kind of a court I like to deal with. That's the court you maintain in your own mind. You select your own time, place, and technique for dealing with people. If you do that, you put a lot of people at disadvantage when they try to injure you.

33. Desire for Revenge

Thirty-three: *desire for revenge* for real or imaginary grievances. Which is the worse, to have a desired revenge for a real grievance or for or an imaginary grievance?

Think that one over. What happens to you when you express or desire revenge for any reason?

Does it hurt the other fellow? No. It hurts you. How does it hurt you? It makes you negative. It poisons your mind. It even poisons your blood if you maintain it long enough. Any negative mental attitude will get into your blood and interfere with your sound health.

34. Producing Alibis Instead of Results

To what extent do you immediately begin to look for an *alibi* when you make a mistake or when you do something and it doesn't turn out right or when you neglect to do the thing that you should have done? To what extent do you come across and say, "It was my fault"? Do you lay it on the line and face the music, or do you begin to conjure up a set of alibis to justify what you've done or neglected to do?

That's the point on which you're grading yourself. What is the pre-ponderance of your habits on that subject?

If you are an average person, the chances are that in the majority of cases, you will look for an alibi to justify what you do or refrain from doing. If you're not an average person—and I'm sure you'll not be if you become properly indoctrinated with this philosophy—you will not look for alibis, because you know that's only weakening. It's a crutch that you're leaning on. You will face the music. You will acknowledge your mistakes. You'll acknowledge your weaknesses. You'll acknowledge your errors, because self-confession is marvelous. It does something to the soul when you really know what your faults are and confess them honestly. You don't have to spread them to the whole world, but confess them where confession is necessary.

35. Lack of Dependability

This perhaps will be a bit hard to grade yourselves on, but generally you know whether you're dependable or not. You know whether your words are dependable, you know whether your performance in your occupation is dependable, you know whether you're a dependable family man or woman. You know whether you're dependable or not in your credit relations.

I've known some alcoholics in my time. I used to try to cure them. I don't anymore. Instead I put in the time on behalf of those good fellows that are not alcoholics, and I get much better results. If I find an alcoholic now, I turn him over to Alcoholics Anonymous. They do a better job than I do.

I've known some men who were wonderful when they were sober but were absolutely no good at all when they were not sober, because they weren't dependable. Most business firms would never give that kind of man a responsible job, because they can't depend on him.

14

Creative Vision and Imagination

Next we will cover the creative vision. The imagination, said someone, is the workshop wherein is fashioned the purpose of the brain and the ideals of the soul. I don't know of a better definition than that.

There are two forms of imagination. The first one is *synthetic imagination*, which consists of a combination of old ideas, concepts, plans, or facts arranged in a new combination.

New things are few and far between. As a matter of fact, when you speak of somebody having created a new idea or anything new, the chances are a thousand to one that it's not anything actually new. It's a reassembly of something that's old and that's gone before.

Number two is the *creative imagination*, which operates through the sixth sense in the subconscious mind. It's based in the subconscious section of the brain and serves as the medium by which new facts or ideas are revealed.

Any idea, plan, or purpose brought into the conscious mind and repeated and supported by emotional feeling is automatically picked up by the subconscious section of the brain and carried out to its logical conclusion by whatever natural means that are practical and convenient.

I want to emphasize one important fact: any idea, plan, or purpose that is brought into the conscious mind and repeatedly supported by emotional feeling comes into fruition. Ideas in your mind that are *not* emotionalized or over which you are *not* enthusiastic or in connection with which you *don't* have faith seldom produce any action.

You've got to get emotion, enthusiasm, and faith into your thoughts before you get action.

Synthetic Imagination

Here are some examples of applied synthetic imagination. First of all, Edison's invention of the incandescent electric lamp. There was nothing new about Edison's electric lamp. Both of the factors which combined made up the incandescent electric lamp were old and well-known to the world long before Edison's time.

It remained for Edison to go through ten thousand different failures and to find a way of marrying these two old ideas, bringing them together in a new combination. One idea was that you could take and apply electrical energy to wire, and at the point of friction, the wire would become hot and would make a light. A lot of people had found that out before Edison's time. Edison's problem was in finding some means of controlling that wire so that when it was heated to a white heat to make light, it wouldn't burn up.

He tried over ten thousand experiments, and none of them worked. One day, as was his custom, he lay down for a catnap to turn the problem over to his subconscious mind. While he was asleep, the subconscious mind came up with the answer. (I've always wondered why he had to go through ten thousand failures before he could get his subconscious mind to give him the answer.)

He had half the problem solved already. He saw the solution to the other half in the charcoal principle. To produce charcoal, you put a pile of wood on the ground and set it on fire, then cover it over with dirt, allowing just enough oxygen to percolate through to keep the wood smoldering, but not enough to permit it to blaze. It burns away a certain part of that wood, leaving the rest, which is charcoal. Of course, where there is no oxygen, there can be no combustion.

Taking that concept, with which Edison had long been familiar, he went back into the laboratory. He took a wire that he'd been heating with electricity, put it in a bottle, pumped the air out, and sealed the bottle, cutting off all oxygen. No oxygen could come in contact with the wire. When he turned on the electrical power, it burned for eight and a half hours. To this very moment, that's the principle on which the incandescent electric lamp operates. That's why when you drop one of those bulbs, it pops like a gun: the air has already been drawn out of it. No oxygen can be permitted to be inside of that bulb, because if it were, it would quickly burn the filament up.

Two old, simple ideas were brought together through synthetic imagination. If you will examine the operations of your imagination or the imagination of successful people, I think you'll find that in a large proportion of the cases, what has been used has been synthetic imagination and not creative imagination.

Clarence Saunders' Piggly Wiggly grocery store system was nothing but a use of synthetic imagination. He didn't create anything. All he did was to take the idea of the cafeteria by the ears, drag it across the street, and introduce it into the grocery store. That's all he did. Was that valuable? Yes, it was—$4 million worth in the first four years. Rearranging old ideas and concepts can be very profitable.

You may have discovered that there's only one new principle in this philosophy that you may not have been familiar with before. I have only made one contribution to it; everything else is as old as mankind. But what did I do? I used my synthetic imagination, and I reassembled. I sorted out the salient things that go into the making of success and organized them in a way that they had never been before—in a simple form, where anyone can take hold of them and put them to practical use. Yet that simple use of synthetic imagination is destined to influence more people probably than any other thing that's been done in my field in the last five hundred years. It is destined to help people that are not yet born.

I often wonder why somebody else smarter than me didn't think of that a long time ago. When we get hold of a good idea, we are always inclined to think, "Why didn't I get it a long time ago, when I needed the money?"

Henry Ford's combination of the horse-drawn buggy and the steam-propelled threshing machine was nothing but the use of synthetic imagination. He was inspired to create the automobile when he first saw a threshing machine being pulled along by a steam-propelled engine. This threshing outfit, with the machinery attached to the locomotion of the steam engine, was going down the highway, and Mr. Ford observed it. Then and there he got the idea of taking that same principle and putting it onto a buggy instead of the horse and making the horseless buggy, which eventually turned out to be known as the automobile.

Creative Imagination

Now for examples of creative imagination. All new ideas originate through a single or Master Mind application of creative vision—generally, through the Master Mind. When two or more people get together for the solution of a major problem, think along the same lines in a spirit of harmony, and work up enthusiasm, all the people in the group begin to get ideas. Out of that group will come an idea pertaining to the problem. Somebody will find the answer depending on whose subconscious tunes into the infinite storehouse and picks the answer out first.

Oftentimes the answer will not come from the smartest or best-educated man in the group. It'll come from the least educated and least brilliant person, because it seems that the subconscious mind and formal education do not have much in common. That is bound to be true when we see what great achievements have been brought about by men like Henry Ford, who had no formal education to speak of, Mr. Edison, who had very little formal education, and me. I had just a high-school education, and yet I had the privilege of giving the world the first practical philosophy of achievement, which is now benefiting millions of people all over the world.

Here are some examples of creative imagination. Take radium, for instance, which was discovered by Madame Curie. All she knew was that theoretically there should be radium somewhere in the universe. She hoped it would be on this little ball of mud that we call the earth. She had a definite purpose. She got a definite idea. She worked it out mathematically and determined that there was radium available somewhere. Nobody had ever seen any; nobody had ever produced any.

Imagine Madame Curie starting out to find radium in comparison with the proverbial story about the person looking for a needle in a haystack. I'd take the haystack and the needle every time in comparison with her task. By some strange process of nature, she came into contact with the first radium and had it refined. It is now available for medical purposes.

How did she do that? How did she go about searching for it? What gave her the first cues? Don't think for a moment that she went out with a spade to dig for it in the ground. She wasn't that foolish.

She conditioned her mind to tune in on infinite intelligence, and infinite intelligence directed her to the source—the exact process that you use in attracting riches or practically anything else you want. You first condition your mind with a definite picture of the thing you want, you build it up and support it with the faith and your belief, and you keep on wanting it even when the going is hard.

Take also the Wright brothers' flying machine. Nobody had ever created and successfully flown a heavier than air machine until the Wright brothers produced theirs.

When they started out, they were ridiculed. They had flown it successfully, and they announced to the press that they were going to demonstrate it again at Kitty Hawk, North Carolina. The newspapermen were so skeptical, they wouldn't even go down there. Not one single, solitary newspaperman went down there for the biggest scoop in the last hundred years. They were smart alecks, wise guys; they knew the answers. How many people do you see like that when somebody comes up with a new idea? Smart alecks, wise guys, people who don't believe that it can be done because it's never been done before.

There is no limitation to the application of creative vision. The person who can condition his mind to tune in on infinite intelligence can come up with the answer to anything that has an answer—no matter what it is.

When inventor Elmer R. Gates was sitting for ideas, he used his direct communication with infinite intelligence through the subconscious mind, based on application of definiteness of purpose. There was also Marconi's invention of wireless communication and Edison's talking machine, or recording device. As far as I know, Edison's one idea that came out of creative vision was his talking machine.

Before Edison's time, nobody had ever recorded or reproduced sound of any kind. Nobody had ever done anything even resembling it.

Edison conceived that idea almost instantaneously. He took a piece of paper out of his pocket and drew a crude sketch of what became later the first Edison recording machine, which had a cylinder on it. When they modeled it and tried it, the thing worked the very first time. You see, the law of compensation paid him off for those ten thousand failures while he was working on the incandescent electric lamp.

Don't you see what a generous, fair, and just thing the law of compensation is? Where you seem to be treated unfairly in one place, you will find that it will be made up in some other place in proportion to your deserts. That works with penalties too. When you run a red light and escape the cop at one corner, next time he'll catch you on two or three counts.

Somewhere out in nature, there's a tremendous cop and a tremendous machine recording all of our good qualities and all of our bad ones, all of our mistakes and all of our successes. Sooner or later they all catch up with us.

Achievements of the Creative Vision

Creative vision also enables us to evaluate the great American way of life. We still enjoy the privilege of freedom in the richest and freest country ever known to mankind, but we need to use vision if we are to continue to enjoy these great blessings. If you look backward and see what traits of character have made our country great, here they are.

First of all, the leaders who have been responsible for what we have, the American way of life, made definite application of the seventeen principles of the science of success, with emphasis on the following six.

At that time they didn't call these principles by these names. They probably weren't conscious that they were applying these principles. (One of the strangest things about all of the successful people that I worked with: not one single, solitary one of them could sit down and categorically give me step-by-step the modus operandi by which he had succeeded. They had stumbled upon these principles by sheer accident.)

1. Definiteness of purpose
2. Going the extra mile and rendering more service
3. The Master Mind principle
4. Creative vision
5. Applied faith
6. Personal initiative

The makers of American way of life did not expect something for nothing. They did not regulate their working hours by the time clock. They assumed full responsibilities of leadership even when the going was hard. That definitely applies to any successful person that you find today in any business. You will find them applying the principles laid right down here.

Looking backward over the past fifty years of creative vision, we find, for instance, that Thomas A. Edison, through his creative vision and personal initiative, ushered in the great electrical age and gave us a source of power the world had not previously known. That one man ushered in the electrical age, without which all of the industrial improvements that we've had—radar, television, radio—would not be possible. What a marvelous thing that one person did to influence the trend of civilization all over the world!

What marvelous things Mr. Ford did when he brought in the automobile! He brought the backwoods and Main Street together. He shortened distances. He improved land values by causing roads to be built through them. He gave employment directly and indirectly to millions of people who would not otherwise have had employment and to millions of people who now today have businesses supplying the automobile trade.

Then Wilbur and Orville Wright arrived. They changed the size of the earth. They shortened distances all over the world—just those two men operating for the good of mankind.

When Mr. Stone and I were talking about our operations and our future, we both came to the conclusion that (1) we have been blessed with the greatest opportunity that any two men living anywhere today have ever had in taking this philosophy to the world; (2) along with that opportunity comes the responsibility to one another and to our Creator for carrying out our assignment faithfully and continuously. That's exactly what we intend to do—devoting our lives to that.

Through his creative vision and personal initiative Andrew Carnegie ushered in the great Age of Steel, which revolutionized our entire industrial system and made possible the birth of myriad industries which could not exist without steel. Not satisfied with accumulating a vast fortune of his own and raising scores of his associate workers into sizable fortunes, he finished up his life by inspiring the organization of the world's first practical philosophy of personal achievement, which makes the know-how of success available to the humblest person.

Carnegie's personal initiative and creative vision created the largest number of jobs ever accomplished by one man in the history of civilization. The philosophy of success that he inspired will go marching down through the ages to benefit millions of people not now born. What a marvelous thing one man could do, operating through one other man!

When you begin to analyze what's happened here, you see what a marvelous thing can take place when an individual gets together with another individual, forms a Master Mind alliance, and begins to do something useful. There's nothing impossible for two people working together in the spirit of harmony under the Master Mind principle.

Without that alliance, I could never have created this philosophy, even if I'd had a hundred lives to live. The inspiration, the faith, and the confidence and the go-ahead spirit that I got by having access to a great man like Mr. Carnegie enabled me to rise up to his level, something I never could have done otherwise.

What a marvelous thing it is to be able to tap that thing called creative vision, and through it to tune in on the powers of the universe! I am not making a poetic speech; I'm citing science, because everything that I'm saying is practical and is being done, and it can be done by you.

To look back over the past fifty years of the great American way of life, here is a brief bird's-eye view of what men and women with creative vision and personal initiative have given us. First of all, the automobile, which has practically changed our entire way of living.

Those of you who have been born in the last few decades have no concept at all of what the vibrations of this nation were under the horse-and-buggy age in comparison with today. In those days, you could walk down the road safely. Nowadays, you can't even cross the street unless you are very alert of limb and eye. The whole method of transportation, the whole method of doing business, has changed as a result of the automobile. I daresay that if tomorrow morning the government announced that each of us would have to turn in his automobile, we wouldn't be permitted to use it anymore, there'd be consternation. There'd be a racket going up if you took automobiles away from people today: they just couldn't do without them.

Then airplanes, which travel faster than sound and have shrunk this world, whereby the peoples of all countries know one another better—what a marvelous thing they are! Perhaps the Creator intended it that way: that instead of all the wars that we've been having in the past, by reducing the world in size and bringing the peoples of all nations together within a travel distance of twenty-four hours or so, they would become better acquainted and finally become neighbors and brothers under the skin.

If the brotherhood of man ever comes about, it will be because of these things that the imagination of man has uncovered. They bring us together and make it more convenient to assemble and to understand each other all over the world. You can't carry on a war with the person that you are doing business with or the neighbor that you're living near. At least you can't do it and have any peace of mind. Try to get along without the people that you have to come into contact with.

Then radio and television, which give us the news of the world almost as fast as it happens and provide the finest entertainment without cost to the log cabins of the mountain country and the city mansions alike. Quite an advance over the days of Lincoln, as he learned to write on the back of a wooden shovel in a one-room log cabin.

It is a marvelous thing to know that down in the mountains of Tennessee and Virginia, where I was born—famous only at that time for mountain views, corn liquor, and rattlesnakes—you can turn a little knob and tune in to the finest operas and music and know what the world is doing almost as fast as it's doing it.

If we'd have those conveniences when I was growing up, I doubt that I would have had as my first definite major purpose becoming a second Jesse James. I probably would have wanted to become a radio operator. How these things have changed those mountain people and all those throughout the country and throughout the world! But they're just the result of what the mind of man has brought forth to introduce people to one another.

Then there is the development of electrical energy, which ushered in the push-button age. It now makes possible the performance of all sorts of labor, which formerly were done by hand. I don't know whether that is a good thing or not. Certainly we know that this is a push-button age.

After I grew up, I operated the first automobile school in the United States and personally taught over five thousand people to drive an automobile. Now children are born with steering wheels in their hands.

Then radar, which gives us advance notice of approaching hazards by both air and sea long before they are visible to the human eye. You can look out into the distance and see what's taking place long before the human eye can pick it up. Mankind has gone way beyond even the Creator and extended the possibilities of sight far beyond the range of the human eye. I don't know what final good or final evil will come out of radar, but I know that right now, it's a great protection to this nation, because we can pick up the presence of enemy planes long before they get to the point where they might do the greatest damage.

By our personal initiative and creative vision, we have at long last uncovered the secret by which the energy of the atom has been released and harnessed for the benefit (we hope) of mankind.

The Seventeen Principles in Labor

Let's take up some suggestions for the exercise of your imaginations and see if we can plant a few million-dollar ideas in your mind. Go back in your subconscious mind where you stored away that idea you had five, ten, or fifteen years ago because you thought you couldn't create a good idea and it was no good because you created it. Bring it forth, dust it off, and see if we can't find something useful in it.

Maybe we can eliminate all labor disputes, strikes, lockouts, and misunderstandings among the workers of business and industry by the use of the seventeen principles of the science of success. They were designed to provide equal benefits to all individuals and all human relations. This single achievement alone could provide extra profits in business and industry, which would make it possible for all workers to share in the earnings over and above their wages, equal, perhaps, to the profits allotted to those who supply the working capital.

This profound human relationship can be brought about only by the personal initiative and the creative vision of men and women engaged in business and industry who sincerely desire to see the present waste caused by friction and misunderstanding converted into dividends instead. Here is the take-off point from which many leaders of both labor and industry may make themselves something only a little less than immortal to the eternal benefit of our great American way of life.

Might I add that here is a marvelous opportunity for students in this class to become connected with some outstanding industrial or business concern and by the application of this philosophy do such a swell job in industrial relations that you will wipe out all of this friction.

We have one such firm organized down in southern Illinois, and it's working out beautifully. It is a business engaged in making steel tanks. Two of my outstanding students are at the head of that business. They organized and are developing and operating it 100 percent on the seventeen principles. I hope to see the time come when every labor contract that's written between any labor organization and any business concern will contain a provision that the service rendered by the labor members will be based on the seventeen principles.

I've had that done in a great many instances, and the returns have been so astounding that I wonder why other industrialists and labor leaders haven't awakened to the opportunities. I don't wonder too much, because I know why. There are too many fat rackets in the labor business for some leaders to want to change their system. Their system doesn't exactly coincide with mine. They don't exactly believe in going the extra mile. That's why.

Some day that fallacy will be shown up. Some outstanding man in the field of labor is going to come over and tie in with Napoleon Hill, and he's going to become the dominating factor in the labor field. I don't care who he is; he'll do it. I tried to get William Green to do it when he had his break with John L. Lewis. I told Mr. Green that if he would follow the formula I laid down, I would guarantee to eliminate John L. Lewis from the labor world and to make him its king. I would guarantee to sign up every business and every industry in the United States for the AF of L. I wouldn't charge him a penny for doing it.

Mr. Green sent me a word to come down to see him. When I got there, he said, "Napoleon, I suspect I owe you an apology. I've heard a lot about you, but I had some curiosity to see what you look like. I must confess you don't look like what I thought you did, because I thought you'd look like a nut. You don't look like a nut at all. Now about this formula: I thought if you wanted to come down at your own expense, the least I could do would be to invite you. What is this formula?"

"All right, Mr. Green, I'll give it to you," I said. "I want to present the American Federation of Labor with some substance of my life work. I want to turn my philosophy over to them and start schools all over the United States teaching this philosophy to all members of the American Federation of Labor."

"What are the principles? What's the philosophy? Let's hear it."

"All right," I said. "Seventeen principles: number one is definiteness of purpose."

Mr. Green said, "Why, it seems reasonable."

"Number two is applied faith."

"That's reasonable."

"Number three is enthusiasm."

"Well, that's all right."

"Number four is imagination."

"I see nothing wrong with that."

"Number five is going the extra mile."

"What's that?" he said.

"Mr. Green, that means the rendering of more service and better service than you're paid to render, doing it all the time, and doing it with a friendly, pleasing mental attitude."

"I knew there was a catch in it," he said. "That's our big stick. You know very well that we couldn't even operate if we followed that route."

Listen and think. Some labor leader is going to find out how to operate with the principle of going the extra mile, and when he does, he's going to be tops. When he starts the pattern at the top, other labor leaders are going to have to fall in line or get out of business.

When business and industry and workers have gotten to be more into partnership, they will work on a more friendly basis. There will be a better distribution of income and profits. But before there can be a better distribution of profits, there have to be more profits to distribute. Certainly going on sit down-strikes and that sort of thing is not going to make more profits.

If you don't think this idea is good, you go down to Baltimore, Maryland, and talk to my student Charles McCormick. Take a look at his books. What was happening in the way of profits up to the time he adopted this plan, and what has happened every year since? You would know beyond any question of a doubt that it pays off handsomely to let workers participate in the profits.

It does not cost the business anything to do that; in fact, it enables it to make more. It does away with all of this quarreling, friction, discouragement, hatred, and anger between men, which I want to help wipe out as far as I can with my philosophy. I want to make this a better world in which we live. I want to see us start trying out Christianity once. It might work if we gave it a chance. Who knows?

Creative Possibilities

One creative possibility is a series of flood control dams across the major streams of the Ohio, Missouri, and Mississippi rivers, where the silt will be caught, extracted from the water, and redistributed over the soils of these valleys, thus saving rapidly deteriorating soils and providing flood control at the same time. Here is an idea to inspire creative vision among engineers and soil conservationists. Think of that—the best part of the soil going down the Mississippi and the Missouri and all the other rivers. It could be caught, trapped, brought back, and put on the soil again at the government's expense.

If I knew that some of my income taxes were going for that, believe you me, I wouldn't squeal so hard at tax time the way I do. Nor would I be cutting corners in making out income tax returns, if I were sure that some of that money was going into doing something for an evil that's creeping up on us. That Mississippi River, Old Man River, is getting bigger and more dangerous all the time. He's taking more and more of the wealth of our soil down into the ocean. Millions and millions of tons of silt, which is the fertile part of the soil, are going down the river every year. In addition, floods come constantly. We could control them very easily if we had the proper dams at the proper locations up and down these rivers.

Here's a pet idea of mine. Somebody's going to make himself governor or mayor and take this one on: a citizen traffic cop system to slow down highway accidents and lower automobile insurance rates. It would deputize automobilists of good reputation and give them authority to make arrests and give out traffic violation tickets.

Wouldn't it be wonderful if, when you go on the highway and see these morons endangering their own lives and the lives of everybody else, you could pull them over to the curb, take their driver's license away, and give them a ticket? They could only get that license back by appearing at the nearest police station. I never go on the highway without wishing I were a policeman with authority to make arrests. If reckless drivers knew that the fellow in front of them or in back of them was a cop, they'd be a little more careful.

How about a new political party made up of the men and the women who are becoming dissatisfied with all of the present parties? Some smart fellow with personal initiative and creative vision will embrace this one sooner or later, and it won't be Colonel McCormick, owner of the *Chicago Tribune*. (I've heard it said that when Colonel McCormick backs a candidate, all the employees of the *Tribune* vote for the other side.)

There could also be the development of a system of therapeutics for curing ailments and bad habits during sleep using directives given directly by phonograph to the subconscious mind. Such a machine is already in existence, and many doctors and educators are experimenting with it. I have one of them myself.

At Napoleon Hill Associates, we're going to start making records for the attainment of any purpose that you want, like wiping out poverty consciousness and giving you a prosperity consciousness while you sleep, or eliminating any ailments that you may have.

Not too long ago, if I had a made a statement like that, you would have given me a horse laugh, but experiments are going on in many scientific circles today proving that marvelous things can be accomplished by simply turning on a machine and dealing with your subconscious mind while you're asleep.

There isn't a single person who, if I had the time to sit down with them one hour a day and deal with their subconscious mind, couldn't attain any goal they set their mind on. Any goal that you set your mind on and believe, you can achieve.

What do you suppose I would do with that one hour? I would repeat to you the thing that I wanted you to do. I'd repeat it until you couldn't resist it. No, I'm not going to do that. I'd get a machine to do it just as well and much more cheaply. About six different firms have commenced making these machines since I started talking about this some ten years ago.

When you understand the basis of this system, you'll understand the importance of having a definite major purpose and repeating that purpose until your subconscious mind can't resist it any longer, until you have hypnotized yourself with belief in the fact that you not only know what you want but that you're going to get it.

Of course, you can do this through autosuggestion, self-suggestion, or repetition, but that's laborious. I want something you can use while you're asleep. Let's economize. Let's make some use out of those eight hours of sleep. As a matter of fact, if you made scientific use of your sleep, you could accomplish more in the way of success while you sleep than you could when you're awake. That's a fact, because when you're awake, your conscious mind is on duty and it won't let you get through with ideas that will lift you up. You have too many reasons why it can't be done, too many impediments, too many obstacles, too many false beliefs. Your subconscious mind accepts anything that's handed over to it. If you had a method of pouring into your subconscious mind only the things you want it to do, keeping out of it the things you don't want, don't you see what could happen in your life?

As it is now, when you go to sleep, you turn your subconscious mind over to dreaming foolish dreams. It wastes time all night long, annoying you with nightmares, dreams, and things of that kind. Well, it has to have something to do, so it might as well pester you a little bit.

Sound foolish? It's not foolish at all; it's real. Any time you wake up with a nightmare, you know that your subconscious has been out strolling around to see what mischief it can get into.

Then there could a new type of religious philosophy without a sectarian brand, to teach people how to live harmoniously with one another regardless of race, color, or present religious views. It would be the antithesis of communism, which now threatens to undermine all religions and all human freedom. If you are using your synthetic imagination or your creative imagination, you know right now that we have that religion and that you're studying it. You know that there isn't a blessed thing in this religion that the Catholic can't accept, the Protestant can't accept, the Jew can't accept, that anyone can't accept. In other words, it's a universal series of truths, more or less embraced by all religions, but under different brands.

This philosophy in its present form, without any additives of any kind, is sufficient to make anyone's religion more vital, operative, and effective. There's no denying it. We have the religion that doesn't permit jealousy springing up between those who operate it. It induces friendly cooperation on the Master Mind principle rather than opposition and jealousy.

We could also create a school system for educating men and women for public office, with the adoption of regulations based on grades, which all seekers for public office must pass, rather than the present system of electing people to office merely by vote. Oftentimes voters are not qualified to judge competent men for public office. This system will specialize in training people for higher offices such as the presidency, Congress, the presidential cabinet, ambassadors, and diplomats. Educators with personal initiative and creative vision may find an outlet for other talents in connection with this suggestion.

Someday a person with an outstanding formal education is going to take over this idea and start this kind of school, and he's going to get more free publicity for it than he could get for anything else that I could mention at present. It would be something that's needed, it would be commercially profitable, and it would give him an outlet for his talent such as he could never find in any other direction. It might be of untold value to the people of this country.

I'm not starting it, because I have a big job already. Believe you me, if some of you brilliant students don't grab that idea, it may well become a department of Napoleon Hill Associates in the years to come. Right now we have a lot to do in taking this philosophy to the people through tape recordings, moving pictures, home study courses, books, and classes like this for training teachers.

A School of Marriage

Here's another one: a school for the education of men and women for marriage. Wouldn't it be marvelous if you could send your children, while they're still in their teens, to a nice school of training, preparing them to know how to select a mate, how to deal with that mate after he or she has been selected, how to run a home, how to economize, and how to Master Mind?

If you don't pick that one up, I'm going to pick it up myself one of these days, because that is a honey—a school to train people for marriage instead of this hit-and-miss system. There's this idea of marrying a gal because she has beautiful eyes and beautiful ankles and wears nice hats. The time may come when her eyes are not so beautiful and her ankles may get out of shape, but if you select a mate on the right basis and live with that mate on the right basis, the chances are she'll never become anything but good. She'll always be beautiful.

When I speak of Annie Lou, I call her beautiful. She will say, "Now you know you don't mean that."

I say, "Listen, Annie Lou. My definition of beauty includes every-thing on the surface and everything beneath the surface; remember that. To me, you are very beautiful. You always will be." I think she's beautiful on the surface, and I know she is underneath the surface.

Some people might criticize me for speaking of my wife so much, but when you have something that you're really proud of, and on merit, why not holler it out to the whole word and let them know? It's a whole lot better for me to be interested in my wife than it is to be interested in somebody else's wife. Maybe a good way of keeping myself from being interested in somebody else's wife is to keep my attention on the one I have.

Here's another pet of my mind: education in soil feeding, which will make it obligatory for farmers to feed the soil with all the neces-sary minerals to give food the values that nature intended it to have. Much has been done in and is being done along this line already, but the work must become mandatory for those who raise food products for sale.

Bad teeth and many physical ailments are the result of malnutri-tion caused by improper foods, and, I must say, bad dispositions too. The time will come when the food that you buy in the market will have to have the contents marked on it, just like the vitamins that you buy now for food supplements. The time will come when if a farmer doesn't feed the soil with all the elements necessary, his food will not be salable; people won't buy it. That'll be the best way of enforcing that rule.

Next: the functions of the federal government that have been taken over from the states will be taken back by the people through a better recognition of the importance of voting intelligently and the elimination of many of the present pressure groups, which work only for the benefit of a limited number of individuals. Pressure groups running the government in this country have gotten to be a very dangerous hazard. Somebody's got to break that up.

Another idea is talking pictures that will make the science of success philosophy available to children in homes and schools. Now believe you me, that's coming sooner or later; you'll be able to go down to the library for television, radio, and talking pictures and you'll have lessons on, for example, definiteness of purpose that will be done up in terminology that children will understand and that will interest them. Think of what that would do to the home, and think what a great commercial product that is. A lot of people now have projectors in their home. The time is coming, and if it doesn't come voluntarily, we have ways and means of making things happen. Things don't just happen at Napoleon Hill Associates. We make them happen.

We want to give our students a chance to develop some of these ideas. Nevertheless, if students don't get around to it, we have ways and means of doing it ourselves. The time is coming when these principles are going to be reduced down to entertainment and education for adult and child alike in the homes. Maybe I'll go into competition with Roy Rogers and Bob Hope.

You may be interested in knowing that a program based upon the seventeen principles was carried on KFWB in Los Angeles, one of the large stations out there, for three continuous years, summer and winter. That program led every other program on that station and produced more mail than all the programs combined.

Warner Brothers, who owned that station, called a staff meeting and devoted one whole afternoon to analyzing this program. They first monitored several of my programs, and they repeated them there in the staff meetings. One of the Warner Brothers people asked, "What has this Napoleon Hill fellow got that enables him to go on our station with a thirty-minute commercial and lead all other programs in listener interest?" They called my program a commercial. I guess in a way it was. Nevertheless, it was of interest to people.

Interstellar Communications

Next is a system of interstellar communications which will enable us to communicate with the people of other worlds, if any, throughout the vastness of the universe. If someone announced in the press tomorrow that they had made contact with Mars and they were exchanging communications, I wouldn't doubt it in the least. I will be one of the first to believe it, because I believe with all my heart and soul that if anyone lives on Mars or any other planet throughout the universe, the time will come when we will be able to communicate with them. When we do, we will be able to learn something from them about a better way of living with one another than we have here on this planet. It couldn't be any worse than the way we relate ourselves and probably will be better.

The Creator of this universe is not idle. He's on the march, and he's revealing stupendous ideas of great benefits that are available to people if only they would have the initiative to take advantage of it.

Another idea: public highways engineered so as to greatly reduce the hazards due to reckless driving. Radar devices will intercept speeders by automatically controlling roadblocks, where traffic officers will be stationed. That's coming as surely as anything, because this enormous death rate has got to be controlled in one way or another. Killing thirty-six thousand people a year and maiming several times that number is just something that can't go on forever. That is, if we are to continue to call ourselves civilized.

15

Maintaining Sound Health

It's wonderful to have a physical frame in fine condition so that you can do anything you want to do anytime you want to do it. If I hadn't had a system for keeping myself healthy and full of energy, I couldn't have done the amount of work that I've done in the years past. I couldn't do the amount of work I'm doing now.

I have to keep myself in this condition for several reasons. In first place, I enjoy living better if my body is responsive. If I make demands on it for enthusiasm, I want the physical basis for that enthusiasm to be there. I don't want to get out of bed in the morning ailing. I don't want to look in the glass and see my tongue coated. I don't want my breath to smell bad.

There are ways and means of avoiding all that, and I hope that you'll get some suggestions out of this lesson that will help you keep your physical body in fine condition.

Mental Attitude

Mental attitude comes at the head of the list, because without health consciousness, the chances are that you're not going to be healthy.

I never think of ailments. As a matter of fact, I can't afford them. They take up too much of my time. They hurt my mental attitude too much.

You may ask, "How are you going to help having ailments?" When you get through this lesson, you're not going to have them as often as you did before. There is a way of controlling ailments: mental attitude. You will notice that every one of the following things in connection with conditioning a mental attitude is something that you can control if you want to.

First of all, there must be no griping in family or our occupational relationship. It hurts the digestion. You say, "Well, my family makes it necessary for me to gripe and complain." All right. Change the circumstances so you won't have any reasons for griping and complaining.

I mention family relationships because, along with occupational relationships, you spend most of your life there. If you're going to allow those relationships to be based upon friction, misunderstandings, and arguments, you're not going to have good health, and you're not going to have peace of mind. There must be no hatred, no matter how much a person deserves to be hated. You can't afford to do the hating, because it's bad for your health. It produces stomach ulcers and worse. It produces negative mental attitudes, which repel people instead of attracting them to you, and you can't afford that. Hatred attracts reprisals in kind. If you hate people, they'll hate you. They may not say so, but they will.

There must be no gossip or slander. That's a pretty hard one to comply with because there's so much material in the world to gossip about. It's a great pity to cut you off from all that pleasure, but let's transmute that desire into something that's more profitable to you. No gossip or slander, because they attract reprisals, and they also hurt the digestion.

There must be no fear, because it indicates friction in human relationships and, again, hurts the digestion. Also, if there's any fear in your makeup, it indicates that there's something in your life that needs to be altered.

I can truthfully say that there isn't anything on the face of this earth or in the universe I survey around me that I fear—nothing at all. I used to fear everything that the average person fears, but I had a system for overcoming those fears. If I had a fear now, I'd have it out with myself. I would eliminate its cause, no matter what it took or how long it took.

I will not tolerate fear in my makeup. I just won't tolerate it, because you can't have good health. You can't be prosperous, you can't be happy, you can't have peace of mind if you're going to fear anything at all, even death, most of all death.

Personally I'm looking forward to death with great anticipation. It's going to be one of the most unusual interludes of my whole life. As a matter of fact, it'll be the last thing I'll experience. Of course, I'm putting it off a long time—I've got a job to do and all that—but when the time comes, I'm going to be ready. It's going to be the last thing I'll do, and the most wonderful thing of all, because I'm not afraid of it.

There must be no talk about disease, because it leads to the development of hypochondria or imaginary ailments, the thing that most doctors live on.

There must be no envy, because it indicates lack of self-reliance, and again hurts the digestion.

The way you use your mind has more to do with your health than all other things combined. You can talk all you want about germs getting into the blood, but nature has set up a marvelous system of doctoring inside you. Germ or no germ, if that system is working properly, the resistance within your physical body will take care of all those germs.

I discovered a long time ago that hardly anybody reaching the age of thirty-five does *not* at one time or another carry tubercular germs. A large number of people carry tubercular germs and other germs all the way through life. Why don't they have tuberculosis? Because bodily resistance keeps the germs from multiplying. The minute you become worried, annoyed, or afraid, you break down that bodily resistance. The germs begin to multiply by the billions and trillions and quadrillions. The first thing you know, you really are sick.

Eating Habits

Prepare to eat with peace of mind. There must be no worries, arguments, or unpleasantness at mealtime. The average family selects mealtime as the hour of discipline of the husband, wife, or the children, as the case may be. At the one time when you get them all together and they're not inclined to run away, you're giving them a tongue lashing. Believe you me, if you could see what happens to the digestion and bloodstream in a person who eats while he's undergoing punishment, you would know that's the wrong time to do it. The thoughts you have while you're eating go into the food you eat and become a part of the energy that goes into the bloodstream. The best evidence of this is women who have nursed children at their breast. They know very well if a woman becomes worried or annoyed as the child nurses at the breast, it'll have colic in a matter of minutes. The mental attitude poisons the milk.

There must be no overeating. It overworks the heart, the lungs, the liver, the kidneys, and the sewer system. Most people eat twice as much as they could get along with. Look at the amount of money you'd save nowadays, with grocery bills what they are. It's astounding how many people overeat. I mean people who engaged in sedentary occupations. Of course, a man who's digging ditches has to have a certain amount of meat and potatoes or something equal to them, but a man or woman doing office work or working in a store or the house doesn't have to have the same amount of heavy food.

You must eat a balanced ration with fruits, vegetables, and plenty of water or the equivalent of water in the form of juices. In California,

I have a system of making at least one meal a day of nothing but live food. That is to say, vegetables, berries, nuts, melons, and things of that sort—all alive, nothing that has been canned or processed in any way, shape, or form. I have all the difference in the world in my energy while I'm at home following my established diet.

Don't eat rapidly. It prevents proper mastication and shows that you've got too much on your mind. You're not relaxed. You're not enjoying yourself. A meal should be a form of worship. While you're eating, you should have your thoughts on all of the beautiful things that you want to do, your major purpose, or the things that please you most.

If you're eating with someone else and engaged in conversation, it should be a pleasant conversation, not a fault-finding job. When a man is sitting across the table from a beautiful woman, I don't see why he shouldn't talk about her beautiful eyes, her hairdo, her lipstick, and all the things that women like heavy talk about sometimes (if you're the right man). Even if you're sitting across the table from your wife, I don't know why it wouldn't help you and her too. Say something beautiful about her while you're eating. Tell her how nice the toast is or how well the coffee has been made this morning. I never go to the table without complimenting Annie Lou on everything that comes onto the table, because she prepared it. (I help her a little; I squeeze the orange juice, but she does everything else.) We make a ceremony out of eating. It takes two hours in the morning to eat breakfast, not because we eat very much, but because of the way we eat. When we're through eating, our two little dogs, who are sitting there, are waiting for their attention. One gets up on my lap and one gets upon her lap, and they have a session with us. We talk some dog talk to them and have a grand time. The dogs enjoy it, we enjoy it, and it does something for our health.

I suppose I have people in my following who, if they found out the way I live, would think I was a little bit eccentric. Well, eccentric or not, I've learned how to live, and that's important, isn't it?

Don't eat candy bars, peanuts, or snacks between meals or drink too many soft drinks. I know people that make a whole lunch of candy bars and snacks that they get from the newsstand and a bottle or two of Coca-Cola. A young person's stomach can stand that for a while, but it's not being treated properly. Sooner or later nature makes you pay up for that mistreatment of your stomach.

It'd be far better if an office worker got a head of lettuce, put some nice salad dressing on it, and ate that, or some fruit or grapes at the fruit stand. That'd be far better than eating candy bars.

Liquor in excess is taboo at all times, but liquor in reasonable amounts is all right. I can take a cocktail; I can take two cocktails; that's about my limit at one time. I could take three, but if I did, maybe I'd say some things that I shouldn't say, or do some things that wouldn't do me any good. I like to be in control of my mind all the time.

What's the sense of tickling your stomach and your brain so that you're not yourself? People find out too much about you that you don't want them to know. You look silly, don't you? Don't you think that a person whose tongue has been loosened up with liquor makes a spectacle of himself that doesn't do him very much credit, no matter who he is?

I don't believe in being a prude. If I go into a home where they take a cocktail, as I often do, I don't say, "Oh, no. I don't take that. I don't touch this stuff." I take the cocktail, and if I'm not in the mood to drink it, I carry it around the whole evening. Sometimes, if I'm to give a speech that night, I'll dump the cocktail into the sink so they think I drank it. It would be silly to get all het up with liquor before making a speech.

With liquor or smoking, as with everything else, if it's moderate and if you take it instead of it taking you, I'd say it wouldn't be too bad, but the better plan is to get over using it at all.

Now you see I have pleased all of you. I've told some that I don't believe in drinking, some others that I do believe in it. I fix it so that each one of you can take whatever you want out of this story. You're going to do that anyway, so I might as well make it easy for you.

Take vitamin tablets if needed to supplement food deficiencies, but only on the prescription of a doctor or somebody who is familiar with vitamins. Don't just go to the drugstore and say, "Give me the brand that will do the whole thing at one shot." That's bunk. There's no one vitamin that's going to supply you with everything you need. I've got a string of vitamin bottles in my room; each one has a different function.

Relaxation and Play

You need play to ensure sound health, so balance all work with an equivalent amount of play. That doesn't mean an equivalent number of hours, because it doesn't work out that way. I can offset one hour of work with five minutes of play. I'm an inspirational writer, as you may have guessed. I write when keyed up; I'm up on another plane entirely. It's intensely hard on the physical constitution, and forty minutes is all I can stand of it. Then I go to my piano and sit down and play for five or ten minutes, and I completely balance out that intense activity. I can go back and do another forty minutes of work.

I can't play the piano, but I can make an awful lot of noise on it. Annie Lou says the only one who enjoys my piano playing is Sparky, my little female Pomeranian dog. She comes in and sits on the stool beside me, looks up at me, and says, "Hello, Mr. *Paderewski*." She thinks I really play the piano. She's really fine.

Then sleep eight hours out of every twenty-four, if you find time to do it. It might be a fine habit to get into—to get some good sleep. Don't turn and twist or groan and snore. Lie down and sleep peacefully. Get into such good rapport with yourself, your conscience, and your neighbors that you don't have anything to worry about. When you hit that old pillow, you can go right smack to sleep.

Train yourself not to worry over things you can't remedy. It's bad enough to worry over the things you *can* remedy. I wouldn't worry over them any longer than it took me to remedy them. One of my students some time ago asked if I didn't worry a lot about people who came to me with their problems. I said, "Other people's problems? Why, bless your life! I don't worry over my own problems. Why should I worry over somebody else's problems?"

It's not because I am indifferent; I'm far from indifferent. I'm very sensitive to the problems of my friends and my students, but not sensitive enough to let them become *my* problems. They're still *your* problems. I'll do all I can to help you solve them, but not enough to take them over myself. That's not my way of doing it, and don't you get into that habit either. A lot of people not only make room in their makeups for their own problems, but take on the problems of their relatives, their friends, and the neighborhood, and sometimes the problems of the whole nation.

A lot of people now are worrying about the atomic bomb. I'm not worrying, because whenever it hits, I won't know it anyway. Why should I worry about it? I'm going right ahead. I'm going to do my job just as if this whole world was in the process of being corrected. If it doesn't come out right, I will have done my best. That's all anyone can do, no matter what's expected of him. Worry was made for somebody else, not for me. Don't look for trouble. It will find you in its own way too soon anyhow.

Now because the circumstances of life have a queer way of revealing to you the thing you're searching for, if you're looking for faults in others, for trouble, or for things to worry about, you'll always find them, and you don't have to go very far. You don't have to go out of your own house to find a lot of things to worry about if you're looking for them.

Hope

Sound health inspires hope, and hope inspires sound health. A person without hope is lost. By *hope* I mean some yet unattained objective in life, something that you're working toward, something that you're trying to do. You know you're going to do it, and you're not going to be worried because you're not doing it fast enough.

A lot of people in this world start out to be rich. They want to make a lot of money. They're very impatient; they become nervous and work themselves into a fury because they don't get the money fast enough. Sometimes this desire to get money quickly influences people to get it the wrong way, and that's not good.

Develop hope by daily prayer. Express prayer every day in one form or another, in your own words, or you don't need to use any words at all, just in your own thoughts. Pray not for more blessings, but for those you already have, such as freedom as an American citizen.

I suspect it's rather hard for us Americans to fully recognize the benefits that we have in the freedom that we enjoy in this country—freedom to be ourselves, to live our own lives, to have our own objectives, to make our own friends, to vote as we please, to worship as we please, and to do pretty much anything else we please, even abuse ourselves by wrong living, if we want to do it that way.

Then there is the privilege of acting on our own initiative and a job that is secure from hazards at the present time. There's no danger of war at this time. There may be some time later on, but right now there isn't.

Express gratitude also for the opportunity to secure economic freedom according to your talents, for sound physical and mental health, and for the time that lies ahead of you. The richest part of my life and my achievements is still ahead of me. I'm still just a youngster. I've been going to kindergarten. I'm going to grade school now in my profession, and I'm going to do some really good work. I am making better use now of my time than I used to.

Then there's the hope of a better world now that the war is over and another war is not imminent. You can help make this world better by applying this philosophy, first in your own life and then in the lives of those around you. You can make your world a better world. There's no two ways about that.

Avoid Drugs

Avoid drugs and nostrum habits. It's all right to take them on doctor's orders, but avoid making them habits; throw away your aspirin and your headache tablets first thing you can. Headache is nature's way of warning you that something needs correction. Headache is nothing in the world but nature telling you that there's some trouble somewhere, and you'd better get busy and do something about it.

Did you know that physical pain is one of the most miraculous of all of nature's creations? It's a language that every living creature on earth understands. Every living creature begins to do something when physical pain begins to clamp down on it, because it's a form of warning.

Take no purgatives of any sort at any time. That's a bad habit. Remember, sound health does not come from bottles, but it may come from fresh air, wholesome food, wholesome thinking and living habits—all of which are under your control.

Watch your weight. Fat people may be good-natured, but they generally die too young. I don't like to see people dying too young.

Fasting

If you want to know one of the main secrets why I have such marvelous health, lots of energy, with no ailments, it's because twice a year, I go on a ten-day fast. Ten days without any food of any nature whatsoever. I condition my physical body through two days of preparation by fruits and fruit juices: nothing but live, vital elements going into the body. Then I go on my fast of water, nothing but just plain water, all the water I can drink. I put flavoring or lemon juice or something in it, just a few drops to take the flatness out, because believe you me, when you're fasting, water will taste mighty flat. When I come out of my fast, for the first two days afterwards I take a very light diet. The first day I have only one small bowl of soup with no grease in it and one slice of whole-wheat bread.

Now don't you start fasting just because I said so.

Don't start fasting at all until you learn how to do it and why to do it from the directions of a doctor or somebody skilled in fasting. I first learned the art of fasting from Bernarr MacFadden when I had the flu in 1928. Even after it was over, I had recurrent spells of it. It would come back every two weeks or thereabout in a light form. I told Bernarr about it and he said, "Why don't you get rid of it?" I said, "How?" He said, "Let's starve it to death." He sold me on the idea that if you could stop feeding it, it'll have to die. He sold me on the idea of cleansing my body thoroughly and giving the flu bug nothing to live on.

Of course, the flu did die, and I had no recurrent spells of it. Since that time, it's only this year that I've had anything even resembling a cold. I immunize my body against these things by going on a fast twice a year.

When you go on your first fast, you will have one of the most marvelous spiritual experiences that you'll ever have had in all your life. You will remember things that happened when you were wearing three-cornered pants. I did. I remembered the conversation that I had with my mother when I was out in the yard playing wearing three-cornered pants, and that was all I had on. It was a warm summer day. She came out and asked me a few questions, and I gave her a few answers. I remembered exactly what the questions were and what my answers were, just as plainly as if it were a few minutes ago. A lot of other things that had happened to me when I was quite young also came back to me. In other words, my whole memory system was revitalized.

If I'd had worries before the fast, I couldn't have carried them through, because your worries dissolve into thin air when you're fasting. Another thing: when you gain victory over your stomach, when you have old man stomach absolutely under control, it gives you a victory over many other things after you come out of the fast.

I know people who have fasted for forty days. I know doctors that cure cancer by fasting. I've seen it done. There is tremendous therapeutic, spiritual, and economic value in fasting.

Healthy Work

On work: work must be a blessing because God provided that every living creature must engage in it in one way or another. The birds of the air and the beasts of the jungle are neither spinning nor sowing nor reaping; nevertheless, they have to work before they can eat.

Work should be performed in the spirit of worship—as a ceremony. How wonderful it would be if you would look at your work as the rendering of useful service, instead of what you're getting out of it! Think of the people you're helping as a result of what you are doing in life.

When you're engaged in a labor of love, when you're doing something for somebody just because you love that person, you never think it's hard. It does something for you. You get your compensation as you go along.

Going the extra mile is the most wonderful thing in this philosophy. It makes you feel better—better towards yourself, towards your neighbor—and it gives you better standing in the world of health.

Work should be based on the hope of achievement of some definite major purpose in life Thus it becomes voluntary: a pleasure to be sought and not a burden to be enduring.

Work with a spirit of gratitude for the blessings it provides in sound physical health, economic security, and for the benefits it provides to one's dependents.

Faith

Learn to communicate with infinite intelligence from within, and adapt yourself to the laws of nature as they are in evidence all around you. That's one of the greatest systems of therapeutics that I know. It's an abiding and enduring source of faith. It does wonderful things to your physical body, and if ailments do happen to creep in, I know of no better medicine.

Believe that you can cure yourself. If anything became wrong with my physical body, I believe I could go out, live in the desert, strip down to the skin, and work out there. God's sunshine and his dirt and I can whip anything that might be interfering with my body. I know I could do it.

Habits

All habits are made permanent and work automatically through the operation of the law of cosmic habit force, which forces every living thing to take on and to become a part of the environmental influences in which it exists. (I will discuss cosmic habit force in the following lesson.) You may fix the patterns of your thought habits and your physical habits, but cosmic habit force takes these over and carries them out. Understand this law and you will know why the hypochondriac enjoys poor health. Health begins with a health consciousness, and in the foregoing paragraphs, you have a brief summary of the factors that may give you such a consciousness. If you are not health-conscious, you are not healthy.

16

Cosmic Habit Force

We're on a wonderful lesson now. To me, it's the most profound of all of the seventeen lessons. If any of you happen to be students of Emerson, if you read his essay "Compensation," you will get the sum and substance of this lesson much more quickly, and you'll also get more out of it.

After I had read Emerson's essays for ten years, especially the one on compensation, I finally interpreted what he was talking about. I said that someday I would rewrite that particular essay so that men and women could understand it the first time they read it. This lesson is that rewrite.

We call it the law of *cosmic habit force*, because it is the controlling force of all natural laws of the universe. We have many natural laws, and obviously they work automatically. They are not suspended for one moment for anybody. They are laid down so that the individual who makes it his business to understand and adapt himself to them can go very far in life. Those who do not understand or adapt themselves to them go down in defeat.

You've often wondered about habits: how we happen to have habits, how we get them, how to get rid of the ones we don't want. I hope that from this chapter you will get a fleeting glimpse of the answer to these questions.

As I have repeated time and time again, man has control over one thing and one thing only, and that's the privilege of forming his own habits—tearing down those habits and replacing them with others, refining them, changing them, doing anything he wants to do with them. He has that prerogative, and he's the only creature on the face of this earth that has it. Every other thing that comes into life has its life pattern and its destiny fixed for it. It cannot go one iota beyond that pattern. We call it *instinct*.

Man is not bound by instinct. He's bound only by the imagination and the willpower of his own mind. He can project that willpower, that mind, to whatever objective he pleases. He can form whatever habits he may need in order to take him toward his objectives, and this chapter deals with that subject.

The science of success, which you've been studying, is designed to enable one to establish habits that lead to financial security, health, and peace of mind necessary for happiness.

The Law of Nature

In this lesson, we briefly examine the established law of nature which makes all habits permanent to everything else except mankind. Now there's no such a thing as a permanent habit for a man, because he can establish his own habits; he can change them at will. It's a marvelous thing to consider that the Creator gave you complete control over your mind and a means of making use of that control. The law of cosmic habit force is the means by which you set the pattern of your own mind and direct it to whatever objective that you choose.

Some of the patterns that are fixed by cosmic habit force and are not subject to suspension or circumvention have to do with the stars and the planets. Isn't it a wonderful thing to contemplate all those millions, billions, and quadrillions of planets and stars out there in the heavens, all going along according to system, never colliding? The system is so precise that astronomers can determine the exact relationship of given stars and planets hundreds of years in advance.

If the Creator had to hang out those stars and watch everything every night, he'd be a very busy fellow. Now he's not going to do that. He's got a better system. He's got a system that works automatically, something like my system of eight princes—imaginary entities, and they're not so imaginary either—that look after me for all of my needs. I don't need to worry; they take care of everything.

I don't claim to be as smart as the Creator. I imagine he is smart enough to fix the system so that it automatically works all the time throughout all of the universe or universes. This system works for, or against, all people alike. If you learn those laws, you can adapt yourself to them and profit by them. If you don't learn them, you will probably suffer by them through ignorance or neglect.

The majority of people, not recognizing that there is a law of cosmic habit force, still go all the way through life using this marvelous law. What for? To bring prosperity, health, success, and peace of mind?

No. They bring poverty, ill-health, frustration, fear, and all the things that people do not want by keeping their minds on those things. Cosmic habit force picks up those habits of thought and makes them permanent. That is, until I come along and break them up with this science of success philosophy.

Mr. Stone and I had a very charming lady in our office wanting to sell us some space in a book that she was getting out based upon the birth dates of people, and she wanted to know what my birth date was.

Mr. Stone didn't let her get very far. He told her that he would have nothing to do whatsoever with any system or book that presupposes that a birth date has anything to do with what happens to one in life. When he got through, he said, "Now, I can't speak for Napoleon Hill, but that's my decision."

"Well," I said, "you've just made my speech now, Mr. Stone."

I don't care what star you're born under. I don't care what unfavorable circumstances you may have met with in life. I don't care what happened to you in the past. I do know that I can take you, and, if you follow my instructions, you can get from where you are now to where you want to go, and you will get there easily. I know that you can set up habits that will make your success so easy you'll wonder why you worked so hard in the past and didn't get far. Most people work harder at failing in life than I work at succeeding—a lot harder. It's much easier to succeed when you learn the rules, and there's a lot more pleasure in it than there is in failing.

You certainly are not going to succeed unless you understand cosmic habit force and start building habits that lead to where you want to go. There are no ifs or ands or maybes or buts about it. You must form habits that will lead you in the direction of the way you want to go.

The seasons of the year come and go with regularity. Everything that grows from the soil of the earth reproduces and grows. Each seed precisely reproduces its own kind without variation, as does every living thing from the microscopic infusoria up to man.

Strictly speaking, what I have just said is not correct. There *is* variation according to the environment, weather conditions, and location. For instance, I lived down in Florida, and I went out rabbit hunting with some gentlemen. Up north I'd always been accustomed to seeing rabbits with a gray coats. These rabbits had black coats, and I thought they were cats. They were all killing rabbits, but I didn't kill any, because I thought they were cats.

There is variation. Luther Burbank discovered that he could take the variations in flowers and blend them together and breed new specimens.

Habit is found too in the chemical reactions of matter, from the smallest particles of matter, the electrons and protons, to the largest objects, such as the stars. All actions and reactions of matter are based upon the fixed habits of cosmic habit force.

Have you ever stopped to think that the very smallest particles of matter all exist as a result of habit? Each seed reproduces its own kind, but each individual reproduction is modified by the vibrations of the environment in which it exists.

Thought habits of individuals are automatically fixed and made permanent by cosmic habit force. These thought habits are automatically fixed, whether you will it or not. The thoughts that you give expression to are going to be fixed in habits. You don't need to worry about it if you keep your mind on the things that you want to become habits. Cosmic habit force will take over from there on out.

The individual creates the pattern of his thoughts by repetition of thought on a given subject. The law of cosmic habit force makes these patterns permanent unless they are broken up by the will of the individual.

Breaking the Habit of Smoking

When I see the number of people smoking cigarettes nowadays and when I see the publicity in magazines and newspapers about the high death rates of lung cancer from using cigarettes, I wonder whether or not people can break that habit.

If you want to go ahead and get lung cancer by smoking cigarettes, that's your business. I have nothing to say about it, but I want to give you a taste of something that might be helpful. If you cannot start out tomorrow morning and prove that your willpower is stronger than a little piece of tobacco and a little piece of silk paper, you want to begin working on your willpower right away and reeducating it.

I don't have any habit that I can't break instantly. When I quit smoking, I laid my pipes down. I told Annie Lou to take them and throw them away; I wouldn't be needing them.

She said, "I'll put them away until you call for them."

I said, "Throw all of them all away. I'll not be needing them."

If you can't get control of the habit of smoking, it's going to be very difficult for you to get control of the habits of fear, poverty, and other things that you're allowing your mind to dwell upon.

When I have some enemies to deal with, I always take the biggest guy first. When I lick him, the rest of them take their tails between their legs and run. If you've got some habits you want to break, don't start with the little, easy ones. Anybody can do that. Start with the big ones, the ones you want to do something about.

Take that pack of cigarettes that you have half smoked, and when you go home, put it up on the dresser. Say, "Look here, fellow. You may not know it, but I'm more powerful than you are. I'm going to prove it by not going into that package again. I'm going to let you sit there for forty days. After which I won't need cigarettes anymore."

No, I don't think that I am talking against the cigarette business. I am just giving you some ideas through which you may start testing your capacity to build the kind of habits that you want by starting with the tough ones.

I'll give you another habit. Go on a week's fast without any food. Tell your stomach that you are the boss. It may think it's the boss, but you are. Don't do this on your own. Do it under the direction of a doctor, because fasting is not child's play. But get control over your stomach, and you'll be surprised at how many other things you have control over.

How can we expect to be successes in this world if we let these myriads of habits, which come along through everyday circumstances, take hold of us and rule our lives? We can't expect to be successes. We have to form our own habits long enough until cosmic habit force takes them up automatically.

Physical Health

Let's take up the question of how the individual may apply the law of the cosmic habit force in connection with physical health.

The individual may contribute to the healthful maintenance of his physical body by establishing four habit patterns. It's not very difficult to do this. If you want to prove the soundness, potency, and effectiveness of this law of cosmic habit force, here is a fine way to start in, because I don't know of anything in this world that men and women want more than to have a good, strong physical body that responds to every need in life.

I couldn't do the kind of work that I do, I couldn't write inspirational books, I couldn't deliver inspirational lectures if I didn't know that when I put my foot on the gas, so to speak, there was going to be power there. No matter how steep the hill or how long the drive, I know that I've got plenty of power to go the full distance, because I keep my body in that kind of condition.

First of all, your thinking is the place to start in connection with applying cosmic habit force to develop sound health. A positive mind leads to the development of a health consciousness. A consciousness is a continuous awareness of a condition. Health consciousness is a predominating tendency of your mind to think about health, and not about disease or ailment.

Most people have a wonderful time telling about their operations. About six months ago, a very good friend of mine visited me; he had just come out of the hospital. His description of his operation was so vivid that I could feel the surgeon's scalpel turning in my back. I finally turned around and rubbed my back. It began to hurt back there where he was describing before I got myself under control.

When he left, I didn't ask him to come back to see me again. Most people don't like to hear you talk about your ailments. They're not interested in your ailments, and you ought not to be either, except to get rid of them. The best way to get rid of them is to form a health consciousness: think in terms of health, talk in terms of health.

Look in the glass a dozen times a day and say, "You are a healthy man," or "You are a healthy woman." Talk to yourself. You'd be surprised at what will happen. Go into the medicine chest and take out all the bottles, the aspirin and the purgatives. Throw them all down the sink. Say, "From here on out, I'm starting to get my health out of God's fresh air, good thinking, good exercise, and good food, and not out of bottles."

A positive mind leads to the development of health consciousness. Cosmic habit force carries out the thought pattern to its logical conclusion, but it will just as readily carry out the picture of an ill-health consciousness created by the thought habits of the hypochondriac. It can even produce the physical and mental symptoms of any disease on which the individual may fix his thought habits through fear.

If you think about a certain ailment or disease long enough, nature will actually simulate it in your physical makeup. Down in Wise County, Virginia, I knew an elderly lady in the mountain section. When I was a small boy, she used to come over to my grandmother's every Saturday afternoon. She would sit on the front porch and entertain us all afternoon with the operations on herself, her husband, with what her husband died of, what her mother died of, what two of her four children died of. After about three or four hours of this, she always wound up by saying, "I know that I'm going to die of cancer," putting her hands on her left breast.

I saw her do that a dozen times. I didn't know what cancer was at the time. I found out later. Years later, my father sent me a copy of the county paper, and I saw an announcement of Aunt Sarey Anne's death from cancer of the left breast. She had finally talked herself into it.

That's not an exaggerated case at all. It happens to be one that I know about. You can talk yourself into a headache; you can talk yourself into a stomach condition. You can talk and think yourself into anything if you allow your mind to dwell upon the negative aspects of your physical body.

Correct Eating

The mental attitude and thought patterns established while one is eating and during the following two or three hours, while the food is being broken down into liquid form for introduction into the bloodstream, may determine whether the food enters the body in a suitable form for the maintenance of sound health. The mental attitude that you're in when you're eating becomes a part of the energy that goes into the bloodstream.

As I've already pointed out, if a woman is disturbed, upset, or afraid while nursing a baby at her breast, the baby will have colic immediately after taking the milk. If you've been married and had have babies, you know this. You know that the mental attitude of the mother changes the chemistry of the milk in her breast. It also changes the chemistry of the food in your stomach before it ever gets into the bloodstream.

You can't afford to eat when you're disturbed or when you're too tired physically. Sit down, rest, relax. As a matter of fact, food should be a form of a religious exercise, a religious ceremony. When I get up in the morning (at least when I'm home), the first thing I do is to go out to the kitchen and squeeze a nice, big glass of orange juice. Then I step over to where I can look out and see deer coming down over the mountains to get water. I have my ceremony by saying, "Bless this orange juice. But look up, fellows: here come your brothers and sisters. Those little brothers and sisters are coming down to enter my bloodstream to pick me up, help me, and make me enjoy my breakfast." I worship every ounce of that orange juice as it goes down. I don't just turn up the glass and let it all go down. I let it go down little by little and worship every mouthful of it.

If you think I am kidding, perish the idea, because I'm telling you something that's very important. If you get into the habit of blessing your food, not only when you sit down on the table, but as it goes into your body, it will go a long way towards keeping you healthy.

Work as a Religious Ceremony

In connection with your work, here are two mental attitudes that can be vital allies of the silent repairman that is working on every cell of the body while one is engaged in physical action. Work should also become a religious ceremony, in which only positive thoughts are mixed.

One trouble of this civilization consists in the fact that there are so few people in the world at any one time who are engaged in labors of love. That is, doing the thing they want to do because they want to do it, not just because they have to eat. I am hoping and praying that before I shall have crossed over on the other side, I will have made valuable contributions to the end that individuals may find labors of love in which to make a living and earn their way. And I'm hoping and praying that those of you who are going to become associated with me as teachers will also look forward to the time when you can make valuable contributions to that end.

What a grand world this would be to live in if it weren't for some of the people who live here! What's wrong with them? Nothing; it's just their habits that are wrong. They think wrong. My mission in life—and your mission in association with me—is to help change the thoughts of people and give them a better set of habits than they have now. Let them think in terms of good health, opulence and plenty, and fellowship and brotherhood instead of setting man against man and nation against nation and thinking in terms of war instead of cooperation.

There's plenty in this world for everybody, including the animals and birds, if only some people wouldn't try to get too much. I honestly don't want any advantage and ability that can't be shared with all people everywhere. I want no advantage over other people. I want only the opportunity to share with them my knowledge and my ability to help them to help themselves.

The famous Mayo brothers have discovered that four vitally important factors must be observed to maintain sound physical health: an equal balancing through thought habits of work, play, love, and worship. That comes from the great Mayo Institute, where they have had thousands of people pass through their clinics. They have found out that when those four things are out of balance, almost inevitably it results in some physical ailment.

Here is a sound explanation of one major reason for going the extra mile. This habit not only benefits one economically but enables one to work with a mental attitude that leads to sound physical health. When you're doing something out of a spirit of love, of desire to help other people, it tends to give you better health. And of course it tends to give you other advantages, because every time you render useful service to other people, you put them under obligation to you. If you have enough people under obligation to you, when you ask them for something, they are not in the position to say no. They don't want to say no.

By comparison, consider the person who has the habit of performing all work grudgingly and in a negative frame of mind. Nobody wants to even work with him, and nobody wants to employ him. He damages everybody around him. Mr. Andrew Carnegie told me that one single negative mind in an organization of ten thousand could more or less poison the minds of everyone within two or three days, without even opening his mouth, just by releasing thoughts.

If I go to a home where there is fighting between members of the family, I can tell when I get in the front yard whether I want to go in or not. And for certain, I can tell after I go in.

We have an experience in our home that may illustrate this better than anything I can tell you about. Almost invariably, when a person walks into our home for the first time, they look around and make some complimentary expression such as this. A publisher came to see me not long ago, and when he walked into our living room, he said, "Oh, what a beautiful home!" Then he looked around again and said,

"It's just an ordinary home. It's not anything outstanding. What's beautiful is the way I feel when I get in here. The vibrations are good."

"Now you're getting hot," I said; "you're getting up my alley." This home is charged and recharged constantly with positive vibrations. No disharmony is permitted inside this house. As I've mentioned, even our little Pomeranians pick that up. They respond to the vibrations in that home. They can tell when a person is not in harmony with that home. If they go up to a person, sniff him, and find he is in harmony, they'll kiss his hand. If they're not pleased, if they find he is not in harmony, they bark at him and back away.

Homes, places of business, streets, cities, all have their own vibrations made up of the dominating thoughts of those who work and go that way. If you go down Fifth Avenue in New York City, with those big, prosperous stories like Tiffany's, you'll catch the feel of that crowd and you'll feel you're prosperous too, no matter how much or how little money you've got in your pocket. If you go just four blocks over to Eighth or Ninth Avenue, in Hell's Kitchen, I defy you to walk one block there without feeling as poor as a church mouse, even though you may have all the money in the world, because the people there are poverty-stricken. They think in terms of poverty, they live in poverty and squalor, and it dominates that whole part of town.

You could blindfold me and take me over there, and I could tell you the moment we got to Fifth Avenue and when we got to Eighth or Ninth Avenue. I would get the sensation of that vibration just as easily as I would have gotten it through my eyes.

Economic and Financial Benefits

Let's see what we're going to get out of cosmic habit force in connection with money. One may hand over to cosmic habit force the exact picture of the financial status he wishes to maintain, and it will automatically be picked up and carried out to its logical conclusion by an inexorable law of nature, which knows no such reality as failure.

I have observed that people who are successful think constantly in terms of things they can do, never in terms of the things they can't do. I once asked one of them if there was anything he wanted to do but couldn't. He said, "I don't think about the things I can't do. I think about the things I can do."

Many people, however, are not like that. They think about the things they can't do, worry about them, and consequently they can't do them. They think about the money they don't have and worry about it. Consequently, they don't have it and never get it.

Money is a peculiar thing. Somehow or another, it doesn't follow the fellow around that doesn't believe he has got a right to get it. Money is inanimate, so I don't believe it's the fault of the money. I think it is in the mind of the person who doubts that he can get it.

I have noticed that when students of mine start believing that they can do things, it starts to change their entire financial condition. I have also noticed that when they don't believe they can do things, they don't do them.

The whole purpose of this philosophy is to induce students to build up habits of belief in themselves and in their ability to direct their minds to whatever they want in life, and to keep their minds off the things they don't want.

If you don't know too much about Mahatma Gandhi, it'd be a good idea to get a book and read up about him. There was a man who didn't have anything to oppose the British except his own mind. He didn't have any soldiers. He didn't have any money. He didn't have any military equipment. He didn't even own a pair of britches, and yet he put out the great British Empire just by resisting it with his mind power. He didn't want them, he didn't accept them, and the British got the big idea and got out.

It's surprising how many individuals will do that when you set your mind against them. You don't have to say or do anything. You just have to say it in your mind—"I don't want that person in my life"—and eventually he'll get out, sometimes very quickly. I have a little black book that I carry with me. Anytime anybody gets in my way that I don't want to, I'll write his name in it. That's all I do, so help me, and I have never yet written a name in that book when the person didn't get out of my life and stay out.

Mind power definitely is powerful. It's potent, it's marvelous, it's profound. And it is well to call attention to the fact that no one has ever been known to become financially independent without first having to establish prosperity consciousness, just as no one may remain physically well without having first to establish health consciousness.

It is a fact well-known to psychologists that poverty-stricken people maintain a poverty consciousness, some of them from early childhood on through life. I remember so well my greatest difficulty when I started out with Andrew Carnegie. It was forgetting that I was born in poverty, illiteracy, and ignorance. It took me a long time to forget the little mountains of Wise County, Virginia, where I was born. When I'd start out to interview an outstanding man, I'd think, "I'm insignificant when I come into his presence. I guess I'll be ashamed and afraid," because I remembered where I came from; I remembered my poverty. It was a long time before I could shake that poverty off. But finally I did it and I began to think in terms of opulence. I began to say then, "Why wouldn't Mr. Anderson see me, because I am just as big in my mind as he is?" I not only felt that, but I saw the day when I made it come true.

This philosophy has spread and is spreading all over this world, and it is destined to spread still faster and still farther and deeper. And I say that's an achievement equal to those of Mr. Anderson, Mr. Wanamaker, Mr. Carnegie, or anybody else. It's an achievement when you can reach out and influence the lives of millions of people all over the world beneficially. It couldn't have been done if I hadn't changed the habits and thoughts of Napoleon Hill.

My biggest job was not getting in to see the men of affairs and getting their collaboration. That was easy. My biggest job was to change the habits of thinking of Napoleon Hill. Had I not changed those habits, the books that I have written never would have had the effect that they had. But before I could write books of that kind, I had to completely build over my thought processes and learn to keep my mind automatically on positive things.

Fixations of Fear and Faith

There is nothing that a doctor dreads more than a fixation on the part of his patient. A patient has a fixation when he has become so empty and subdued by fear that he is afraid that the doctor cannot remove the ailment. The doctor knows very well that without the cooperation of the patient's mind, he is never going to get any results. I don't care what kind of medicine he gives. He's got to have that mind power.

Each one of us came over to this plane with a marvelous doctoring system of our own, a chemist that breaks up our food and distributes it. If you think right, eat right, exercise right, and live right, this doctor inside of you will do everything else automatically. They call it *bodily resistance*. I don't care what you call it. It's a system that nature gave you for balancing everything that you need to keep your body in fine condition all the time, but you have to do your part. If the food that you take out of the soil does not have the vital elements, nature can't take that kind of food and give you a healthy body, so we have vitamins.

Fixations don't have to be negative, but you want to look out for fixations of fear and self-limitation, the belief in things that you can't do, fear of criticism or fear of anything else.

If you want to make use of fixation and benefit by the law of cosmic habit force, go to work on the fixation of applied faith. How do you go about making a fixation on anything? By repetition: applying it in everything you do, think, and say. Some of you are old enough to remember the formula, "Day by day and every way, I'm getting better and better." Millions of people all over this country were saying that, and it wouldn't have amounted to a tinker's damn unless the first man who said it believed it. It was in what he said and what he thought while he was saying it. A lot of people said it over and over again and finally turned thumbs down. It didn't work for them because they didn't believe in the first place. You can understand why. It makes no difference what formula you use as long as your thought patterns are positive and you repeat them over and over again.

You can always transmute any negative energy into something that will benefit you and the person that you come into contact with. Cosmic habit force working on me down through the years has conditioned my mind so that by a snap of the fingers, I can change it from one state to another. You can do the same thing too, and that's what I want you to do. I want you to follow the habit of thinking in positive terms until cosmic habit force takes up your mental attitude and makes it predominantly positive rather than negative.

The circumstances of life are such that the minds of the majority of people are predominantly negative all the time. I want you all to change all of that and make the mind predominantly positive all the time. No matter what you want, you can turn on the power and get some response from infinite intelligence.

Infinite intelligence is not going to do anything for you while you're in a state of anger, no matter how much right you have to be angry. Infinite intelligence is not going to do anything *for* you, but she is going to let you do something *to* yourself if you keep yourself in a negative state of mind.

You can't afford to go into action, you can't afford to have human relationships while you're in a negative mental attitude. The best way to avoid this attitude is to build up positive habits and let cosmic habit force take them over and make them predominant in your mind.

Here are the negatives that you should avoid making into fixations: poverty, imaginary illness, laziness. You know what a lazy man is? He is a man who hasn't found his labor of love. That's right: there are no lazy people except those who haven't found something they like to do. Some men are pretty hard to please. They'll go their way through life and have an alibi: they don't like this, don't like that; as a matter of fact they don't like anything, period.

Other negative habits to be avoided are envy, greed, anger, hatred, jealousy, dishonesty, drifting without aim or purpose, irritability, vanity, arrogance, cynicism, and the will to injure others. These things become fixations in the lives of most people, and you can't afford to have that kind of a fixation; it's too expensive.

Here are the positives that you can afford to have, and you can't afford *not* to have them. Definitely have a major purpose in life; make it a fixation by all means. Eat it, sleep it, drink it. Every day of your life, indulge in some act leading in the direction of your overall major purpose. Other positives are faith, personal initiative, enthusiasm, willingness to go the extra mile, imagination, the traits of a pleasing personality, accurate thinking, and all the other traits recommended in this philosophy of individual achievement.

Those are the things that you can afford to make into fixations so that they dominate your mind. You live by them, you think by them, you act by them, you relate yourself to people by them, and you'll be surprised at how quickly you can change your life. You'll be surprised at how quickly the people who have tried to injure you will fall away of their own accord and become ineffective or impotent. You'll be surprised how you'll attract new opportunities to yourself. You'll be surprised how quickly you solve your problems. You'll wonder why, instead of worrying about your problem, you just didn't get busy and solve it—all as the result of having made fixations out of these positives.

You'll notice that every one of these is subject to your control through repetition of thought. That's all you have to do. Just keep repeating it over and over and over again, and put some action behind the thought: words without deeds, you know, are dead. Engage in some sort of action.

How does a professional man, like a dentist or lawyer or doctor or engineer, go about attracting a lot of patients that are agreeable to get along with and pay their bills promptly?

The effects start with the professional man himself. His mental attitude towards his clients or patients determines what they do toward him. There's no getting away from that. That's absolutely true. It happens to a merchant, to a man or woman in any job or any other person.

In other words, if you want to reform people, don't start with the people. Start with you. Get your mental attitude right, and you'll find that the others will fall in line. They can't do anything about it. As a matter of fact, if your mind is positive, a person in a negative state of mind cannot influence you in the least. A positive-minded person is always the master of the negative-minded person.

Social and Physical Heredity

We are what we are today because of two forms of heredity. One of them we control outright, and one we do not control at all. Through physical heredity, we bring into this world a sum total of all of our ancestors. If we happen to be born with nice brainpower, nice, well-developed, bodies, fine, but if we happen to be born with a hunchback or some affliction, there's nothing much we can do about that. In other words, we have to take physical heredity as it is.

Of course we can go a long way toward adjusting ourselves to an afflicted body. Charles P. Steinmetz, for instance, was born with the curvature of the spine, but he adjusted himself to that in such a way that he became an outstanding genius. Another man would have used that as an excuse to have a tin cup and some pencils down on the corner of the street. As I said, I knew a man afflicted with the loss of his legs through polio who sold pencils within two blocks of the White House, while in the White House, a man afflicted with the same thing was running the biggest nation in the world. He made an asset out of his affliction instead of a liability.

Social heredity, however, is another thing. Social heredity consists of all of the influences that enter into your life after you are born, and maybe even back to the prenatal stage, before you're born.

The things you hear, the things you see, the things you're taught, the things you read about, the legends that influence you constitute social heredity. By far and away, the most important part of what happens to us all through life is due to our relationship to social heredity, or what we get out of our environment and how much we control it.

It's a good idea for all of us to go back and reexamine ourselves about the things that we think we believe and find out just what right we have to believe them. Where do we get our beliefs? What is there to support any belief? So help me, I don't think I have any beliefs that are not supported by good sound evidence, or at least what I believe to be evidence.

When voting time comes, I think ultimately, who will do the best job? Who's the most honest and the most capable? In 1928, Al Smith ran for the presidency. I'm not a Catholic, but I voted for Al Smith, because I thought he'd do a bang-up good job. In my book of rules, it doesn't make any difference what a man's religion is. If he's a good man, and he wants public office, I want to help put him in there.

I didn't arrive at that open-minded state of tolerance overnight; I'll tell you that now. There was a time when I was just about intolerant as the next one, but I found out that that was a bad thing for me. By responding to the law of cosmic habit force, I finally built up a set of habits whereby I don't believe that I have any unfair biases or prejudices against anybody in this world or anything.

17

Budgeting Time and Money

This last lesson, on budgeting time and money, is not as poetic as some of the others, but it's just as important. If you're ever to have financial security in this world, you've got to do two things at least. You've got to budget the use of your time, and you've got to budget your money, your expenditures and your receipts, so that you have a definite plan to go by.

Budgeting Time

Let's take up time first. You have twenty-four hours divided into three eight-hour periods: eight hours for sleep, eight hours for work, eight hours for recreation, spare time, and activities.

You have no control over the eight hours of sleep; you have to give that over to nature. And you don't always have too much control over the eight hours that you put into work. But there are eight hours of the rest of your life; they're yours. You can waste them if you want to. You can play, you can work, you can enjoy yourself, you can relax, you can develop by taking a course of instruction, you can read— you can do anything you want.

Therein lies the greatest opportunity of the whole twenty-four hours. Back in the days when I was doing my research, I worked sixteen hours a day, but I was engaged in a labor of love. I reserved eight hours a day for sleep and worked for the other sixteen. Part of the time, I was training salesman in order to make a living, but it was mostly spent in research in order to give this philosophy to the world. Had it not been for the fact that I had at least eight hours of free time, I never could have done the necessary research.

Another thing happened early in my career, and it was very fortunate. I built a bridge across the Monongahela River, down at West Virginia. That one transaction produced enough money to take care of my family for the rest of their lives. I'm still taken care of to this day, so I've had to make no more financial contributions from that day to this. The hand of destiny reached out and gave me a wonderful break early in life, when I needed it badly.

At any rate, in those eight hours of spare time, you can practice developing all of those habits if you choose. Whatever else you may do with any portion of those eight hours, by all means work out a plan for conditioning your mind to be always positive. You don't have to follow my plans, but you will get some mighty good ideas in the lessons on applied faith, cosmic habit force, and the Master Mind.

Of course you know what my plan is: it's about the eight guiding friends I have working for me. Maybe you want a different technique. Work out a plan of your own, and if it's better than the one I gave you, follow it. But have some plan whereby at least a part of those eight hours of free time every day of your life are devoted to conditioning your mind to be positive. When unfortunate adversities come up, you will be equal to them.

Budgeting Income and Expenses

The first thing on your list: your monthly or weekly amount of income should be put down in a budgeting book. It should be distributed as follows.

First, a definite percentage, generally less than 10 percent of gross income, for life insurance. If you have a family or if you don't have a family, life insurance is a must. You cannot afford to be without it. If you brought children into this world to whom you are responsible for an education, it's up to you to insure yourself so that if you pass out of the picture and you're no longer earning, they have enough money to educate themselves with. If you married a wife that's entirely dependent upon you, it's up to you to carry insurance to give her a down payment on a second husband if you should pass out of the picture.

When I get on the plane and start back to California, I always go to one of those machines and purchase a life insurance policy for the largest amount that I can get, which is $50,000. In addition to that, I carry some additional accident insurance policy. Life insurance gives you wonderful protection in case you're taken away from social production.

A man who's in a business where his services are a large portion of the assets should be insured for a sum of money large enough to fill up the chasm left by them if he should be taken out.

Life insurance comes up the top of the list. The next is a percentage for food, clothing, and housing. Don't just go out and blow the works. You can go to the grocery store and spend five times as much as you actually need if you don't have a system to go by. Personally, I buy whatever I fancy, but I happen to be in a position where a budget on food and clothing is not necessary. There was a time when it was necessary, however, and I imagine that in the lives of most people, it is necessary to have a budget.

Then there is a definite amount to be set aside for investment, even if it's only a small amount, only a dollar or fifty cents a week. It's not the amount that you set aside; it's the habit of being resourceful and frugal. It's wonderful to be frugal, not to waste things.

I've always admired the German people so much on account of their frugality. They are frugal people, who just don't waste things. I have always admired anybody that doesn't waste things, like my grandfather. He used to go around picking up old nails, strings, and pieces of metal; you'd be surprised at the collection of things he had.

My frugality never went to that extent. It ran more to Rolls-Royces and six-hundred-acre estates. But believe you me, I've long since learned that no matter how much of this philosophy you have, if you don't have a system for saving a part of what goes through your hands, it makes no difference. And if you don't have that system, you will go through all of it. Saving money is a very difficult thing for most people, because they don't have any system to go by.

Whatever amount remains after you have taken care of those food, clothing, and housing should go into a current checking or savings account for such things as emergencies, recreation, and education. You can draw on that; you don't have to follow your budget on it. In other words, it's a petty cash account, and if you're really frugal, you'll let it get up to a pretty good size. Isn't it a wonderful thing to know that you have a good nest egg lying in the bank so that no matter happens, you can go down and get the money? You may not need it, but if you don't have it there, believe you me, you'll have a thousand needs, and you'll be afraid in connection with all of them.

Perhaps the thing that gives me the most courage to speak my piece, be myself, and demand that people keep off my toes is the fact that I no longer have to worry where my money is coming from. People try to worry me sometimes, but it's as Confucius say: "When rat tries to pull cat's whiskers, rat generally ends up in honorable cat's belly."

With this system of tapping a little percentage of what goes through your hands, it's not the amount that I am so interested in as the fact that you're establishing a habit of frugal savings. If your income is so low that you can't cut your expenses anymore and you can only take out one cent out of every dollar, take that one cent and put it away in some place where it's hard for you to get at.

I am a great believer in having money invested in an investment trust. These represent a great variety of well-known stocks, so if one goes bad, it doesn't affect your investments at all. There are a lot of investment trusts; some are good, some not so good, perhaps. If you invest in an investment trust, go to your banker or somebody is qualified; don't try to do it on your own judgment. The individual as a rule is just not qualified to do that.

Get some of your money working for you, and you'll be surprised at what a nice game it is when you know that you're setting aside a certain amount every month or every week and that that amount is beginning to work for you.

When I go to the bank, I always take out a $20 bill and put it in a special pocket in my wallet, just in case. I'll always have $20, and the other day I needed it too; it came in very handy.

Analyze Your Habits

Analyze yourself and find out exactly what your habits are in regard to the things that are important to you. You can grade yourself. The grading runs all the away from 0 up to a 100.

First of all, the choice of a profession or occupation. How much time are you giving to that? How much time have you given to getting yourself adjusted in an occupation or a business or a profession that can be a labor of love? If you haven't already found the profession or the occupation that can constitute a labor of love, you should put in a lot of time searching until you do.

In regard to habits of thought, how much do you put in on the can-do sort of thinking, and how much do you put in on the no can do? In other words, how much time do you put in on what you desire and on what you don't desire? How much time goes in on the things that you don't desire in life: ill-health, frustration, disappointment, discouragement? I'll bet you'd be surprised if you had a stop watch to record the time that you put in every day on worrying. The first thing you know, the predominant part of your time is going to thinking about the things don't you want.

Have a system of budgeting whereby you keep your mind definitely fixed on the things you do want. I have three hours a day set aside for meditation and silent prayer, three hours. No matter what hour I get home, I'll put in three hours of meditation, giving and expressing gratitude for the marvelous opportunity that I have had to be a minister to other people. If I don't get to it at the end of night, I get it in sometime during the day.

The finest prayer on the face of this earth is not to pray for something but to pray for what you already have: "O divine Providence, I ask not for more riches, but for more wisdom with which to make better use of the riches I already have."

You have many riches. You have health, you live in a wonderful country, you have wonderful neighbors, you belong to a wonderful class, you're learning a wonderful philosophy. Believe all the things you have, and be thankful for them.

Think of the things that I have to be thankful for. It's no wonder I am rich, is it? Why? There would be something wrong with me if I weren't rich. If I couldn't stand here and tell you that I have everything in this world that I want, there would be something wrong with me and this philosophy. I would have no right to teach it to you whatsoever if I couldn't say that about myself. If I found somebody who could run me out of my own office, take my philosophy away from me, and convert it over to their uses, I wouldn't deserve to have it. I can be the master of my fate, captain of my soul because I live my philosophy, because it's designed to help other people, because never under any circumstances do I do anything to intentionally hinder, harm, or endanger another person.

In regard to your personal relationships with others, how much time do you put into goodwill in your relationships with other people in business or your job? Do you spend some time cultivating people? If you don't, you're not going to have friends. Out of sight, out of mind. I don't care how good the friend is: if you don't keep contact, he'll forget about you. You've got to keep contact. Someday I'm going to get up a series of postcards. I'll have a beautiful motto of friendship on each one so that my students can mail out one a week to each of their friends, just to keep in contact.

It wouldn't be a bad idea for a business or a professional man to do that, and he would not violate the ethics of his profession by doing it. There'd be no commercial atmosphere in it at all. You only send out one a month. You'll send out twelve cards a year with the right kind of message on the back of it, signed by yourself. Believe you me, it would be the best thing in the world to build up your practice.

Then there are the habits of health, physical and mental. How much time are you putting in to building habits that give you health consciousness? Health consciousness doesn't come without some effort on your part.

How much of time are you putting into living your religion? I'm not talking about believing; I'm not talking about going to church and putting a quarter in the basket now and then. Anybody can do that. How much are you living it in your bedroom, your drawing room, your kitchen, your place of business? Those are the places to grade yourself, not in church. Chances are that you go to church once a week. It's not how many times you go that counts. It's not how much you contribute to the church in the way of money. It's what you do to live that religion in your everyday life. I don't know of a religion on the face of this earth that wouldn't be wonderful if people lived by it.

It may seem trite to ask you to grade yourself on how much time you're spending on living your religion, but unless you are very different from most people I know, you need to reflect on this subject.

And then the use made of your spare time: that is where you really need to go to town and examine yourself. Really give yourself an accounting on that one. Just how much of that eight hours of spare time are you devoting to some sort of advancement of your interest, improvement of your mind, or benefiting by association?

And then, the budget thing: spending money.

Have you got a system for doing that? If you haven't got a system, work out one. You can make that system flexible.

Accurate thinking: how much time are you putting into learning how to think accurately, following the rules I've laid down in that lesson? Did you just read that lesson while doing nothing about it? How much are you doing to put that lesson into actual practice, thinking accurately, doing your own thinking for once?

Then the use made of the power of thought, whether controlled or uncontrolled. Are you controlling your thoughts, or are all of your thoughts uncontrolled? Are you letting the circumstances of life control you? Are you trying to create some circumstances that you can control? You can't control all of them. Nobody can do that. But you certainly can create some circumstances that you can control.

And how about the privilege of voting? Do you say, "I don't go to the polls. Crooks are running the country anyway, and my little vote is not going to count"? Do you say that or do you say, "I have a responsibility. I am going to go to the polls and vote, because it's my duty"? Do you put time in on that? A lot of people don't, and that's why there are so many crooked politicians and others in public office that shouldn't be there. Too many of the decent people don't vote. I've been guilty of that myself now and then. I'm not creating any alibis; I just say that I'll take my punishment along with the rest.

Then family relationships: are they harmonious?

Have you a Master Mind relationship, or are you letting that one slide by? How much time are you giving to building and improving your family relationship? You have to do something about it. Somebody has to give in, and if the wife won't, why don't you give in, gentlemen, and vice versa? If husband doesn't give in, start a little Master Minding; why don't you give in? Why don't you make it interesting for him? You made it interesting for him before you married him; I'm sure you did.

Are you happy in the marriage? Why don't you try it all over again and renegotiate your marriage so that you have a wonderful relationship? It'll pay off. It will pay off in peace of mind. It will pay off in dollars and cents. It'll pay off in friendships. It'll pay off in every relationship.

In your job or business or profession, are you going the extra mile, and do you like your work? If you don't like your work, find out why.

If you're going the extra mile, how much are you going the extra mile? In what ways are you doing it, and are you doing it with the right sort of mental attitude? I don't care who you are or what you're doing; if you're making it your business to go the extra mile in connection with every person possible, the time will come when you will have so many friends that whenever you want to carry out something through them, they'll be there at your beck and call.

Annie Lou takes life a little more seriously than I do. She works on many things that she doesn't really like. I don't do that, I won't do anything I don't like to do, but we are in a wonderful situation. We have wonderful health. She's just the woman I should have playing opposite of me in this great theater of life. We have everything in the world we can use or need. If we don't, we only have to click our fingers and it will come running from a million different sources.

Don't think for a moment we could have that on any other basis than that of deserving it. We earned it. We couldn't have it otherwise. Nobody can have anything in this world worth having without earning it.

This marks the end of the Master Course. It is not a short program. Just remember one thing always: in order to get cooperation and get a friend, you have to be a friend.